Humanistic Studies in the Communication Arts

CRITICIZING THE CRITICS

A TAXONOMY OF
CONCEPTS IN COMMUNICATION
by Reed H. Blake and Edwin O. Haroldsen

COMMUNICATIONS AND MEDIA
Constructing a Cross Discipline
by George N. Gordon

ETHICS AND THE PRESS
Readings in Mass Media Morality
Edited by John C. Merrill and Ralph D. Barney

DRAMA IN LIFE
The Uses of Communication in Society
Edited by James E. Combs and Michael W. Mansfield

INTERNATIONAL AND INTERCULTURAL COMMUNICATION
Edited by Heinz-Dietrich Fischer and John C. Merrill

EXISTENTIAL JOURNALISM
by John C. Merrill

THE COMMUNICATIONS REVOLUTION
A History of Mass Media in the United States
by George N. Gordon

COMMUNICATIONS ARTS IN THE ANCIENT WORLD
Edited by Eric A. Havelock and Jackson P. Hershbell

EDITORIAL AND PERSUASIVE WRITING
by Harry W. Stonecipher

ENTERTAINMENT
A Cross-Cultural Examination
Edited by Heinz-Dietrich Fischer and Stefan R. Melnik

CRITICIZING THE CRITICS
by John W. English

Humanistic Studies in | H S / C A | the Communication Arts

CRITICIZING THE CRITICS

by

JOHN W. ENGLISH

COMMUNICATION ARTS BOOKS

HASTINGS HOUSE, PUBLISHERS

New York 10016

Dedicated to Emery L. Sasser, who got this ball rolling. And to the others who kept it and me going.

Library of Congress Cataloging in Publication Data

English, John Wesley, 1940–
  Criticizing the critics.

  (Communication arts books)
  Includes bibliographical references and index.
  1. Art criticism—United States. 2. Arts—United States. I. Title.
NX640.E53 1979   700'.973   79-16245
ISBN 0-8038-1270-1
ISBN 0-8038-1272-8 pbk.

Published simultaneously in Canada by
Copp Clark Ltd., Toronto
Printed in the United States of America

CONTENTS

FOREWORD

A friend of mine, now deceased of natural causes, served for many years as a critic on an influential New York newspaper. (Never mind which one and what he criticized.) He was a good critic and took his responsibilities seriously. The future of many a struggling performing artist lay almost entirely in hand by virtue of the frown or smile he would bestow upon them after their premier performance in the big-time New York world of the performing arts.

At one point in his life said friend, as peaceful and defenseless a creature as one could imagine, applied to the proper authorities of New York State to carry a pistol for purposes of self defense, so often was his life threatened by irate victims of his critical disdain. Not only did he receive such permission immediately by telephone from this agency, he was requested to pick up his gun permit in person and as soon as possible. "We cooperate with the homicide boys any way that we can," he was told. "And the sooner you buy your piece, the safer you will be!"

He never had to use his pistol—happily, because he might well have blown off his own toes had he attempted to defend his person with firearms about which he knew nothing. New York State did not care. He was a critic and therefore fair game for somebody else with a gun, bomb, poison dart or Karate blow to the jugular.

Critic baiting, like riding to hounds, is an old and honorable sport that has its roots in Periclean Athens, if not before. Its antiquity derives from the fact that artistic criticism is certainly as old as the arts—possibly older, because the absence of anything to criticize has never stood in the way of the confirmed and devout critic. Note today's television critics and Martin Mayer's observation in the October, 1979 issue of the obscure publication *American Film* Writes Mayer with a characteristic jocular shrug, "(S)ometimes I wince at the thought of all the power we (television critics) have!" Mayer, of course, has *no* power and his criticism for all its cleverness and sharpness is rarely about television. What can an intelligent man say about the subject to readers he presumes also are intelligent? Instead, Mayer centers upon institutional and legal matters relating to broadcasting, and his criticism, when sum totals are drawn, centers on trends and fads in American culture as they are spread to the masses.

The trouble with criticizing critics is that it is all too easy to do poorly. Critics are vulnerable, and they may be "proved" wrong in too many ways. A movie that receives a negative critical reception can make monkeys out of the most prestigious reviewer simply by pleasing a large or notable audience. George Roy Hill's *A Little Romance* is a recent example. All television critics—Mr. Mayer included—have to buck the gods of numbers: the cold facts that even program failures (in dollar and cents terms please) have enormous mass audiences of millions, which is exactly what they were created to do in the first place, even if they are cancelled after a pilot showing or their first season. Press critics with few exceptions (Bob Wood and the people who operate the *Columbia Journalism Review*) tend to hit and run. Criticizing journalists is a perilous business, mainly because a man or woman given a press card turns immediately into a super-patriot defending the American Constitution, the First Amendment, motherhood and apple pie and should, he or she thinks, be immune to most environmental and judicial perils through which we mere mortals must survive.

A critic is, however, a man or woman who must enjoy living dangerously. My late friend is not the only one who has carried a gun. Some have even had to hire bodyguards. Their antagonists may come from all or any parts of the public. I remember what I consider a justified explosion in print from the late, dignified and scholarly playwright Maxwell Anderson, when one of his plays was chewed to ribbons by the Broadway scribes working for the New York press in the 1940's. Anderson called them (a group consisting of such legendary figures as George Jean Nathan, Brooks Atkinson, Burns Mantle and Louis Kronenberger) the journalistic

"Jukes Family," doubting not only their integrity but also their intelligence and proclivity towards collusion. Never mind what lesser writers, actors, directors, producers have said about. The fact remains that, for many reasons, only a handful of drama critics survive to this day, and I myself have my doubts about them—particularly those who have been recruited from the world of ballet and atonal music, to say nothing of obituaries and book reviewing.

Criticizing critics is dangerous work too, but safer than being a critic. This peril stems from misinterpreting standards of evaluation, finding biases and misconstructions that do not exist and from I. A. Richards' famous motivation (in *Practical Criticism*) "politeness or spleen."

Not so many years ago a music critic, so an entirely reliable story goes, wrote in a review printed in a journal devoted to this art that a concert singer went flat in a certain phrase or aria of a certain song. The singer challenged the criticism. Unknown to the critic, the entire recital had been recorded, and an evaluation session was arranged to which were invited various experts on the roundness and flatness of singing. On one side, if the critic was wrong, lay a ruined literary reputation and a law suit for defamation that involved many hundreds of thousands of dollars. On the other hung the integrity, ego and future professional life of the singer. The tape was played in a sound proof studio. The vocalist *was* unquestionably flat at the disputed moment, but the critic's nerves had been short circuited! He became an editor and retired from the judgmental world of critical journalism just in time to save his sanity.

I make no claim that John W. English has committed no such sins in the book you are about to read. English, however, understands both the need and function of good critics in a culture where it is impossible for one to judge for himself the value of all the movies, books, television shows, plays and works of art that swirl around in an enormous marketplace. A good critic is like a good wine taster. Because he has studied and developed sensitivities that are sharper and more acute than yours or mine, he sips the available output and ranks it according to criteria that are significant for lovers of the grape: taste, aroma, color, dryness and, of course, price. He can be trusted because of what he *knows*, not because of his personal likes or dislikes or color of his attitudes or ability to write clever English.

We live in a time, unfortunately, when authentic wine tasters are all too few. In their place, we discover "wine tipsters," cousins of the public relations fraternity, who know little if anything except what they like or dislike. As critics, they are less

than worthless because they share the guilt of a man who know-
ingly prints road maps on which the route numbers and place
names have been inaccurately drawn. Their stock in trade is the
bum steer, but they are peculiarly insulated from discovery and
disgrace because, all too often, they control the same market that
they criticize. *One* film critic—not a very good one—in New York
City effectively controls whether or not certain independent
and/or foreign films receive national distribution. The make-or-
break power of drama and art critics for less than a handful of
newspapers and magazines is not only legion, it is a national disgrace that smears its fundamental corruption into culture at
large and affects millions of people who are unaware that bad
decisions have been made for them in distant places long ago.

John English insists simply that we get to know our critics
better and that we attempt to understand the caprices of reviewing of all sorts—from rock music to restaurants—a good deal better. I have never met a critic who has not claimed that whatever
power he has was and is unasked for and that his readers look to
him for sagacities of judgment that he doubts he delivers—in
other words, that he has found himself in a hot spot and wishes it
were cooler. Maybe so; maybe not. What *is* irrefutable is that critics of all kinds, in print and on radio and television, will continue to exercise their (possibly inevitable) sharp tyrannies upon
all of the rest of us. I hope that *Criticizing the Critics* will blunt
some of these razors' edges a bit by means of enlightenment,
analysis and reason. I think it may.

GEORGE N. GORDON
Muhlenberg College
Cedar Crest College

PREFACE

One unstated consequence of the social turmoil of the 1960s was the split between the middle class and intellectuals at the same time as popular culture began to emerge as the dominant force in the arts. Pop journalist-sociologist Tom Wolfe goes so far as to say: "Art today is the religion of the educated classes."

For years, critics working for Establishment media, with their stiff-shirted elitism intact, had generally berated the popular arts as mediocre, false, shallow and bad. They espoused the dictum that any fare achieving popular and commercial success was contemptible without further examination. Dwight Mac-Donald, for instance, pompously allowed that "homogenized" popular art didn't even have the "theoretical possibility of being good."

Some contemporary critics still echo that sentiment. A noted television critic of a major newspaper recently said: "How does the mind that considers itself serious deal with popular culture, which generally does not consider itself serious, except perhaps at the soiled 'bottom line' of success or profit?" The nation's leading drama critic also takes an aloof line: "There are things that are beyond criticism and things that are beneath criticism."

Phooey! This writer is convinced that such arrogance only alienates critics from the broad communities they seek to serve.

As artists themselves began holding up a mirror to the majority American culture, so too, a few pluralist-oriented critics became interested in T. S. Eliot's profound proposition: that which
is easiest to consume probably has the most influence.

Some critics of the popular arts—those who reject cultism
and snobbishness—not only share the belief that all the arts enhance the art of living, as I do, but also contend that the popular
arts have essential entertainment value in themselves. These
egalitarian critics support the theory that discriminating consumers can slowly be guided toward improved tastes through
selective exposure to quality popular fare. While persuading consumers to embrace increasingly complex fare in order to gain
more pleasure from their arts experiences, these critics also seek
to help the public sample and appreciate new segments of the
wide spectrum of culture available in America. They know that if
audiences are encouraged only to read pulp science fiction, or go
to action movies or listen to *reggae* music, few will ever know
what joys lie beyond.

Admittedly any cultural change—like the one I'm suggesting
here—is difficult to puzzle out while it is still evolving. New reports flash across the public consciousness and tend to confuse
more often than clarify everything. For example, when *Newsweek*
published its special issue on "The Arts in America" on December
24, 1973, writer Arthur Cooper heralded in "the era of the critic
as superstar." One theory to explain that media phenomenon at
the time went: the influence of and interest in criticism increases
as the quantity and quality of new art declines. In the early
1970s, the arts were said to be in a cultural lull and audiences
reportedly had become passive, asking to be spoon-fed and worry-
ing over whether their views conformed with the ephemeral
"they" (translate—critics).

Cooper rightly implied, however, that this age of the critic
might be short-lived, though I quarrel with his elitist explana-
tion: "As the arts become increasingly synonymous with popular
culture, the critic will have to go into the snake pit of all the all
too 'lively arts' at increasing danger to his effectiveness—and his
soul."

Nonetheless, his conclusion lends strong support to the
populist or pluralist approach to culture, which I also advocate:

> Who shall criticize the critics? To ask the question is to
> realize that criticism is not the function of an enlightened or
> unholy few but a human faculty that plays an important part in
> everyone's reading of and relation to the world. "Criticism" is,
> perhaps, the central faculty that distinguished the effective op-
> eration of the human consciousness in the world it shares with

less-developed, uncritical consciousnesses. The critic criticizes art, but as Matthew Arnold said, art itself is a criticism of life. By showing us how art works, the great critic shows us how life works—or isn't working.

If Cooper's final point is right, and I am convinced it is, then readers are obliged to learn a great deal more about critics and criticism than is now common knowledge. This study aims to prepare the public—those attuned to the arts and to criticism—to criticize critics.

Since the media are the main forum of continuing adult education, responsible citizens must be aware of how the press system works so they can evaluate and assimilate new information and opinions. Because critical writing is such a specialized form of subjective journalism, it has largely been ignored by writers on the media.

Yet, while no one would dispute that the arts are important to one's quality of life, few give critics credit for their role in verbally supporting the arts and in seeking to improve them. The negative connotation of the word "criticism" is a clue to the prevailing sentiment toward its practitioners.

The word "critic" actually comes from the Greek *kritikos*, which means "able to discuss." This implies both positive and negative comments to me. Thus, I have tried to moderate the text by citing exemplary practices of some critics and corruption by others. In each instance, names are named, events are chronicled and examples corroborate generalizations.

Though critics are often called "assassins of culture," this writer takes no such negative view. In fact, the bulk of the text is given to the critics themselves in order for them to state their views. I have intentionally not studied just one critic or a handful of one type—as previous scholars have attempted—but sought an overview of the profession and a multiplicity of opinions. I have kept the focus on the primary sources—the critics—and what they say about their jobs, their problems and pressures, standards and networks of influences, effects and even their future. Chapter 6 also attempts to assess the state of criticism in each form for the close-up perspective, while Chapter 7 supplies 13 key questions readers might ask of any critic.

Though certainly selective and subjective, I have sought to make my points through accurate and complete reporting and to let the reader participate in the evaluation process. To help others criticize critics effectively, I have sought to present all relevant facts and opinions. I have not assumed that all critics have integrity; for instance, I tested the premise with investigation. If critics said they believed in the principle of social responsibility, I have sought examples of how they serve readers and reported them.

In short, I have tried to hold critics, like all public servants, accountable for their performance. Criticizing critics—subjecting them to the same scrutiny they apply to the arts—is a necessary route to establishing a more functional form of criticism that will aid both the arts and their audiences.

Why is all of this important? Because the popular arts contribute to everyone's sense of the quality of life and critics are an integral part of the arts system.

Former film and book critic Wilfred Sheed has said, "I would rather see inferior talk about the arts than none at all." I disagree. Rather, I subscribe to the Brechtian notion that if "Bad theatre hurts all theatre," then weak or second-rate criticism, too, is destructive in the long run.

The goal of this study, then, has been simple: to inform the public about critics and criticism so it can better interact with the arts and media coverage of them. Thus, everyone improves from the exchange. If I succeed only in raising a few new intriguing questions, even though I may fail in supplying satisfying answers to them, I will consider this pioneering work a small step in the right direction.

June 1979   JOHN W. ENGLISH
                                               Athens, Georgia

INTRODUCTION

Greenhorn critics often get the jitters because they don't know what they are going to say about a given work *before* they experience it. I admit I also fretted about criticizing critics *before* I began this study.

My professional and academic credentials helped ease my initial anxiety toward the task. I had already worked six years as a professional journalist, including more than a year as popular arts critic for the *Wisconsin State Journal* in Madison. And, I had written scores of free lance articles on art and artists for daily newspapers, Sunday supplements and various magazines.

My education in journalism was extensive. After an A.B. from the University of Tulsa, I later obtained a Master's from the Columbia University Graduate School of Journalism. And, I had a year's worth of doctoral studies from the University of Wisconsin School of Journalism and Mass Communication and had studied film criticism at the Department of Cinema Studies at New York University one summer.

Additionally, I had earned some valuable first-hand arts experience. Collaborative creative efforts had resulted in three short, experimental films. I had also run a kinetic light show company which presented multi-media projections for rock music acts, fashion shows, dance concerts and even a symphony performance. Further, I'd studied video at the Global Village in New York and animation at Zagreb Studios in Yugoslavia and helped found a professional ballet company in Hong Kong.

In June 1973, with the support of a Moss Fellowship, I took a leave of absence from my faculty post at the University of Georgia (where one of my courses was teaching critical writing) to begin studying the field of criticism.

Under the aegis of the interdisciplinary doctoral program of Union Graduate School (Yellow Springs, Ohio), I laid out an extensive, multi-faceted research strategy to investigate the field. My study was guided by a knowledgeable committee of five: Roger Ortmayer, a former art and religion specialist for the National Council of Churches of Christ in New York; Robert Lewis Shayon, former television critic for *Saturday Review* and now a professor at the University of Pennsylvania's Annenberg School of Communications; Benjamin DeMott, social critic and intellectual journalist for the *Atlantic Monthly* and a professor of English at Amherst College; and fellow doctoral students Ms. Ruth Lovald, a sociologist now studying law in Washington, D.C., and Andrew Potok, an artist, scholar and teacher at Goddard College, Plainfield, Vermont.

My research began in earnest when Frank Pollock, editor of the journalism review *Media & Consumer*, invited me to coordinate a special issue to be called "The Journalist as (Consumer) Critic." I accepted the offer and moved to Connecticut, where I spent nearly two months reading hundreds of newspapers and magazines looking for critical articles to reprint, commissioning a score of free lance writers to produce original articles, editing the pieces and organizing the format of the magazine.

My contribution to that project describes its philosophic thrust, as well as my own viewpoint:

> It is true that in their regular critical assessments of politicians, government programs and the performing and visual arts, the media offer criticism that is both necessary and useful, helping the public to make decisions based on first-hand reporting and carefully considered judgments. But generally speaking, critical journalism has dealt with political and cultural aspects of life, neglecting economics and everyone's basic needs—food, shelter, transportation.
>
> Signs are cropping up, though, that the media are becoming more concerned about issues related to the quality of life. Consumer-oriented criticism is also catching on: the major distinction between consumer reporting and criticism is that critics must include their just estimate of a subject's worth. Critics state their evaluations directly. In defining his or her position on

a subject, the central question a critic must resolve is, "What is my relation to all this?" and *not*, "What is my opinion of all this?" An effective critic assumes the role of a consumer so readers can identify with that view and respond accordingly.

The value of criticism—whether it deals with a film or a new car— is assumed to be educative and constructive. Critics exalt the good and condemn the bad and thus guide the public toward improving its potential for pleasure and civilized progress.

In pursuit of this mission, critics obviously run into conflicts with those being criticized. But consumer critics have only to judge their writing in terms of whether it reflects reality or truth, not whether someone else's interests are helped or hindered. A critic's responsibility also differs from that of journalist-advocates in the partisan press; critics have only to serve the public interest, striving to be free of special biases and causes and to be fair in their evaluations.

In the past, journalism has too often treated its audience as a passive market for its advertisers and its content as packaged information or entertainment requiring only consumption, not responsive action. Critics of the marketplace, to be effective agents of change, must convince others to push beyond surface stimulation or outrage, must teach its audience to become critics in practice of everything they buy and use. Developing a critical attitude in one's everyday life means the difference between merely surviving life and enjoying it. The best criticism is based on the notion that there is something more, something beyond. A critical perspective is a way of life.

From my established base in Ridgefield, Connecticut, I also conducted a national survey of professional critics employed by media in 18 selected cities (Los Angeles, New York, Atlanta, Chicago, Detroit, Seattle, Minneapolis, Dallas, Washington, D.C., Boston, San Francisco, Winston-Salem, N.C., Tulsa, Okla., Denver, St. Petersburg, Fla., Des Moines and New Orleans). A pretested questionnaire (see sample in Appendix) was sent to 226 identifiable critics and nearly 50 per cent of them sent back usable responses, 107 in all. A few resisted the form, but their views, contained in letters and, in one case, a cassette recording, were utilized in my text.

Not only did the survey generate information that could be tabulated for a general overview, but it also produced some highly interesting statements that could be quoted directly. The critics' views could not easily be dichotomized since their explanations for their stances on issues raised covered a wide spectrum. The lack of unanimity about anything became one of my central discoveries in polling the critics. Selected personal interviews and wide reading of critics later confirmed the idiosyncratic nature of the practitioners of the craft.

In addition, I enrolled and attended three courses in criticism available in New York City. At New York University's School for Continuing Education, I took copious notes as John Simon lectured on his brand of highbrow criticism, as Andrew Sarris and Roger Greenspun extolled auteurism, as Molly Haskell explained the feminist perspective and Stuart Byron, the gay vantage point. But I was most impressed with David Denby, film critic for *New York*, who cited the pleasures of eclecticism and the social experience of movies, while warning of the limitations of a single critical theory and cultural categories.

At the New School for Social Research, I gained additional critical aesthetic experience from Faubion Bowers, a scholar-writer on the traditional arts of Japan and Russia (and a fellow former Tulsan). The course covered a range of artists from classicists Scriabin, Ashkenazy and Noguchi to experimentalists such as composer Peter Lieberson, choreographer Alwin Nikolais, and Merrill Brockway, former director of CBS's arts showcase "Camera Three." Bower's vision of the arts was expansive, eccentric and enlightening.

Stimulated by my work in Hong Kong with ballet, I also decided to study dance criticism and took the Dance Theatre Workshop course offered by Deborah Jowitt, the *Village Voice* critic, and Marcia Siegal, *New York* columnist. The critic-instructors assigned reviews of such dance programs as Martha Graham, Twyla Tharp and the Harkness Ballet and taught students the difficult process of describing dance movement so readers can visualize it.

Because of my own disillusionment with the productiveness of many one-on-one interviews and yet recognizing the need for what Ernest Hemingway called a good "shit detector," I decided to try an innovative research method. Working with Dr. Herbert London, of NYU's University Without Walls, I formulated the program for a public symposium, entitled "Criticism and Popular Culture," and invited 19 professional critics to discuss the aesthetics of popular culture, techniques and standards of criticism, occupational hazards and pleasures and other major issues of criticism of the performing and visual arts. (See Appendix.) The day-long symposium was held on a snowy Saturday, March 30, 1974, at NYU's Vanderbilt Hall and the results of the interaction were fascinating. Excerpts of those four sessions appear in the text of this work.

Four professional meetings encountered in my research also contributed significantly to my understanding of the field. At the National Critics Institute, which meets for four mid-summer weeks at the Eugene O'Neill Memorial Theatre Center in Waterford, Connecticut, I was tutored in the how-to's and why's of drama criticism by Ernie Schier of the *Philadelphia Bulletin* and Larry DeVine of the *Detroit Free Press.* In addition to writing reviews of about 20 new plays and getting detailed critiques of same, I learned a great deal about the process of theatre production from playwrights, directors, actors, set and lighting designers. Visiting critics Julius Novick, Norman Nadel, Martin Esslin, Judith Crist (I took her workshop in film criticism at Columbia as a graduate student), Michael Feingold, Clara Hieronymous, Elliott Norton and Marilyn Stasio led seminars and bull sessions sharing insights, experiences and gossip. In the relaxed shore setting, conversations were intimate and lively. From my fellow critics, I regained an appreciation for how difficult the process of expressing one's views about a work is for some people.

Much less valuable to me was the Robert Flaherty Film Seminar, which was held in early summer on the campus of Bradford College in Haverhill, Massachusetts. This eight-day gathering was mainly a screening and critique of new documentary films, in the tradition of ethnographer Flaherty, attended by about 75 filmmakers. The few film scholars and critics there remained peripheral to the discussions. As I listened to the various filmmakers talk about their work, I realized anew how inarticulate most of them were about their own work. Even singer Judy Collins could add little to my understanding and appreciation of her "Antonia," one of the hits of the seminar. Conversely, I sensed repeatedly that critics were much more adept at dissecting an artist's work and explaining it to others than were most artists. It was an important lesson.

Finally, I was able to participate in the formation of two new critics' organizations: the Dance Critics Association and the American Theatre Critics Association. The contrast between the two foundings was especially telling: the traditional drama critics fretted about the exclusivity of their membership while the dance critics sought to include anyone writing in the field. One sensed the theatre folks were banding together from a desperate fear of extinction, while the dance critics ambitiously sought to lobby for more space in the media to cover increased dance activity. Both groups looked for the collectives to solve individual frustrations. Yet an operational dilemma frequently surfaced in both meetings: critics have their jobs because of the individuality of their opinions; thus, many don't want to be associated with group views on anything. Perhaps the most refreshing comment heard at these formative sessions came from Dan Sullivan, of the *Los Angeles Times:* "Critics exist to make theatre better." Few others—many bent on satisfying their need for ego attention —seemed to agree with such a simple objective.

Throughout my year in the New York area, I was able to hear a number of critics in public lectures. For example, art critic Harold Rosenberg, of the *New Yorker,* defended his paeans for post-WW II action painters at the YHMA; Judith Crist told a Hunter College audience to be their own critics; John Simon argued that critics need more space to write their opinions in full at a New York Cultural Center convocation; Anna Kisselgoff, dance critic of *The New York Times,* explained her standards to a Dance Society meeting; *The Nation*'s Lawrence Alloway complained about the narrow-mindedness of most art critics at a seminar at the Whitney Museum of American Art; *Newsweek*'s Douglas Davis told a Museum of Modern Art meeting that many critics were uneasy with video art because of its ephemerality; and (the late) Thomas Hess, of *New York* magazine, bluntly told students at the School of Visual Arts that artists are no longer "visionaries."

At a Columbia University colloquium, film critics Vincent Canby, Roger Greenspun, James Murray, Richard Schickel and Andrew Sarris deliberated over the question "Is there an art to film criticism?" and hedged on the answer by insisting that it was both an art and a complicated craft. TV critics Neil Hickey, John J. O'Connor and Les Brown agonized that the quality of television programs was tied to business conditions at a drop-in dinner of the National Academy of Television Arts and Sciences. Six art magazine editors talked about a new sense of cooperation among their publications, which reflected how the art world itself was settling down, at a panel at Donnell Library Center. And, at SoHo's Artists Space I listened to *Artforum*'s John Coplans herald the rise of pluralism, while Barbara Rose sniffled over her demoralization with the current art scene.

Elsewhere, TV critics Ron Powers and Norman Mark told a Popular Culture Association group in Chicago they left criticism because they were worn out. At Agnes Scott College in Atlanta, Stanley Kauffmann, of the *New Republic,* defended his "moralist" stance in light of abhorrent film trends. *Time*'s Robert Hughes told a University of Georgia class that critics should only write about art that turns them on; while at Emory University, Pauline Kael told another class that Bernardo Bertolucci had joined her list of favorite filmmakers because of his sensuality.

Transcripts of critics' meetings also came to my attention. At the founding meeting of the short-lived Rock Writers Association, members debated such conflicts of interest as doing public relations for record companies and then turned right around and proposed that big-name rock groups be asked to play benefits for their organization because they "owed us a favor." Participants in the annual Music Critics Association's summer institutes detailed how the sessions had helped them improve their critical judgment and writing skill. And Stuart W. Little's report on the First American Congress of Theatre contained some details on the drama critic's role in calling for action to improve theatre.

Numerous informal interviews with critics—a beer with Ron Butler in Tulsa, lunch with Linda Winer of the *Chicago Tribune* in Stratford, Connecticut, a friendly visit with *Variety*'s Carroll Carroll in his Los Angeles apartment, or a phone chat with David Denby in Manhattan—were also useful along the way.

Colleagues in academe were also an enormous help in gathering material and shaping my work. Larry Aldridge of Georgia told me about a "Tomorrow" show featuring television critics. Bill Rivers of Stanford let me rummage through his files on West Coast critics. Don Dodson, also of Stanford, sent me a copy of a master's thesis titled "Standards for Theatre Criticism" by Donald S. Altshul. New York University undergraduate Janet Rose shared her notes from her criticism class with Clive Barnes. The late Charles Steinberg of Hunter College sent me a complete report on his study of television critics. John Johnstone of the University of Illinois at Chicago Circle answered questions about the number of critics that showed up in his media manpower study. Henri Peyre of City University of New York wrote about the difficulties of studying critical vocabulary.

Charles Martin, also of Georgia, patiently worked with me in devising computer programs to tabulate the data from my two major studies and to enrich their interpretation. Gerald Kline of the University of Minnesota spent a day going over the original raw data of a critics' study he had directed under the sponsorship of the Twentieth Century Fund. (John E. Booth of the Fund and Sandra Schmidt Oddo, who also worked on the project, also contributed to my effort by sharing its heretofore-unreported findings.)

Andy Schwartzman released a copy of the Louis Harris survey of critics commissioned by the Communications Office of the United Church of Christ. Joseph T. Klapper of CBS's research division gave me some unpublished studies he had conducted on the effects of mass communication, which helped me in that section of this work.

This list seems endless, but it only highlights the support I received. Friends in the arts often expressed constructive opinions. My own students reported articles they had read that seemed pertinent. In short, this study was really a collaborative effort, only directed and written by an individual.

Another important part of my research involved witnessing arts events first hand so I could then read critical reviews of same with greater understanding. Thus, I became a peripatetic patron of movies, plays, musical and dance concerts, art shows, television specials, fine restaurants, and an observer of architectural landmarks. As I attempted to sample America's rich cultural fare, I gained a greater appreciation for the diversity and quality of the arts available. The arts in America truly enhanced my life. And, the media—through their resident critics—served as a guide to those pleasures.

The activity—readers comparing published reviews to cultural events and testing their own reactions to both—was essential in assessing what a critic's standards were and in later criticizing the critic. From my own experience, I learned how to separate the different elements of a review (see Chapter 1 and Chapter 7) and even how to glean something of value from a critic whose judgment I fundamentally disagreed with.

Finally, in sharing the discoveries of my exploration, I have relied on honest and fair reporting, selective quotations that make important points with more credibility and flair than I was capable of and on direct and implied criticism. I have made special effort to praise certain aspects of critics' work, as well as to knock those that don't contribute to building the ideal relationship (see Model 5, page 95).

I have used a pluralistic perspective, intentionally rejecting one theoretical framework of analysis over another. My working aesthetic no doubt stemmed from the definition of popular culture I use, one proposed by Russel B. Nye, professor of English at Michigan State University and co-founder of the Popular Culture Association: popular—that which is widely dispersed, purchased, used, accepted and practiced and which reflects the values of the majority of people in a society; culture—acquainting ourselves with the best that is known or said in the world, as Matthew Arnold put it. I recognize that this definition not only neglects the synthesized meaning of the two terms but it also contains an inherent contradiction. Yet I have not been able to come up with a more suitable alternative, so will leave that problem for other scholars or readers.

In addition to pluralism, I have deliberately written this work in a fragmented style in order to cover a sweeping range of material. Naturally, I believe this approach makes the material easily accessible. In keeping with this spirit of mixing forms of communication, I have also included a scholarly report of an original research project I conducted to test reader evaluation of critical reviews.

Throughout my work, I have assumed that readers of this book are dedicated enthusiasts of the arts and intelligent readers of criticism. I also acknowledge that anyone seeking to learn about life through the popular arts must make commitment to that goal. I did and found that the best arts experiences, while vicarious, are only slightly less "real" than their sources of inspiration. Critics certainly did play a pivotal role in guiding me toward worthwhile arts experiences, as I suspect they do for most consumers of culture. However, once evaluative judgment or discrimination is offered, everyone—readers, critics and artists—is obligated to be fully aware of just what is taking place and why. This book attempts to probe for such information and understanding.

1

CRITICS AND CRITICISM— PROFILE AND PROCESS

How did criticism become part of American journalism?

Critical journalism has a long tradition in America. In the mid-1730s, for example, *The South Carolina Gazette* began publishing reviews of Otway's "Orphan," Farquhar's "Recruiting Officer," and other popular plays offered in Charleston's theatres. Book reviews also appeared in early newspapers and journals.

As the American press grew and diversified through the years, the range of criticism expanded and reviewing the arts became more accepted and institutionalized. While early movies were regularly reported and reviewed, film criticism only became an accepted practice in 1924 when *The New York Times* named Mordaunt Hall as its first regular, full-time critic. A few years later, architectural criticism was initiated when the *New Yorker* panned the Fred F. French building on Fifth Avenue.

"Instant criticism," a form that began about the turn of the century, developed because of the great newspaper rivalries of the Penny Press—Hearst, Pulitzer, et al. Criticism was treated as news and competitive news operations were bent on being first in print with a "scoop." Critics for morning newspapers were expected to rush back to their offices after an evening performance and pour out their views in time for the deadline of the next edition, then usually past midnight. (Since reviews were considerably longer in those days, often 3,500 words for major events, critics could prepare some sections of their "review" in advance—such items as plot synopsis, biographical data on the author or cast notes or other such details.)

Today, in the few remaining competitive newspaper cities and elsewhere, instant criticism is still practiced. But rush-to-print policies are beginning to diminish as press deadlines have moved up to 11:30 p.m. and few critics can produce creditable work in less than 30 minutes. Some publications, like the *New York Times*, intentionally delay reviews of some events 24 hours, so critics have a reasonable amount of time to write after a late performance. The only alternative, insists music critic Harold C. Schonberg, is to leave part of many events unreported for history.

The concept of reviews as news remains intact.

What is the legal basis for criticism?

Despite explicit protection by the First Amendment, many publishers and editors have been reluctant to criticize any subject—including the arts—for fear of libel suits or losing advertising or an overriding sense of decency. Bold editors early took the risk of offending subjects and published criticism, thus establishing, in practice, the theory that the freedom of criticism is essential to a free people, guaranteed by the Bill of Rights.

The doctrine of "fair comment and criticism" developed slowly both in England and the United States, observes New York libel lawyer and author E. Douglas Hamilton. In one landmark English case in 1808, where suit was brought against a book review, Lord Ellenborough decided in *Carr v. Howard*: "They (authors) should be liable to criticism, to exposure and even to ridicule, if their compositions be ridiculous." This case didn't express the full limits of the law, Mr. Hamilton says: "One should be able to express his opinion that something is ridiculous without accountability to anyone."[1]*

A 1929 case (*Hoeppner v. Dunkirk Printing Co.*) was more concise in expanding the doctrine:

> Every one has a right to comment on matters of public interest and concern, provided he does so fairly and with an honest purpose. Such comments or criticisms are not libelous, however severe in their terms, unless they are written maliciously.

---

* Footnotes throughout this book are tabulated in special sections at the ends of chapters.

Thus, it has been held that books, prints, pictures and statuary publicly exhibited, and the architecture of public buildings, and actors and exhibitors are all the legitimate subject of newspaper criticism, and such criticism fairly and honestly made is not libelous, however strong the terms of censure may be.[2]

In the turn-of-the-century heyday of "yellow journalism," a famous case of libel resulted when a *Des Moines Leader* critic wrote this severe and satirical review of a vaudeville song-and-dance trio known as the Cherry Sisters:

> Effie is an old jade of 50 summers; Jessie is a frisky filly of 40; and Addie, the flower of the family, a capering monstrosity of 35. Their long, skinny arms, equipped with talons at the extremities, swing mechanically, and anon, waved frantically at the suffering audience. The mouths of their rancid features opened like caverns, and the sounds like the wailings of damned souls issued therefrom. They pranced around the stage with a motion that suggested a cross between the *danse du ventre* and fox-trot—strange creatures with painted faces and hideous mien. Effie is spavined; Addie is stringhalt, and Jessie, the only one who showed her stockings, has legs with calves as classic in their outlines as the curves of a broom handle.[3]

The court ruled that the critic's strong words were justified and that sarcasm, ridicule and gross exaggeration, when based on facts, could be used to criticize a public performance if malice was not apparent. The case also reaffirmed the newspaper's right and duty to publish criticism as "privileged communication."

However, the law retains one important protection for artists. Critics may not make personal attacks on any artist or performer in their reviews. In the precedent-making (1904) case of Prof. O. L. Triggs versus *The New York Sun* (*Triggs v. Sun Printing & Publishing*) the court wrote:

> The single purpose of the rule permitting fair and honest criticism is that it promotes the public good, enables the people to discern right from wrong, encourages merit, and firmly condemns and exposes the charlatan and the cheat, and hence is based upon public policy. The distinction between criticism and defamation is that criticism deals only with such things as invite public attention or call for public comment, and does not follow a public man into his private life or pry into his domestic concerns. It never attacks the individual, but only his work. A true critic never indulges in personalities, but confines himself to the merits of the subject matter, and never takes advantage of the occasion to attain any other object beyond the fair discussion of matters of public interest and the judicious guidance of public taste.[4]

While the 1964 case of *The New York Times v. Sullivan* again broadened the interpretation of the law, today the major elements of the "fair comment and criticism" privilege include:

1. The art form or subject matter being criticized must be one of public interest.

2. Critical comments or opinions about any popular art form must be based on facts or factual situations.

3. Critics may not overstep the line laid down by the law to comment on the private life of the individual whose work or qualifications are being considered.

4. The critic's comments are a fair and honest expression of opinion, regardless of what others may think of such views.

5. Unless malice is proven, the right of critics to criticize is practically unlimited.

How many critics are active and which media do they represent?

A reasonably accurate profile of who is doing what where can be constructed by piecing together the small body of survey research that has been done on critics.

The landmark study describing the field nationwide was conducted by Louis Harris and Associates for the Office of Communication, United Church of Christ. The church agency commissioned the survey of critics as part of its efforts to improve the quality of broadcasting, especially television, and as director Rev. Everett C. Parker explained, "in recognition of the indispensable role of criticism in modern society."

> In the arts, man attempts to express his highest aspirations and deepest devotion. The good critic seeks out what is banal and untrue. As he contributes to the healthy condition of the arts, we in the church must be concerned for the health of his profession,

Rev. Parker said with idealistic optimism.

While the Harris survey emphasized the television interests of its client, it did offer much valuable information on cultural criticism in all mass media. A thousand mail questionnaires were sent out to identifiable critics—500 working for newspapers, 100 in magazines, 200 on TV and 200 on radio—in all geographic areas of the country as well as a sample of metropolitan areas and smaller cities. Five hundred editors were also surveyed.

From all media, a total of 269 critics responded to the questionnaire and Harris analysts estimated that this sample represented about one-third of all working American critics in 1970. Nearly three-quarters of all criticism is published in newspapers, Harris said. Respondents also indicated that 95 per cent of the newspapers sampled had four or five critics on their editorial staffs, but two-thirds of the other media—magazines, TV, radio— had no critics at all.

How much editorial content is devoted to arts criticism?

Very little. A survey, conducted by the University of Minnesota School of Journalism and Mass Communications for the Twentieth Century Fund, sampled 67 randomly selected newspapers in 1966 and found that the editorial space devoted to the performing arts was 1.6 per cent of the total news hole (or space given to news). More specifically, 1.2 per cent of that total was arts news and a minuscule $4/10$ of one percent was reviews, criticism or critical essays. Of the more than 10,000 news items on the arts examined in newspapers large and small, the vast majority were straight local news stories, mostly about theatre, instrumental and vocal music events. Of the 2,323 critical pieces the researchers read, about 85 per cent were locally written reviews. The performing arts events covered were music (52 per cent), theatre (36 per cent); opera, cabaret and dance comprised the rest. Reviews from the Associated Press (4.5 per cent), United Press International (2.3 per cent) and The New York Times News Service (1.8 per cent) made up the rest of criticism.

(The director of the 1966 Minnesota study, Dr. Gerald F. Kline said he believes its factual data and interpretation remain valid and that any changes would only be "glacial shifts" or minor differences.)

Which popular arts do media generally cover?

Arts coverage in the media has a fairly consistent order of priority. Eighty-nine per cent of all media have some criticism of drama, three-fourths criticize motion pictures and music and more than half cover books and television. Somewhat less than half include criticism of painting, sculpture and dance.

• • • •

Biographical footnote: A music critic for *The Los Angeles Times* has a most apt moniker: Melody Peterson.

• • • •

How does the number of critics compare to other news personnel?

It is easy to understand why cultural reportage and criticism are a tiny fraction of media content when the personnel statistics are known. In a Manpower and Public Communications survey conducted by the Academy for Educational Development, Prof. John Johnstone reported that the culture beat engaged only 2.2 per cent of the total editorial manpower pool in the American news media, which includes broadcasting, the wire services, news magazines and weekly newspapers as well as dailies. In comparison, sports personnel were an impressive 10.7 per cent of the total or nearly five times as many, and those covering politics and government were a staggering 26.9 per cent.

These statistics, while certainly disproportionate considering the much higher business volume the arts industry annually records over the sports world, are most out of balance in medium and small-sized cities where critics are non-existent and sports staffs are large. Even in a major city such as Atlanta, the *Journal's* sports staff has 13 full-time writers while the culture corner includes four full-time reviewers and one regular free lance. At the zenith, *The New York Times'* cultural staff of 32, of which 17 are critics, doesn't rival the 41-member sports staff.

Yet the coverage of the arts is growing in some places. Alfred V. Frankenstein, art critic of the *San Francisco Chronicle,* said the development of criticism on his newspaper is an important story:

> I came here as music and art critic in 1934, and for 15 years I covered all the music and all the art there was around here. Then for 16 years I had a full-time associate music-and-art critic. But in 1965, we split the department into two departments and I became art critic full time. I also have a full-time associate art critic. There are now four full-time music critics on our staff and two full-time reviewers of the jazz and rock scene, which we formerly ignored. All this signifies an enormous growth in the art life of the Bay Region plus an ever-increasing emphasis on the arts on the part of the paper.

Where does most critical writing appear?

In geographic spread, nearly one-third of all reviews were published in the press of New York, New Jersey and Pennsylvania, followed by the upper North Central states, the West Coast and the Southeast.

Newspapers in the centers of the performing arts—cities of 500,000 or larger—published about 80 per cent of all critical writing. The top three newspapers in reviews were *The New York Times, Los Angeles Times,* and *Boston Globe.* Small city dailies were found to contain almost no critical writing.

The most competent reviews come from the big newspapers in centers of culture, the Minnesota study concluded. Many newspapers slight or ignore the arts, it said, even though the press has a two fold obligation: to report and to illuminate the arts. "A newspaper that makes any pretense at reflecting the life of the community it serves has no option as to whether it will cover the arts—its only choice is whether it will cover them badly or well," the final report submitted to the Twentieth Century Fund boldly stated.

Is there an archetypal critic?

Not really. Critics are a diverse group, though some general characteristics are known. A typical critic is a 45-year old male. Although 20 per cent of critics were female at that time, it's likely that women have made some small gain in this area as the percentage of women in the media has increased slightly in the last few years to 24 per cent in 1974. Two other exceptions are worth noting: book critics tend to be older than other groups and critics in the South are generally younger than those in other regions.

Is there a difference between critics and reviewers?

Yes, but . . . the label of critic is a misnomer for the vast majority of journalists writing about the arts, though the distinction between critics and reviewers is generally blurred.

Reviewers write white-hot reactions to cultural events, relying heavily on descriptive reporting of the scope of the event as well as some of its detail. If interpretation is required, the reviewer tends to generalize and summarize. Evaluation tends to be specific—this particular work is interesting and worth attending or it isn't. Reviewers most often deal with the content of the arts, rather than their formal aspects, because the content is the most accessible outer layer. A reviewer works under the pressure of deadlines and for those on morning newspapers that often means only an hour or less to write a complete review.

The critic, however, takes a wider perspective of cultural fare and emphasizes the value of a particular event in a larger context. Criticism may attempt to place a work of art in history by comparing it with previous similar works. Or it may comment on the merit of a new work in view of other efforts by the same artist. Critics, though, are less tied to the work than the reviewers.

Critic H. L. Mencken further delineated the difference between reviewers and critics by insisting that "catalytic critics" promote a reaction between the artistic work and its spectators so everyone can understand, appreciate and enjoy the work, which is precisely what the artist intended.

"Criticism—like art—should have no *a priori* assumptions," Mencken wrote in his essay "Criticism of Criticism of Criticism."

> A critic must consider a work of art by the clarity and sincerity of expression, the force and charm of its ideas, the technical virtuosity of the artist and their originality and artistic courage.
>
> A critic must be able to get into the mind of his artist, to feel and comprehend the vast pressure of creative passion before he can understand or interpret him. The best criticism is written by those with reflective and analytical faculties and the gusto of an artist,

Mencken said.[5]

What is the difference between criticism and reviewing?

Reviewing and criticism require different disciplines and whether a daily reviewer can switch gears to criticism depends on the critic's role preference. *New York Times'* book critic Christopher Lehmann-Haupt explained the difference between daily reviewing and Sunday book criticism like this:

> I can enjoy a book and talk about my enjoyment without feeling obligated, at least as a reviewer, to say, 'How important is this book?' To a degree, that's our role, but I don't think it's our primary role. I think you want to let readers know what a pleasant, exciting, aesthetically pleasing experience it is. You don't even have time to reflect on where it fits into the broader spectrum of aesthetic developments, or the significance of the novel. I don't think it's the function of the daily review to do that.[6]

If daily reviewers have difficulty with the demands of critical essays, that chore is surely compounded if one covers more than one field, as most do.

What do most readers have in mind when they think of critics?

The critic's image seems to be widely distorted.

A few of the major critics are more famous than most of the celebrities of show business they write or talk about. One such Superstar for the majority who depend on the tube for their news and views is Gene Shalit, film and book critic on NBC's "Today" show. Shalit also appears on more than 100 of the network's affiliated stations with his nightly 90-second reviews heard also on network radio. He claims an audience of some 45 million Americans which makes him the most widely exposed critic in the country.

Shalit's formula is simple and appealing: all comments stem from his bottom-line verdict—thumbs up or thumbs down. Compared to most TV personalities, Shalit looks "funny" with his bushy hair and outlandish mustache. And he's full of wisecracks, puns and one-liners. For example, a transcribed portion of his Ten Best and Ten Worst of 1974 lists went:

> In *The Longest Yard*, Burt Reynolds wins the tight pants award for his appearance in this prison football game between inmates and the guards, two teams of interchangeable thugs. Almost every aspect of this picture is out-of-bounds, so I suggest you pass it.
>
> Lucille Ball showed up in a cement version of *Mame*, and by the time the heavy footed dancers and clumsy direction were done with, they changed the spelling to M-A-I-M.

At the other extreme, readers know of, even if they don't read, the high brow critics who write gobbledygook displays of erudition in specialized journals. Such pretentiously intellectual verbal gymnastics, often lacking any real ideas, defy comprehension, as this passage from *Artforum*, the leading periodical of the field, illustrates:

> Task performance assumed through that kind of amplification of hook into elevator cage, and with this functional context, a dramatic quality which stood in paradoxical contrast to its explicit attenuation with the context of performance proper.[7]

What this gibberish says about the art of Robert Morris is uncertain, though it's a safe bet it's not very enlightening for or influential on most consumers of the mass media.

Most critics find themselves looking for an audience with work somewhere in between these two extremes. Critics, like the arts, must relate to and connect with diversified audiences to serve and survive.

What qualities should an ideal critic have?

The drawback of trying to establish what the most important characteristics critics should possess to perform their roles effectively is that any such list is purely ideal and abstract.

Some years ago, this writer asked a number of prominent journalists what qualities newspapers looked for in prospective newsmen and created a model: curiosity, abilities to write and to think, an instinct for what is likely to be true or false, intellectual discipline, physical and nervous stamina, the ability to withstand routine without becoming monotonized, enthusiasm and energy, dedication to complete an assignment no matter how much he dislikes it, empathy and even "hamminess"—the desire to see one's byline over a good story.[8]

If critics are "journalists with a difference," as they say, then this list easily becomes applicable. Assuming that critics must have an affinity or "love" of the arts and that their personal opinions—the "I liked/hated it" verdict—matter little, only two personal attributes are consistently cited as important to performing their roles.

Knowledge of the arts and the ability to perceive and respond to the arts are the first and third choices of attributes critics cited in a recent survey. Being a talented writer—a general characteristic of the profession, similar to those in the newsman model—is the clear second choice.

Perhaps the attributes critics consider of little importance are even more revealing. In decreasing order of importance, those qualities not valued are: consistent viewpoint, responsiveness to reader and community needs, interesting personality, excellent teacher, high moral values, and highly intellectual.

A number of critics—unable to rank these characteristics—believe that all these qualities are equally essential. "It's all of these rolled into one," said Alfred V. Frankenstein, of the *San Francisco Chronicle*. "They're all related," agreed *Newsweek*'s Paul D. Zimmerman. "A thorough grounding in the art is mandatory," insisted *The New York Times'* Schonberg.

Others cite other qualities as essential: integrity, humor, wit, humility, a simultaneous ability to be involved *and* analytical, ability to think publicly and to communicate point of view as a consumer, and an open mind (which is the opposite of consistent viewpoint). Hobe Morrison, *Variety* critic, includes "respect for the art, the artist and the reader."

"A critic has to be a madly self-conscious person, very aware of himself and all of his biases and prejudices, because he has to do that job of sorting out what his particular problems are in any one experience," says Joy Boyum, of the *Wall Street Journal*. "We have to know who we are and how that relates to what's up there on the screen. Whereas the viewer who isn't committed to make comments for other people doesn't have to do that. The ideal viewer will always do that, of course, but very few of us are ideal viewers."

"The ability to be honest—to give an unequivocally personal reaction to the thing—and to know why your reaction is what it is means to know yourself and being honest with yourself is the first step toward honesty in criticism," said Mary Knoblauch, film critic, now with the *Chicago Tribune*.

"The most important thing a critic needs is a standard and it really doesn't matter what its specifics are. A devout commitment to it is the key," added the *Village Voice*'s Michael Feingold. "The public and artist can learn the weak points of a critic they respect and enjoy and even overlook them in light of his virtues. It's like having a friend; the first thing to establish is basic friendliness to the situation, which is that of always striving for the best."

What educational training do critics have?

Nearly 80 per cent of the critics are college graduates and more than a third have higher degrees. Their college educations generally are related to their chosen profession—writing—rather than their eventual critical specialty in the arts. About 51 per cent majored in English or literature, 27 per cent in journalism, 23 per cent in the fine arts or performing arts and smaller numbers in other areas. Generally, Harris analysts found, there was little correlation between a critic's college major and his field of criticism.

• • • •

Biographical footnote: Book and television critic John Leonard, aka "Cyclops," flunked out of Harvard because he spent too much time working on the *Crimson*. Leonard is now the chief cultural correspondent of *The New York Times*.

• • • •

What are the critics' religious affiliations and political viewpoints?

Despite Truman Capote's assertions that "the entire cultural press, publishing . . . criticism . . . television . . . theatre . . .

film industry . . . is almost 90 per cent Jewish-oriented,"[9] Harris reports that religious backgrounds tend to be diverse: 47 per cent of the critics are Protestant, 17 per cent are Catholic, 25 per cent are without affiliation and only 7 per cent are Jewish—although this figure rises to about 30 per cent in metropolitan centers.

Politically, the majority of critics (57 per cent) describe their views as liberal while 27 per cent said middle-of-the-road, 10 per cent, conservative and 5 per cent, radical.

• • • •

Biographical footnote: Rex Reed seems to have earned the distinction of being the only film critic ever to have been hung and burned in effigy. While an editorial writer on the campus daily at Louisiana State University, Reed wrote an editorial attacking segregation that so enraged the Ku Klux Klan that they stoned the journalism building and burned a dummy in his honor.

• • • •

How do most critics get their jobs?

Critics identify themselves basically as journalists with the same basic training, reporting skills, standards and ethics of the press as their colleagues.

About two-thirds of the critics got into the field by working in journalism rather than working in the arts, though 24 per cent reported professional experience in the arts or media which they criticize. Critics in major media tend to have more experience in the arts than others in the national sample, but this was in addition to their work experience in journalism. Critics acknowledge that there are no defined career patterns, backgrounds or prerequisites for becoming a critic.

Editors most often said they hire critics from within their own staffs since proven competence in journalism is of utmost importance. Once a critic is hired, the editors said, they receive little or no special training or supervision on the job, though a few editors said new critics are required to serve an apprenticeship with a senior critic and others encourage critics to attend seminars, lectures and discussions that add some formal training to their background.

• • • •

Biographical footnote: When her master's thesis on Italian architecture was rejected, Ada Louise Huxtable, architectural critic of *The New York Times*, left New York

University without a degree and sold furniture at Bloom-
ingdale's.

● ● ● ●

How important is experience in performing their job?

The critic's job is stable. The study of critics conducted by
this writer generally confirmed Harris' findings that critics remain in their jobs for long periods of service, somewhat of an
oddity for a profession known for its regular turnover of personnel. Harris reported that 50 per cent of critics had been in their
present jobs for six or more years and that 25 per cent had held
their positions for more than 14 years. The 1974 survey indicated
that only 15 per cent of the 107 critics surveyed had been on the
job for less than five years, 48 per cent had written criticism for 5
to 10 years and 37 per cent had worked for 15 years.

Critic Clive Barnes places high importance on arts experience. Writing in *The New York Times*, he said:

> In literature, the visual arts, in movies, even, to an extent
> through recordings, in music, a 25-year-old can become an in-
> stant critic. In the theatre—and perhaps even more in the
> dance—you have to pay your dues. I went to the theatre vir-
> tually every night of my life for ten years before I had the te-
> merity to start writing about it.[10]

Barnes believes that "informed" opinions are backed only by the
"integrity that comes from an overview of experience."

While readers might assume that critics improve in their professional performance with experience, this might not be the case.
Free lance New York theatre critic Sandra Schmidt Oddo, who
also studied critics, argues that too much experience is often as
debilitating to a critic's production as not enough. Oddo believes that most critics go through three distinct stages in their
professional careers:

When a critic first begins, he hasn't seen enough to make really insightful comparisons and evaluations. For the first five
years, then, he functions as a perennial virgin.

After gaining a wealth of experience, critics have probably
seen more work than anyone, but they retain their link to their
readers and can be of real service for a limited number of years.

At some point, they simply have seen too much and have said
all they want to say about art. These critics have become jaded
and cynical and no longer approach their task with a fresh vision
that can be relayed to readers.

Regular readers of critics should be able to tell how long a critic has been in his job by the enthusiasm conveyed in his writing if Mrs. Oddo's theory has validity.

• • • •

Biographical footnote: Clive Barnes, drama and dance critic of *The New York Post,* attended the London School of Medicine with the intention of becoming a psychiatrist.

• • • •

Are critics generally specialists or generalists?

Usually generalists in the arts. The average critic reviews two or three of the arts or media, the Louis Harris survey found, though on large metropolitan dailies critics are more likely to have a specialty and limit their writing to one or sometimes two related fields. The most frequent combinations mentioned in a 1974 survey were art and architecture, film and theatre, music and dance. Photography was covered by both art and film critics, opera mostly by music critics and other areas such as restaurant reviewing and covering cabarets and special events such as circuses and ice shows were handled by a range of critics with special interests. Most critics review books in their arts specialty.

The critic-at-large designation at a few major newspapers is an exception to the trend toward specialization. As Charles D. Champlin, entertainment editor of *The Los Angeles Times,* film critic and critic-at-large, noted, "I occasionally do almost everything."

In addition to reviewing, what other journalistic duties do critics have?

Most critics continue to utilize their journalistic background, the 1974 Critics Project learned. Only 40 per cent of the critics polled were full-time reviewers, 20 per cent of the others spent at least one-fourth of their time on non-critical journalistic duties while the remaining 40 per cent spent less than half their time reviewing. This final group includes some regular free lancers and stringers, who contribute reviews to the newspaper but who earn their major source of income elsewhere, most often teaching in a university.

Many full-time critics said they had to cover a range of the arts in order to have full-time status. Full-time specialists covering only one field were a rarity, generally working for major metropolitan dailies and newsweekly magazines.

Among the other editorial duties critics reported are staff writing, general reporting and rewrites, general feature writing, and general editing, including producing special tabloid supplements (not related to the arts). Typical of other arts stories critics produce are news stories announcing upcoming events, calendars and short fillers, "trend" stories on new developments and roundups of the current scene, interviews and celebrity profiles, features stories on sidelights, backgrounds to enhance one's appreciation of an event, "think pieces," reviews of books in their field, weekly columns and syndicated articles. At least two architecture critics also write editorials on urban development. A Chicago newspaper critic also does weekly criticism for radio and a *Los Angeles Times* critic said he does free lance writing for magazines and encyclopedias.

Some critics also double as entertainment editors and most give assignments and work with staff and free lancers, edit copy, write headlines and layout their assigned pages.

How much influence does a publication's editorial philosophy have on a critic?

Nearly half of the critics surveyed in 1974 characterized their publications as liberal; liberal publications were more likely to have a wider range of critics—including music, art, architecture and television—than others. Theatre and film critics were evenly spread among all types while book critics most often said their publications were middle-of-the-road. Conservative publications represented 16 per cent of the total and others ranged from "confused" or "schizoid" editorial policy to "quasi-radical" to no institutional editorial position (the wire services, for instance).

When asked if the editorial philosophy or tone of their medium ever influenced their writing of reviews, more than one-third of the critics said there was some or a little influence. Five per cent said editorial restrictions did limit their personal expression, while the remainder said editorial policies had no influence on their work whatsoever or at least they weren't aware of any policy affecting them.

• • • •

Biographical footnote: New Yorker film critic Pauline Kael once worked as a seamstress, cook, textbook ghost writer and manager of an art film theatre before becoming a critic. In 1966, she was fired as *McCall*'s film critic after panning "The Sound of Music."

• • • •

Who do critics report to and what kind of institutional conflicts arise from these relationships?

Although a few of the noted critics working for metropolitan dailies and others work independently or without direct supervision in the press hierarchy, most critics are accountable to an editor or editors and this relationship, while generally satisfactory, is a potential source of conflict.

As the Harris study showed, the recent Critics' Project confirmed that critics tend to be responsible to at least one editor—an entertainment editor, news editor, features editor, managing editor, senior editor, editor-in-chief, and, in some cases, the publisher. In smaller city newspapers, the critic usually reports directly to the city editor or managing editor. Critics in television and radio are often under the program director or station manager.

Conflicts arise when editors don't share the same view of the functions of criticism as critics. *The Associated Press Managing Editors' Guidelines* give one indication of the possible gap. One part of the guidelines that tells editors how to cover culture reads:

> The problem of the M.E. is to publicize the good, skip the bad. This requires some space and one or more intelligent reporters willing to devote time and study to the subject matter, and seasoned sufficiently to shun the hokum that permeates so much of the artistic world.
> Beware of the arty staffer. A reporter fresh from the realities of the police beat may do better.[11]

Fortunately, for critics and the arts, most editors are enlightened enough to ignore such hokum from the A.P., though certainly evidence does show that the arts are given meager coverage in many newspapers and virtually none in others, apparently a result of heeding such advice.

Critics, and other reporters too, differ from editors in two other important areas: political viewpoint and religious affiliation, central parts of one's value system. The Harris survey substantiated that critics tend to be less often Protestant, less often affiliated with religion and more often left-of-center politically than their editors, which, Harris suggests, indicates "a potential

strain in the supervisory relationship" and "a process of negotia-
tion or compromise between some critics and their editors con-
cerning the content of reviews."

What kind of restrictions, either institutional or personal, affect critics?

Sexual works, including X-rated and sexploitation movies,
present critics with tricky choices and a range of attitudes to deal
with them. Some newspapers that refuse advertising of X-rated
films also shun editorial copy on them. Others, such as the *Cleveland Plain Dealer*, let the critic decide the matter. Emerson Batdorff reports, "We don't allow display advertising on X-rated
movies but I can review them if they have merit in my eyes or are
newsworthy." Roger Ebert, of the *Chicago Sun-Times*, has similar
flexibility, "I review what I choose to review. In general, I review
all movies of even slight importance, but only 'major' hard-core
stuff."

Despite any editor-imposed restrictions, some critics ignore
some works because they find them tasteless and trivial. "We vol-
untarily shy away from porn," says *New York Daily News* film
critic Ann Guarino.

Not so for others. "Sex, religion and politics are all verbo-
ten," moans Stewart Klein, a drama critic on New York television station WNEW. "Especially comics like David Steinberg or
Mort Sahl. I once filmed a Steinberg routine only to go on the air
with it and discover most of the sound had been erased."

The restriction of using language that reflects the work being
reviewed is another complaint. Grouses *Time* drama critic, T. E.
Kalem, "We can't print the words that are used on stage."

One architecture critic on the West Coast mentions other,
more subtle restrictions that perhaps others choose to ignore or
refuse to report. His four restrictions are: "turf (where is the line
between me and the other critics?), sacred cows (friends of the
publisher), political and business gods and heretical thoughts."
Perhaps these comments only underscore the relative nature and
perception of absolute freedom.

● ● ● ●

Biographical footnote: John Simon and Alan Rich, colleagues at *New York* were classmates at Harvard in the
1940s, where Rich was music director for the college
radio station and Simon led a workshop that presented
plays on the station. Upon graduation, both taught col-

lege for a while and then quit for the same reason—departmental politics. When Simon's first collection of reviews was published (*Acid Test* in 1963), Rich, then writing for *The New York Times*, panned it. Later, Rich admitted, "I honestly forgot who it was, not that it would have made any difference."

• • • •

Do critics have a free rein in reviewing the arts?

All but a few drama and film critics said they had a completely free hand in choosing what to review. "Good taste" and the concept of a "family newspaper" were considered acceptable restraints. But budgetary restrictions and inadequate space for reviews (especially on Monday after a host of weekend events) were cited as serious problems.

Most critics claim reviewing freedom. "My personal taste is the only restriction," says Lawrence DeVine, film and theatre critic of the *Detroit Free Press.* A more socially responsible attitude was reflected by Peter Altman of the *Minneapolis Star:* "Our only guide is that we don't ignore events of wide popular interest."

Cosmopolitan magazine carries reader concern to a saccharine extreme. Film critic Liz Smith says, *"Cosmo* doesn't want critics to be too critical. . . . We are 'lovers' and recommenders."

If given a choice, do critics tend to review only the "best" works available, avoiding the "worst"?

Nearly three-fourths of the critics attempt to review all cultural offerings possible, without making prior selective judgment about the quality of the work.

Of those who try to cover the spectrum of the arts in their communities, a number offered explanations for their catholic approach. "I wish to present a representative picture of current work," says Robert Marsh, music critic of the *Chicago Sun-Times.* *New York's* Alan Rich selects work to be reviewed by a more refined version of a similar criterion, "I try to decide what is important to, or symptomatic of, today's culture scene."

More representative of the majority of critics who try to cover their fields fairly is Robert Jennings, of the *Memphis Commercial Appeal*, who says, "Quality of the work only rarely is a decisive factor in reviewing or not reviewing."

Some book, film and music critics tend to review only the

"best" works and avoid the "worst." Book critics say they have a responsibility to review both good and bad books if the works or authors are "in the news." Several film critics admitted they avoided certain type of low-budget movies, for example: motorcycle pictures, kung fu movies, black ghetto films, drive-in exclusives and exploitation x-rateds.

"Time doesn't permit every film to be reviewed, so I must be selective and consider the likelihood of the film's having quality," said critic Dorothy Smiljanich, of the *St. Petersburg Times.* Jim Shertzer, of the *Winston-Salem (N.C.) Journal*, leans on social responsibility for his selectivity, "I avoid things I suspect will be bad or not worth coverage or of sufficient reader interest."

"I review what I don't like only when it is of general interest, i.e., a big movie. There's no point in reviewing a bad, small film," adds *Newsweek*'s Paul D. Zimmerman.

Village Voice drama critic Michael Feingold observes of his own reviews, "Notices on bad works tend constantly toward being 'cursory notices'." *Milwaukee Journal* art critic James M. Auer is more emphatic on the same point: "I tend not to waste space demolishing the obvious incompetents."

"I try to talk about works about which something useful can be said. Schlock precludes this," insists Clifford A. Ridley, of the now defunct *National Observer*.

Not so, argues television critic of *The New York Times*, John J. O'Connor, who says he reviews everything because "the worst can also be illuminating."

Other critics believe that effective criticism of the bad can improve the whole. "A critic is also a vulture who clears off the bad," says Norman Mark, former TV critic of the *Chicago Daily News.*

"I think it is occasionally necessary to find something that needs to be exposed as a fraud or cheat or worthless in order to warn the public against it," adds the late Ralph J. Gleason, music critic for the *San Francisco Chronicle* and *Rolling Stone* at the time of his death in 1975.

Tulsa Tribune entertainment writer Bill Donaldson says that selecting the best and avoiding the worst is circumstantial. "It, unfortunately, is the tendency for a one-man band responsible for all entertainment criticism in a market this size."

A more stifling predicament was: "In Los Angeles, this is not a problem since almost everything is mediocre," quips architectural critic John Pastier.

A few top critics can be selective for status-tied reasons. "At this stage, I select the things that most interest me," says *The New York Times*' Pulitzer Prize-winning critic Schonberg. Since Schonberg is the first-string critic, he takes his choice of assignments and leaves the rest for other staff critics to cover. Other *Times'* first-stringers are known to follow the same practice.

Do reviews go through the traditional copy flow? What problems stem from editing?

Obviously, the processing of copy is the major source of contention between critics and editors. Nearly half of the critics recently reported that their reviews were generally edited by only one editor or slotman on the copy desk, while an additional one-third of the critics said their reviews went through two editors to get into publication.

The two-editor flow had no consistent pattern but several common combinations were as follows: through culture editor to copy desk; through metro or city editor to copy desk; through managing editor (or assignment M.E.) to copy desk; and through features editor to copy desk.

The copy flow is more complicated on large metropolitan dailies and critics at *Newsday,* the *Los Angeles Times* and *Minneapolis Tribune* said copy had to clear four editors enroute to print.

A healthy 10 per cent of the critics said that they edited their own copy and trimmed it themselves to fit their allotted space.

How much reviews are actually edited and the impact of copy editors on the published work seems to vary widely. Nearly all critics said editors never (65 per cent) or rarely (30 per cent) make major or substantial changes in their reviews. A few critics of metropolitan dailies explained: *"New York Times'* critics' copy is rarely touched unless there's an obvious error. Critics' copy is more or less sacrosanct." A *Wall Street Journal* critic said copy was "edited very little." A *Boston Globe* critic added, "Except for chops for length, which happen in the composing room, my copy is untouched." Several critics said editors made changes only after consultation with the writer and "never without consent."

Nearly half the critics reported that their reviews were occasionally or frequently trimmed to fit the space available, while the other half said their work was rarely or never cut. "We write to fit" was the latter group's standard.

Slightly less than half the critics said editors made minor changes—copy style, spelling, sentence structure and proofreading corrections—in their work either occasionally or frequently, while the others said this rarely or never occurred.

Despite the frequency of any editing done to reviews, about

55 per cent of the critics said that copy editors' contributions made little difference in the final analysis. Only 20 per cent said editors improved or helped clarify copy.

But nearly one-fourth demurred and said editors either weakened the impact of their review or destroyed their personal style of expression. Typical complaints were that editors lopped out a paragraph that was important or changed words that obscured the meaning of the sentence.

When are the peak periods of critical activity?

As one might expect, critics are busiest when the arts are the most active—on weekends and holidays. Thus, reviews are most often published on Mondays, generally light days for hard news. Wednesdays and Fridays are also peak weekdays. The month of December is the busiest month for critics, the Minnesota study learned, followed by October, March and November in descending order of activity.

August, not surprisingly, is the slowest month for reviewers, so those who must meet a regular schedule of articles often resort to "think pieces" or features during that slack review period.

Given this fluctuation, how are critics allotted space (and time) for reviews?

Editorial space for arts coverage is another source of conflict between editors and critics. In fact, one function of every critics' organization is to lobby with editors for more space. The assumption is that the group might influence a stubborn editor that an individual critic can't persuade.

Many newspapers group their reviews in an arts and amusements page or section, often with cabaret, theatre and movie advertising. While some of these sections are substantial—the most impressive is the *Washington Post*'s "Style" section which often runs three to four pages on the arts—the average newspaper allots little more than a single page to arts coverage; and since advertising occupies at least 60 per cent of each page, the amount of space is usually around two full columns, or roughly 1600 words.

Certainly metropolitan papers in Los Angeles, San Francisco, Miami, Chicago, Boston, Philadelphia and New York have more than twice as much space available as the average, but their coverage must be measured against many papers that have little or no regular space for the arts. Another consideration that critics point out is seasonal variation. From October through June, the peak periods of arts activity, the arts section may be allotted much more space than it will for the four off-season months.

The productivity of critics reflects this variation, too. At the height of the arts season, a critic may write six or eight or even ten reviews a week, while in the August doldrums he may write only one review a week, or more sensibly, take a holiday and do none.

Most critics write an average of three reviews a week; just as many write less than three as do more. TV critics are usually expected to produce five weekday reviews. Art critics may review four or five shows in a long review for a weekend edition. A recent survey indicates that architecture and book critics produce the fewest reviews per week while film and art critics are the most prolific. Music, TV and theatre critics follow in order.

Nearly two-thirds of the critics regularly write critiques or analytical articles with longer perspective weekend entertainment sections, usually part of the large Sunday newspaper. (At one recent count, more than 600 newspapers published entertainment sections in their Sunday editions.) Film and music critics are much more likely to contribute critiques or critical essays than theatre or TV reviewers. Art and architecture critics, who are less event-oriented than others, are also regularly featured in these expanded art sections. Book critics often have a separate page or pages devoted to books and a few major newspapers still have a special section for books.

How long is a typical review?

Reviews vary in length, often dependent on cultural news value, editorial policy and lots of complicated factors. In general, though, the average length in the national sample was 11 to 15 column inches or in the 500-word range. Critics on major metropolitan dailies generally have much more space available and reviews run considerably longer, most often from 14 to 23 column inches or from 550 to 925 words.

"Space is more of a concern than the writer's time," art critic James M. Auer, of the *Milwaukee Journal*, was quick to value. A Chicago film critic said her paper gave the music and drama critics on the staff two more column inches for their reviews, which annoyed her but apparently confirms Auer's point.

When Louis Harris asked selected influential critics if more space for longer reviews would improve the quality of criticism, most agreed because they could give more detail, explain the social context, outline historical trends and be more "balanced, fair and objective." Others who disagreed thought longer reviews did not mean better and that the public preferred short reviews that serve as a quick guide and source of evaluation, not merely analysis of the arts.

How much time does a critic have to prepare and write a review?

While it is well known that critics of morning newspapers who review late evening concerts and plays generally have less than two hours to write their reviews before deadline, one also finds that television critics generally have less than two hours for their reviews, though a few TV critics said they needed more time to prepare and write. Film critics work within the two to five hour range and book and architecture critics say their writing often takes more than a single work day to produce.

Los Angeles architecture critic John Pastier says some complex and controversial subjects, such as city plans, may take more than a week to write about. From that extreme to the other, music critic Mary Nic Shenk, of the *St. Petersburg Times*, dreams of having a full hour to write late concert reviews for the next a.m. edition instead of the usual 30 minutes.

How much preparation is necessary to write a review?

Quality reviews that provide readers with in-depth background on a particular work generally require advance preparation and research. A few critics scoff at including background in a review and prefer just to deal with the work itself. More often, though, critics do bone up on any available resource that may help them perform their role with ease and insight.

Voluminous reading on anything that impinges on art is the broad approach. More specifically, some music critics familiarize themselves with a particular work before going to a performance by listening to recordings of it or studying the score. Drama critics often like to read a play before seeing the performance. Movie critics may want to read the original work, if a film is adapted from a novel or play, as a starting point of comparison. If a critic has written about an artist or performer before, he may check on his previous comments to refresh his memory on any strengths and weaknesses, and to be prepared to note any development in one's career.

Generally, critics rely on their own personal experience as background and on common reference works such as "The Filmgoer's Companion." Newspaper libraries, too, are often mined for previous profiles and relevant material. While many critics say they'll use anything that will throw light on the work being reviewed, less than half rely on interviews with the principals involved, press releases and reviews of their colleagues. This material—evidently considered too biased to have any value—is generally avoided.

Critics new to the job and those writing about local artists for whom there are no published references appear more willing to use any available materials than others.

A critics regimen—witnessing the important works in his field every day, week, month, year—quickly causes him to amass an impressive storehouse of (personal and professional) experience. *New Yorker* film critic Pauline Kael sees 600 films each year. Clive Barnes of *The New York Post* usually attends 10 theatre and dance events a week.

"I believe you are what you write, and the better prepared you are, the better you write," says Richard Christianson, a Chicago critic.

● ● ● ●

Biographical footnote: Gene Shalit, film and book critic on NBC's "Today" Show, edited his fourth grade newspaper, "The Forlorn News."

● ● ● ●

Do critics think the time available for writing is adequate?

Yes. As journalists used to working under the pressure of deadlines, critics overwhelmingly say the time they now have to prepare a review is adequate. Their explanations and comments on time reflect different attitudes:

"If you work on a morning newspaper and 45 minutes isn't enough time to do a deadline review, you're in the wrong medium. Write for a monthly. The notion that a newspaper critic does a better job with more time is, for the most part, nonsense," said Chicago film critic Mary Knoblauch.

"There's never enough time to do a job to perfection," quipped *Milwaukee Journal* book editor Leslie Cross.

"I can rarely think of an occasion on which I did not have enough time to do a proper article. From time to time, I have too much time and in my dilatory fashion, will wait until the last minute," confessed Joe Pollock, film critic of the *St. Louis Post-Dispatch.*

Veteran music critic Alan Rich, of *New York* magazine, offered, "A qualified critic with proper educational background needs *no* time to prepare because his lifetime is preparation enough."

Most complaints of needing more time were reasonable enough: Joe Meade of the *San Diego Union* wanted to see some films more than once before writing; Dorothy Smiljanich of the *St. Petersburg Times* said that to do an in-depth analysis she only needed three or four hours and some background research, "but that is seldom possible."

Bettelou Peterson, TV columnist of the *Detroit Free Press,* espoused equivocal pragmatism in not answering how much time she might need ideally, "It varies so much. . . . As in all writing, one review can be easy, another hard."

The *New York Times* solved the problem for its critics when it decided to wait a day after the event to publish the review in order to give critics time to think and write. But *Times'* music critic Harold C. Schonberg says he writes his reviews in less than an hour after a performance. Here's why:

> Criticism is not a matter of snap judgment, yet any professional critic knows almost immediately whether or not he is in the presence of talent. The actual review may be the product of an hour's work, but the critic is bringing to the particular event 10, 20 or in some cases 50 years of experience in his art. He has heard more than most professional musicians, is a better historian than most, and has in his memory a set of performance values established by the important musicians of a generation.[12]

While others would like the luxury of a full day to mull over their ideas and to write, many critics wouldn't. "Without a deadline, I might still be working on my first review 25 years ago," says grinning *San Francisco Examiner* TV critic Dwight Newton.

What do critics consider the most important element of their review?

Certainly, asking for a simple answer to a complex question may not produce any valuable insights into the issue but some tendencies and preferences are discernible. One such probe is asking critics to rank in order of importance the three essential elements of all reviews: description, interpretation, and evaluation. While some critics balked at the "absurdity" of the task and others said that they simply were all vital, about half said that the analysis and interpretation of the work being reviewed was the significant element. The remainder—divided into nearly equal groups—preferred either evaluation or description of the work.

Several individual responses offered divergent views: Joseph Gelmis, film critic of *Newsday*, said that "recognizing talent and supporting it" is the most important part of a review. Another said that the ranking depended on the work under consideration, that it may be more important to evaluate a concert performance than the work performed since it was a classical work.

What is the value of description?

A descriptive overview of a work orients the reader who didn't witness the event and who wants to know what it was like. Many critics write reviews apparently presuming their readers will understand their interpretive and evaluative comments without such a summary statement. But the best critics don't leave out this essential.

Martin Bernheimer, music critic of the *Los Angeles Times*, for instance, capsulized the program of the Los Angeles Philharmonic's Beethoven marathon with this terse paragraph: "The ingredients were familiar: chamber music at the outset, something akin to an orchestral orgy at the end. For the grand climax, there had to be the Ninth Symphony. What else?" [13]

The *New York Times'* television critic John J. O'Connor briefly described "Honor Thy Father," a CBS made-for-TV-movie about the Mafia, with this impressionist overview:

> The basic ingredients are familiar. Black overcoats, ominous family gatherings, conversations sprinkled with Sicilian phrases, bear hugs, emotional outbursts, friendly pats on the cheek, attacks and counterattacks—they are all here, drenched in lush music. [14]

Dance writing requires accurate description for readers to be able to "visualize" the event. Deborah Jowitt, of the *Village Voice*, deftly sets the scene of Alwin Nickolais' "Tribe" with this passage:

> In the beginning the men swim miraculously through a red glow; actually they're belly-down on skateboards. A little later, the women straddle the men and ride with them; some of them stand in rigid positions looking like stone goddesses aboard sacred alligators. The dancers at first wear pale formfitting suits that cover their heads and show you dark, jagged eyeholes, but

later they appear in briefs (the men) and body stockings (the women). . . .[15]

Without such verbal imagery to recreate the dance, further discussion—interpretation or evaluation—exists in an abstract void that's mostly meaningless to those not at the concert.

Can reviewers really interpret?

The interpretation of a work, especially under the pressure of an hour deadline, is exasperating for many reviewers. Complex works are intentionally ambiguous and open to a variety of plausible meanings. Time for reflection to puzzle out intricacies just isn't available, so reviewers who attempt interpretation must go with the most apparent and accessible possibility. Others prefer to present detailed plot summaries and let the reader decide what it means.

Some reviewers simply dismiss any implications of a work. For example, when the film version of Peter Benchley's best-selling novel opened in mid-1975, *The New York Times'* Vincent Canby wrote:

> "Jaws" is, at heart, the old standby, a science-fiction film. It opens according to time-honored tradition with a happy-go-lucky innocent being suddenly ravaged by the mad monster, which, in "Jaws," comes from the depths of inner space—the sea as well as man's nightmares. Thereafter, "Jaws" follows the formula with fidelity. . . .
>
> If you think about "Jaws" for more than 45 seconds you will recognize it as nonsense. . . .[16]

In commenting on works difficult to interpret and assess, *The Washington Post* "Style" section staff writers provide an unusual model for continuing critical dialogue, as well as persistence, to illuminate such work. The *Post*'s coverage of Tom Stoppard's "Jumpers," which played at the Kennedy Center in early 1974, illustrates their efforts:

Drama critic Richard L. Coe, in a mixed review following opening night, devoted one paragraph to interpretation of the play and cited Stoppard's target as "moral philosophy versus pragmatism at a time when men are walking on the moon. It is more than clear that Stoppard is mocking both philosophers and worldlings. . . ."

The following Sunday columnist Alan M. Kriegsman, unimpressed with the flattery heaped on Stoppard by London and New York critics, took a harsher stance and told *Post* readers:

What you'll expect, given a play in which professors double as acrobats, throw wild parties and discuss the existence of God, is an uproarious farce with profound overtones. What you'll get—if you can ignore the packaging and attend to the product—will be a mixture of leaky puns and pseudo-cerebral humbug.

It may be a minority opinion, but it seems to me that Stoppard's reputation has been inflated far beyond the young author's power to sustain it. . . .[17]

A month later, after Coe revisited the play and mused on its meaning, he wrote a much more detailed interpretive response:

"Jumpers" is a play in humorous perspective about our chaotic present, its central figure an endearing deeply-read professor who accepts that everyday existence is as quixotically jumbled as his own intellectual voyagings and who finds that the conflicting minutiae of his philosophical probings are reflected, as in a crazy house mirror, by the complex maze of his personal life. . . .

The working word in my personal definition of the play is "accepts." That is George's essential ebullience, he accepts wherever life leads. He keeps looking for answers, and while, to be sure, there are none, it is up to Remak Ramsay's ringingly spoken Archie to suggest Stoppard's assertion of faith:

"Do not despair—many are happy much of the time; more eat than starve, more are healthy than sick, more durable than dying . . . Hell's bells and all's well . . . wham, bam, Thank you, Sam."[18]

Works of art that provoke bi-polar evaluative responses—ecstatic raves or excoriating pans—often get short shrift on description or interpretation. Writing in *Women & Film*, Michael Shedlin assessed critical reaction to the Richard Rush film "Freebie & the Bean" and found 57 negative reviews and only 15 positive. Among the hostile reviewers, Rex Reed called the film one of the worst of the year, *Variety*'s Murf blasted it as "tasteless" and "funny as a burning orphanage" and *The Kansas City Times*' Giles M. Fowler wretched, "The movie is worse than a blunder; it is an act of barbarism . . . a Christmas stocking filled with razor blades." Of the few favorable reviews, Candice Russell of the *Miami Herald* was the most effusive: "One of the year's funniest . . . a heady mixture of comic-book fantasy and grueling realism." Shedlin's most important discovery, though, was that only one critic (Gar Smith of the *Berkeley Barb*) offered an interpretation that correctly pinpointed the filmmakers' intention: "The director is warning that the average pedestrian is more inane, more aggressively narrow-minded, more abusively racist than Freebie Waters. . . ."[19]

Shedlin wondered why reviewers hated the film and misunderstood its moral/social issues while the public who trouped to the box office (it grossed nearly $5 million in three months) apparently found it communicative and entertaining. Shedlin's answer was

> I think the critics are unhappy because the film upsets them and withholds from them their comfortable liberal/conservative resolutions. It makes them feel ambivalent. It is too real for them despite its lyrical and farcical abstractions, too suffused with contradictions to be rationalized or categorized, so they shut it out like someone who won't get high because they're afraid to lose control.[20]

Whether the ideological posture of critics is any different from the public's is uncertain. A wide spectrum of critical opinion is readily available in periodicals of all persuasions. Anti-establishment social messages have often been heralded in other films and other media, so it's doubtful that "Freebie" was neglected for that reason alone, as Shedlin suggests.

Occasionally, a critic, like Alan Rich of *New York*, will admit his limitations in dealing with a specific work. Writing a review of a new record album by Stanley Silverman and Richard Foreman, Rich concluded by stating: "I don't think I've really told you very much about *Elephant Steps*, and it does defy description. What it doesn't defy, however, is evaluation: it is a great, lovable work."[21]

What is a critic's verdict?

Readers of reviews assume that critics evaluate and will reach a verdict about the work under consideration, even though critics may not think that task is of utmost importance. Nonetheless, nearly all reviews can be lumped into one of three categories of verdicts: favorable, unfavorable and mixed (which includes both positive and negative critical comments).

• • • •

Biographical footnote: Jill Johnston, one-time dance critic for the *Village Voice*, is credited with introducing "WOW" into the critic's vocabulary as a term of aesthetic approval.

• • • •

How do critics estimate their own output of reviews by verdict?

Although a sizable minority of the critics found it impossible (or, in some cases, even ridiculous) to attempt to assess their total critical output over the years by verdicts, more than 80 per cent gave a reasonable guestimate.

By grouping the individual responses into five categories of verdicts, one surprisingly finds that the "Thumbs Up-Thumbs Down" type of critic—those who write mostly favorable or unfavorable and few mixed reviews are in the distinct minority, with only two per cent of the total.

The largest group of critics—about 36 per cent—write mostly mixed reviews with few clearly favorable or unfavorable. This category is typified by one's comment, "Oh well, nobody's perfect!"

The most favorable reviewers made up 26 per cent of the total, while those who thought they wrote mostly unfavorable reviews were 19 per cent. The remaining 16 per cent said their output was nearly divided evenly among the three choices.

By type of critics, book, art and music critics tended to characterize their verdicts more often as favorable or mixed, while drama critics most often said their reviews were mixed. Television, film and architecture critics were divided according to review verdicts.

Obviously, critical assessment of works says as much about the work or the vitality of the arts in a given community as it does about the standards of a given critic.

"A critic will see far more incompetence than competence in the theatre going," states *New York* drama critic John Simon. Simon and Martin Gottfried are reputed to be the most negative critics (they'd argue that their standards are higher than others). Though no proof exists to prove that distinction, the two are often reviled as "vicious" and "indecent," "misdirected," and guilty of "petty fault-finding" and "bitchy nit-picking." Et cetera.

● ● ● ●

Despite the public impression that all critics are cynics, wise guys and hit men, Walter Kerr insists that negative criticism does not come easy:

"It is much, much more difficult to write an unfavorable review than a favorable one. I'll tell you why. To begin with, the reviewer is a human being like any other member of the audience and, like every other member of the audience, he doesn't settle down in the theatre hoping to be bored. He isn't secretly praying to be driven out of his skull for the next two and one half hours, which means that his real hope is that the show will be enchanting or at least tolerable. With the curtain up, he listens, takes notes, bides his time for just as long as the entertainment at hand will let him; he still doesn't want his evening ruined, any more than the backers do. Then the frost sets in. Sooner or later a genuinely poor show is going to display its essential lifelessness, its inability to compel attention or stir emotion. And, as it loses energy, so does the critic. He wants to laugh, and can't. He wants to take a lively interest in the non-characters set before him, and can't. He wants to fortify himself with a drink during intermission, as so many other members of the audience are so intelligently doing, and can't (he still has to write about it, if possible with some degree of accuracy). By degrees, the salt goes out of him, he slumps spiritually and then physically, he frets, rues the day when he ever sought such employment, bemoans the fact that he'll have to write *another* bad notice on top the four he's recently written, feels himself progressively drained. Two acts. Three acts. Lifelessness begets lifelessness."[22]

• • • •

Critical Note: Don't pay any attention to the critics; don't even ignore them."—Samuel Goldwyn.

• • • •

NOTES FOR CHAPTER 1

[1]"Fair Comment Doctrine," by E. Douglas Hamilton, *Media & Consumer*, Vol. 1, No. 10, Sept. 1973, page 14.

[2]*Dangerous Words*, Philip Wittenberg, New York: Columbia University Press, 1974, page 94.

[3]Ibid., page 104.

[4]Ibid., page 117.

[5]*Prejudices, First Series.* H. L. Mencken, New York: Knopf, 1919, page 25.

[6]"Year-End Roundtable on the Arts," *The New York Times*, Dec. 27, 1972.

[7]*Artforum* quotation attributed to Annette Michaelson, in "Is Criticism Necessary," by Ingrid Wiegand, *Art Gallery*, Jan. 1972, page 10.

[8]Master's thesis, *Is Journalism Education Worthwhile*, by John W. English, Columbia University Graduate School of Journalism, 1966, pages 7–10.

[9]"Interview with Truman Capote," *Rolling Stone*, April 12, 1973, page 46.

[10]"Who Has the Right to Write Criticism," by Clive Barnes, *The New York Times*, Section II, Dec. 7, 1975, page 30.

[11]*Associated Press Managing Editor Guidelines*, Fall 1969, page 46.

[12] "Not Every Critic Disliked the 'Eroica,' " by Harold C. Schonberg, *The New York Times*, Sept. 9, 1973, page 15.

[13] "Happy Birthday, Dear Ludwig," by Martin Bernheimer, *The Los Angeles Times*, Dec. 18, 1974, page 26.

[14] "Bologna Portrays Bill of 'Honor Thy Father'," by John J. O'Connor, *The New York Times*, March 1, 1973, page 95.

[15] "How Do You Tell If It's Human," by Deborah Jowitt, *Village Voice*, June 14, 1975, page 79.

[16] "Entrapped by 'Jaws' of Fear," by Vincent Canby, *The New York Times*, June 21, 1975, page 19.

[17] "Crosscurrents," by Alan M. Kriegsman, *Washington Post*, March 3, 1974, page 2.

[18] " 'Jumpers': Further Elaboration on Its Meaning," by Richard L. Coe, *Washington Post*, March 24, 1974, page 2.

[19] "Ideological Massage; 15 Notes on Freebie and the Bean," by Michael Sheldin, *Women & Film*, Vol. 2, No. 7, Summer 1975, page 99.

[20] Ibid., page 100.

[21] "The Lively Arts," by Alan Rich, *New York*, Nov. 4, 1974, page 91.

[22] "Is It Easier to Pan Than to Praise," by Walter Kerr, *The New York Times*, August 14, 1977, pages 3–4.

2

THE MULTIPLE ROLES
OF CRITICS

How has the role of the critic evolved?

The role of the critic is ever shifting. In earlier times, the best critics *were* the great writers, i.e., Plato, Wordsworth, Goethe, Coleridge. In the 20th Century, criticism was separated from the artistic function. Modern civilized society, with its proliferating cultural offerings and saturated media coverage, demanded full-time critics, indeed a range of reviewers, each dealing with only a small part of the whole. Their broadly defined role was, and is, to report, analyze and assess the range of the popular arts.

But the exact role critics play in today's culture is changing, too. *New York Times* art critic Hilton Kramer observes that the recent decline in scholarly journals and literary quarterlies—outlets for serious, highbrow criticism—has pushed criticism in newspapers and mass circulation magazines, which dwell on the popular culture, into playing the role "whether it wants to or not" the more specialized, smaller-audience, highbrow criticism used to play.[1] Psychologist Robert S. Albert, writing in the *Journal of Social Psychology*, believes that the critic's role has become blurred and less direct because many persons now have so much first-hand experience with cultural fare that they now follow the "every man his own critic" ideal.[2] The critic's role is thus reduced

43

to that of a socializer ("one who instructs another in socially prescribed modes of behavior and thought," says Albert) or a reference group for those active arts consumers.

Mass audiences, for the arts as well as sports or the media, are essentially spectators. People are generally seeking diverting entertainment or pleasure, rather than education or enlightenment. Even the highly educated population looks toward critics as guides to fare that will satisfy special interests. As cultural opportunities increased, the task of choosing one experience over another began to involve more risk and critics' previews of works became an institutionalized way of aiding the consumer in the difficult task of selection. Critics had to try to assess "value" to works, to say what was "good," what was "taste" in order to help readers make choices.

Perhaps because of the parasitic relationship between the critic and art, criticism has rarely been considered as creative an act as the production of the art work being reviewed. Heretofore, it has been assigned a secondary value, though, there are hints that this relationship is changing in some fields. Conceptual art, for example, depends heavily on the reportage and documentation by critics because artists are only interested in the "idea" of art and not finished art objects. Conceptual art, too, attempts to be "beyond criticism" since artists never deliver a product that can be evaluated by the usual criteria.

The subject matter of criticism is the critic's reactions to and preferences in art. While standards can be applied to form, they rarely work on content, which, after all, is vicarious social experience as expressed by an artist. So, critics slowly define themselves by selecting who they write about and how they react to the ideas of that artist. Exalting one artist over another also lends credence to one set of ideas, which critics subsume to be "right" and "good" because they are understood and shared.

On *The New York Times*, for example, this approach is practiced by simply assigning critics with an affinity for a certain type of art—let's say Off Broadway and experimental theatre—to its coverage. That critic, Mel Gussow, creates a certain image in dealing with the unconventional. If he began reviewing traditional Broadway plays, he certainly would re-define himself due to both the projective nature of art and criticism.

• • • •

Critical Note: "A critic is a virgin who wants to teach a Don Juan how to make love," said Tristan Bernard.

• • • •

How do critics define their own roles?

A critic is a cultural phenomenon as well as a cultural force. Anyone holding the job in a mass circulation publication and writing regular criticism that reaches a vast audience becomes a recognizable celebrity, by virtue of his position alone. If a critic also performs effectively in that position, he can become a powerful force in the community's arts, an opinion leader to his audience. If he does only a mediocre job, he can still dictate to his audience what to think about, even if he can't convince them what to think about it.

Psychologist Albert concludes that the critic "operates as a cultural mediator or gatekeeper between artists, who may be the 'real' critics in their more highly personal but interpretive communications, and the public, with its own indirect interest in such communications." Of that central role, Albert says, "The critic functions as a channel of cultural products and therefore of culture itself; the flow being through himself and his work."[3] Albert's point is that critics themselves define their own roles and then fulfill them, most often operating without any direct regulation by media management or little social control from the public. The only restraining factors are self-imposed "standards" or accepted values of "taste."

When critics surveyed in 1974 were asked to assign priorities to different aspects of their perceived role, most said they were reporters of artistic events first, educators second and promoters of the arts third. A few conceded that less important aspects of their job were arbiters of taste, sources of feedback to producers and of advice to artists, in that order.

Others had different views of their role. Several thought critics should inform and advise readers about cultural events, so the public could choose what it might want to see. A few thought their major responsibility was to write interesting pieces that would stimulate people to think about the works. Robert Evett, book editor of the *Washington Star-News*, says critics serve as "explicators, entertainers and reflectors of sophisticated taste."

Newsday film critic Joseph Gelmis believes critics must be "aesthetic early warning systems and an interface between artist and audience." Clifford A. Ridley of the now extinct *National Observer* agrees, "The critic is part of a continuing dialogue about the arts that includes the artist and the audience." *Village Voice* drama critic Michael Feingold is even more precise:

> First, I am an artist myself. Second, I'm an informed respondent to works serving as a source of feedback, encouragement and warning to artists. At best, the critic is a help to the artist in

bringing the best out of himself and a bridge between artist and public, who may be alerted by the critic to the fine points (of a work) they might otherwise miss.

"The critic is supposed to be as sensitive a receiver as the artist is a sender," presumes drama critic Dan Sullivan of the *Los Angeles Times*.

In assaying his 44 years with *The Christian Science Monitor*, recently retired drama critic John Beaufort outlined the reviewer's role as

> (1) to convey to the reader as vividly and accurately as possible the nature, character and particular uniqueness (if any) of a given work and performance; (2) to analyze and explain—particularly in the case of new and "difficult" works; (3) to stimulate the reader's interest in the theatre arts; and (4) to evaluate a given work, both on its own terms and in relation to the currents of play-making. Stating opinions is a secondary, though indispensable, function of reviewing. In any case, the reviewer's concern is to serve the reader: he is not telling writers, directors, actors, and other theatre artists how to do their jobs. His principal asset is the capacity to respond. The danger of prolonged reviewing is to become blasé or jaded. This must be avoided—and it can at times require a conscious effort—if the reviewer is to continue to be worth his press tickets and his right to appear in print (or on the air).

Some critics strive for a positive approach, even providing solutions to arts problems. Informing readers of constructive ideas for improving television programming may be an "indulgent fantasy" for a TV critic, whose fare is "dismal and dull," says John J. O'Connor, of *The New York Times*, but, "Constant carping alone will only paint the critic into an unproductive corner, muttering darkly, 'How do I hate thee. Let me count the ways!' " O'Connor is one who occasionally attempts to present improvement ideas in his Sunday column.[4]

New York drama-film critic John Simon has also proposed reforms for an ailing medium, urging a theatre that serves an "enlightened few" rather than one that attempts to compete with film or television as popular art.

Simon eloquently stated his elitist position when he mused on his role:

> A critic writes, first, for himself. Like any artist—and writing criticism is an art, not only because the practice of criticism is, but also because writing is an art—the critic expresses himself as wittily, precisely, elegantly and penetratingly as he can, to get at the essence of what he likes and dislikes, and to explain to himself the wherefores of his endorsement or displeasure. For

a critic is driven by curiosity: like a scientist, he wants to analyze the unknown quiddity before him; like a mechanic, he wants to know what makes this engine run or stall; like a philosopher, he wants to figure out the first and last causes of, say, a work of dramatic art—the meaning of success or failure in a piece of writing, acting, directing. He does not care if the whole world or nobody watches over his shoulder as long as his writing makes his insights concrete and palatable to himself. If, in the end, he has understood something, he trusts that someone else, too, will learn from it.[5]

British drama critic Martin Esslin also emphasizes the educative role of the critic: "The critic's function is to understand what is going on and to explain it to his readers so they can get more pleasure out of the artist's work.

"The reporting of baseball games and in my country, soccer, is superior to drama criticism generally. If you read baseball criticism or soccer criticism consistently, you note fine points of technique which increase your enjoyment tremendously next game you see."

Many people go to the theatre just because it's the thing to do, Esslin said. "They aren't able to understand traditional theatre, much less avant garde theatre."

Good criticism is needed to raise the general level of awareness of an audience and to help people enjoy and appreciate cultural diversity, he told a session of the National Critics Institute at the Eugene O'Neill Memorial Theatre Center in Waterford, Conn.

You'll be doing a very good thing for your readers if you can explain to them what's going on so they can enjoy performances instead of just going because they think they should. Discrimination is the basis for a good life—otherwise everything tastes the same. People who are uneducated are bored in life. They only know two flavors—sweet and sour.

• • • •

Critical Note: "Criticism is the only civilized form of autobiography," Oscar Wilde wrote in *The Critic as Artist.*

• • • •

Should critics also be artists?

While professional arts experience may aid some critics in performing their jobs, it certainly is not a basic requirement.

> I say that being a critic is an art form in itself, and that you get involved with a critic the same way you do with an artist. The only critics I have developed any respect for, at all, are critics who themselves are artists and admit that they are artists, approach their work as such and, therefore, allow me to respond to their work and their personality on equal ground,

said poet Nikki Giovanni, in a discussion reported in *Today's Health.*[6]

Whether critics should also be artists is another issue related to role. Harold Haydon, art critic for the *Chicago Sun-Times*, believes it is important for critics to be professionals in the art they review. (Harris found nearly one-fourth of the critics surveyed did have such professional experience.) For his part, Haydon, like other stringers, is a full-time professor of art at the University of Chicago. His criticism, then, is secondary and an expressive outlet and outgrowth of his role as an artist.

A number of full-time critics do work in the arts part-time. Wayne Johnson, arts and entertainment editor of the *Seattle Times*, has written a play, as has the *Village Voice* drama critic Michael Smith and others. *Newsweek* critic Douglas Davis has been experimenting with video art, while writing about the field.

Yet, as Ivor Brown, a British novelist and critic, wrote in *Saturday Review*, "It is absurd to suggest that the critic should always be creator." Brown, however, believes that critic-creators who know the ardors and endurances of the arts life write with more "warmth" than others.[7]

Psychologists Robert S. Albert and Peter Whitelam said in the *Journal of Social Psychology* that most critics not only believed it was not necessary to practice the art reviewed but that readers gave little positive value to those who did so. They concluded that arts experience did not contribute to a critic's prestige and should not be considered among important credentials for role performance.[8]

Ivor Brown noted some of the pitfalls of the practice:

> It is the proper business of a critic who has to consider a wide range of production, as most journalist critics must, to work with no initial prejudice against any one individual. He must understand, or at least try to understand, what all kinds of artists and authors are attempting and then assess their success or failure in that line of business. To begin by saying that line of business stinks and that all who traffic in it are beneath consideration is not only unjust, it is idiotic.[9]

This writer's observations at two recent gatherings of artists—the National Playwright's Conference and the International

Film Seminar (Flaherty)—confirmed Brown's warning that artists are not likely to make good critics. Some artists proved jealous of their rivals and thus were inaccurate, unjust, and downright bitchy with little consideration of the art involved. Aside from personal antagonisms, the artist-critic often espouses his own aesthetic, school or style at the expense of all others. His arguments, while onesided and passionate, lack scope and fairness, certainly essential qualities for a critic.

• • • •

Critical Note: "A critic is concerned with the end product and not with the means of manufacture. You don't have to be an egg to make an omelette, nor a cook to know a good omelette from a bad one," said British critic Philip Hope Wallace.

• • • •

What's the best part of a critic's role? The worst part?

When critics are asked what aspect of their job gives them the greatest satisfaction, most cite writing about the arts. Typical responses are: "writing well and aiding worthy work," "seeing good art and then writing about it," and "reporting top performances of first-rate music." Others prefer to focus on the art work or experience itself and report their satisfaction comes from "discovering a film that truly entertains," "being paid to listen to music," "getting to see all the new plays," "the initial experience of the encounter with the art form," and "discovering exciting work."

A few critics say it's the mingling with artists that's most satisfying. "Getting to know good artists," "talking with architects," and "circulating in the wild world of movies" are their ways of expressing this phase of their job.

Promotion of artists and their works gives some critics satisfaction. "Writing a favorable review of a worthy film" is the best part of one critic's job. A major book critic says he enjoys "the successful 'promoting' of a good book," while other critics like "the welcoming of new ideas and talent," "discovering and calling attention to deserving new artists," and "being able to say that someone's work has improved."

"People assume that one of a reviewer's greatest pleasures is coming upon relatively unheralded talent and being able to convey enthusiasm to a wider audience. People are right: it *is* a pleasure," writes *New York Times'* music critic John Rockwell.

Some cite the traditional pleasures of daily journalism, such as "a scoop" or "the immediacy of overnight reviews since no other San Francisco publication does them."

Concern for serving their readers satisfied other critics. "Viewing something that gives me personal satisfaction and education that I can pass along to readers," is most important to Lawrence DeVine, theatre and film critic of the *Detroit Free Press.* Drama critic Stewart Klein, of WNEW-TV in New York, says he likes "breaking news about something good that people should see." Other comments in the same vein are: "sharing an enthusiasm," and "luring people to a worthwhile show they might skip."

A handful of critics have more personal benefits. Joseph Gelmis of *Newsday* says he likes "having to stay open and receptive and honest; doing justice to myself and my subject." Another critic says the best part of his job is the respected relationship it earns him with people in the arts and community. Another delights in "knowing that I have expressed my intention clearly." Others say they derive the most satisfaction from "the variety of the material to cover the self-expression," "intelligent feedback from readers," and, perhaps most candidly, "payday."

While several critics said they enjoyed all aspects of their jobs, others cited a range of complaints. Martin Bernheimer, music critic of *The Los Angeles Times,* says the part of his job that gives him least satisfaction is "playing watchdog." For Irving Lowens, of the *Washington Star-News*, it's "arguing with editors." Others also cite "editorial mishandling of my work" and "lack of space" as annoyances.

Just as dealing with good artists and works is an enjoyable part of many's role as critics, relations with "pushy press agents" and "public relations hacks" are grievances. Other critics bemoan having to review mediocre, dull and dreary fare, variously described as "humdrum stinkers," "clinkers," or "pandering and incompetent work."

Others cite non-reviewing chores as the most tedious part of their jobs—"rewriting handouts," "proofreading," "routine editing," and "answering readers' telephone inquiries." A small group of critics complain about the lack of reader response (or feedback) to reviews as the most frustrating part of their role.

Some unsatisfying aspects of the job are beyond categorization. "Reviewing circuses" is the least favorite chore of Elston Brooks of the *Ft. Worth Star-Telegram.* Allan Wallach of *Newsday* says "promotional exploitation of reviews" makes him most unhappy. Another simply says he detests "going out so damn often."

Misconceptions about a critic's work abound. Vincent Canby, writing in *The New York Times'* "Arts & Leisure" section, explained why the critic's life isn't a picnic:

Taxi cab drivers, bankers, academicians and small children invariably react in the same fashion when one identifies oneself as a film critic. What a peculiar way for an adult to make a living! The kids, especially, are wonder-struck. In their minds, it's not much different from being forced to eat popcorn eight hours a day. What a way to go! The job isn't all that simple, however.

Canby then chronicled his past week of filmgoing (12 hours) and writing (three reviews and a Sunday piece) and researching (read filmmaker's autobiography) and office chores (answering mail and telephones). Picnic, indeed![10]

Despite their ability to spot new trends in the arts and to recognize undiscovered talent, critics do not possess a crystal ball for accurate forecasting, as some readers expect. Former *New York Times'* staffer Clive Barnes admits, "Critics are probably the worst people to ask the future of any art form. On the past, critics are splendid (usually), the present they handle O.K. (for the most part), but frankly the future gives us trouble."

• • • •

Critical Note: "To hell with criticism, praise is good enough for me," said Tallulah Bankhead.

• • • •

What are critical standards? Does a double standard apply to some works?

The subject of critical standards always provokes a lively discussion among critics, perhaps because it's an issue on which there is little agreement. And the very raising of the topic seems to question whether critics either have or know what their standards are.

"There are almost no universally accepted standards in the anarchic reviewing community," insists John Beaufort, of *The Christian Science Monitor.*

"Standards are standards," David Richards, of the *Washington Star-News*, counters firmly.

Music critic Paul Nelson, writing in the *Village Voice* about a Bruce Springsteen concert, clarified his enthusiastic reaction by recalling specific examples of experience that illustrated his exacting standards:

On my feet, clapping, never wanting it to end, I ask myself when I've ever been so moved by a concert. Four times: Dylan doing 'Like a Rolling Stone' anywhere in '65 or '66, the Rolling Stones at the Garden in '72, Jackson Browne in Toronto in '73 and a few of the New York Dolls' late shows at the Mercer Art Center that same year.[11]

Martin Gottfried, drama critic of *Women's Wear Daily*, also claims a lofty standard, "As a critic, I must ask for (and demand) the ideal—just as the artist must reach for it—even in a world where the ideal is unlikely and perhaps impossible."[12]

Julius Novick, drama critic for the *Village Voice*, takes a more flexible attitude: "I try to avoid having anything so rigid as immutable standards out there to hang up each work against. My job is to be as open as possible to what the work is giving me rather than to demand from it according to a set of expectations I'd formed in advance. Bernard Shaw said years ago that when a piece of work is an absolute and unutterable failure in giving you X, you need always to consider the possibility that it's offering you Y instead. That's been my primary rule, as far as standards go."

"To 'make allowances' is patronizing and, in the final analysis debasing of art," agrees Clara Hieronymus, of the *Nashville Tennessean*.

"The work should be defined and judged on *that* basis," says Richard Coe, of the *Washington Post*.

"Going easy helps no one," said United Press International drama critic, the late Jack Gaver.

Slightly more than half the critics surveyed say they operate on a single standard for both professional and amateur works. Book and film critics, who daily deal with nationally marketed products, and architecture critics, who never deal with amateurs, most often say they never make exceptions in their judgments. TV and drama critics, who sometimes do review local, low-budget productions, also say that the source of a work generally does not affect their evaluation of it.

"It's unfair and condescending to judge locals by inferior standards," says Al Rudis, pop music critic for the *Chicago Sun-Times*. "Encouraging local talent can be done without abandoning standards," concurs Bernie Harrison, of the *Washington Star-News*.

Yet a few critics committed to a single standard note some exceptions they consider. "Art is constant but I am tougher on high priced rip-offs," says New York television drama critic Klein. "I try not to have double standards, but, of course, one is bound to respond a little differently even between On and Off Broadway," *Time's* T. E. Kalem goes on. And, Emerson Batdorff, of the *Cleveland Plain Dealer*, admits, "It is hard to swing as freely at someone you know will read it as at some distant, faceless entity."

Metropolitan media often ignore all but the most commercial popular arts in their area, leaving amateur work of quality—such as university theatre, concerts and art exhibits and Off-Off Broadway productions and the like—uncovered.

"Many people mistake purity of impulse for quality; others mistake commercial slickness for a standard," observes *Village Voice* drama critic Michael Feingold.

> This constitutes a confusion between a difference in kind and a difference in quality. If you believe the art world has room for many different kinds of art, you have no problem with this, and can accept conscientious commercial craftsmen, pure-hearted amateurs and intentionally "unprofessional" experimenters, all as doing a good or bad work of their kind.

Feingold's colleague at the *Voice*, Arthur Sainer, says of his standards, "My principal concerns are 1. for a socially involved theatre, and 2. for new aesthetics, though I even seem to lose patience for the latter. Is that a narrow view? Absolutely, but it's a vantage point."

A sizable minority of critics adhere to flexible standards, with art and music critics most often acknowledging that approach.

"I carry an aesthetic slide rule," quips *Seattle Times* critic Wayne Johnson. "Everything must be judged in its own creative context," New York dance critic Robb Baker advises. "You ought to meet a performance on its own terms, but you shouldn't lie about the matter," says Clifford A. Ridley, lately of *The National Observer*.

"In dealing with the performing arts in New York, it is obviously unrealistic to work from a single standard," picks up *New York*'s Alan Rich.

> The range of activity, and of the quality of the end product, is vast in this city, and this is a genuine part of the excitement in a life of attending performances. Everything must be evaluated in relationship to its aims. But amateurism is only saintly when the potential at hand is realized.

Marilyn Stasio, of *Cue Magazine*, adds, "One must consider the goals, needs, function, ideals of groups." But Irv Letofsky, of the *Minneapolis Tribune*, perhaps goes too far when he confesses he "gets emotionally involved in their (artists') aspirations."

Other critics share Letofsky's bind. Peter V. Rahn, of the *St. Louis Globe-Democrat*, admits, "Possibly a weakness on my part, but I tend to go easier on a low-budget, local TV effort and hard on a big-budget network flop." James M. Auer, *Milwaukee Journal* art critic, also says, "I have tried steadfastly to expunge provincialism from my coverage, but I fear it is inescapable, at least to a degree."

Many critics cite variables that affect their criticism. When art critic Harold Haydon, of the *Chicago Sun-Times*, writes about esoteric works, he must be accommodating: "African, Far Eastern, Pre-Columbian art requires adjustment to readers' preparation."

Music critic Harold C. Schonberg, of *The New York Times*, uses a "double standard" as he looks for talent and imagination in new performers, "I can't expect a scared kid making a debut to play with the assurance of a veteran." In agreeing, Dwight Newton, of the *San Francisco Examiner*, recalls, "Barbra Streisand as a youngster at the Hungry i had not developed the enormous talent that would flow forth later, yet as an amateur emergent, she earned praise."

Miami Herald critic John Huddy illustrates other variables:

> Money and the immediate environment (in which the work or artist exists) has a tremendous, and sometimes severe, influence on quality and impact. For example, Liza Minnelli working on a scene with Bob Fosse for four days will produce one level of performance. Liza with a directorial hack who has enough money for only two takes per setup will emerge in an altogether different light. Or Liza on the nightclub stage backed by six male dancers, supported by the best sound and light technicians, accompanied by a 34-piece orchestra and wearing $100,000 in costuming, will provide one kind of show. Liza with a second-rate trio and third-rate charts in a noisy room that has a train-station-level sound system, will look and sound quite different.
>
> The critic must take into account these influences. What is the budget. The support? The working conditions? For that matter, how much does it cost the spectator to see the show or artist? Since most films cost about the same, the critic must be less inclined to give the benefit of the doubt in judging a film, but even then matters of budget and time and intent are crucial.

"So my standards are somewhat, but not radically, different," Huddy continues. "When I sometimes review semi-professional or 'community' productions, I assume the reader is aware that this is a local production with local, built-in handicaps."

Other critics are more explicit in their reviews about their criteria. Robert C. Marsh, of the *Chicago Sun-Times*, insists that critics using more than one standard "should make clear in their reviews the sort of standard being applied." When *Newsday* drama critic George Oppenheimer reviews low-budget productions, he cites them as such and makes certain allowances for scenery and other physical elements. *Tulsa World* critic Ron Butler says he always qualifies reviews for his readers with such phrases as "outstanding for an amateur production." But the *Milwaukee Journal*'s Wade Mosby changes the tone of his reviews with his standards: "Amateurs can be chided gently; professionals who err deserve lambasting."

Women's Wear Daily critic Peter Davis Dibble has sliding standards that shift another way: "Of course, one cannot judge amateurs and professionals alike—often the amateur is better!"

• • • •

Critical Note: "Critics—murderers," said Samuel Taylor Coleridge tersely.

• • • •

Is there an optional role for critics?

Yes, says cultural assayer Benjamin DeMott, the writer for *Atlantic Monthly* and *Saturday Review* and author of four nonfiction books and two novels. Critics are not now doing what they *should* be doing, DeMott argues, holding that this fundamental assessment must precede any real evaluation of their performance.

Today's critics lack a clear-cut and commonly shared perception of their role, the veteran professor of English at Amherst College charges. He believes that nothing short of a whole new critical approach to popular culture is needed.

In a public symposium with sociology professor Ernest van den Haag at New York University, DeMott explicated his position:

> The appropriate methodology of the new critic might be to define the experience of popular art as that experience is undergone by the viewer or the reader. I don't think it's right to raise questions about the object or the value of a movie or television program as a self-enclosed item. The right kind of questions go something like this: What is it like to the person experiencing this kind of object? What's it like to be engaged with this kind of managed time? What possible human responses to life are excluded by the nature of this experience?
>
> I want someday to read about the *experience* of watching television, to read a description of that experience from the inside. I've never read anything that touched the nature of those experiences. . . . The job of the critic is to penetrate that area and stop bemusing himself and the rest of the world with trivialities about whether Jane Fonda is or is not a good actress. That is, relatively speaking, a trivial question, a distraction that keeps

us from seeing the ways in which we inhabit our contemporary lives and keeps us from seeing what we are.

The ideal critic is one who would make things—the television experience or the whole world of entertainment—strange enough so I can see it and speculate about it, interpret it and not take it for granted.

When Michael Arlen wrote about television for *The New Yorker*, he did something unusual because of the fundamental strangeness of his own position. The oddity of being a writer about TV for that publication gave him a mode of lateral thinking and a preoccupation with the strangeness of the work did percolate through every sentence he wrote. He never became a person who took any instance of his viewing experience for granted. He didn't take this thing-in-the-living-room as a part of ordinary life, something that naturally belonged there. But I don't think he ever moved on from what I'd call a sense of occupational peculiarity to any fundamental investigation of the experience of the viewer. From the very beginning he was preoccupied by the oddity of his role and that gave to his estimates of what went on in the box an unusual frequency that no other critic matched, at that time or since.

Pauline Kael is the other critic that I think makes reference to a full cultural context and a full psychological context. She is aware that film is an odd communal experience and a different way of behavior.

Other critics have written about the experience of popular culture accidentally and a few who are unusually sensitive and alert have let the surroundings seep into their writing, but nobody has ever done it really, if you consider my emphasis. No critic is doing what I think needs to be done.

van den Haag: I have the feeling you want to reduce the aesthetics of popular culture to the psychology of popular culture. You want the critic to explore what the viewer experiences as distinguished from exploring the intellectual structure of the work. These are two different things that are not mutually exclusive, but I think your emphasis is more one-sided than I would like. Incidentally, I find the only critic who does both is John Simon. He does it at the same time he tries to apply some standards. I think he's always wrong on any concrete thing but he's always right intellectually in some peculiar way, whereas Pauline Kael is wrong on both.

DeMott: I admit it's very difficult to do what I'm asking since we are hung up on the question of good or bad. Perhaps we should go to a play once as a theatre spectator, a member of the audience, set or prefixed to decide whether it's good or bad or to decide what it's about. And then we should go a second time and say to ourself something like this: there ought to be a way to respond to theatre something like the way you respond to life when you're on a superhighway and you've just seen an accident. For about 15 minutes thereafter, you are aware that you are driving a car, that there is metal around you and that your body is soft and that there is danger. You are aware that you are not doing something habitual but that you are in a fundamentally strange relationship with the world, hurtling through time and space in such a way that if one thing goes wrong you're finished. I think the problem for us in relation to the theatre or the popular arts generally is that we are so encased in our ordinary life understanding of going to the theatre that we go through it in the same way that we go through the driving experience. We don't know what to hell we're doing in relation to these phenomena and we don't know where we are in relation to these experiences. We take for granted an extraordinary variety of life without penetrating or knowing it except when something causes a break in our armor.

People who write about our world aren't supposed to keep reinforcing the commonplace non-understanding of events, they're supposed to open up worlds for us and make us see where we are. I assign the critic a very high role indeed and no one fulfills the role. They all take things for what they appear to be. Until critics begin to help us see what is occurring we have no foundation for criticism, all we have is a bunch of people talking in steam baths and all we see is steam. The greatly gifted artists still fulfill their function for society but no one sees what they point out. The critic doesn't analyze or try to get inside the nature of the oddity as it's experienced and to say what it's really trying to put before us.

• • • •

Critical Note: "Pluralism is the word in criticism these days, no matter what the art form," writes music critic John Rockwell in *The New York Times.*

Perhaps it's just that things are happening so fast that critics without the perspective of time find it impossible to sort out their beloved categories and trends. In the jumble of the immediate moment, we appear to be beset by variety of every sort, and so it seems safest simply to label our time as pluralistic, with all the arts marked by extreme diversity of style.[13]

• • • •

Do critics share a common philosophical approach to their craft?

Critics' responses to the philosophical question—"A critic must not be concerned with 'What do I think of this?' but 'What is my relation to this?' "—were intense and controversial enough to brighten any marquee:

"Nuts"—Archer Winston, *New York Post*. "Valid"—William Hogan, *S.F. Chronicle*. "Baloney"—Cecil Smith, *L.A. Times*. "Wholeheartedly agree"—Irv Letofsky, *Minneapolis Trib*. "Preposterous"—Wade Mosby, *Milwaukee Journal*.

Yet, on a closer look, the majority of critics disagrees with the statement, favoring a clear expression of opinion or evaluation in a review. Ann Guarino, of the *New York Daily News*, asserts, "I think a critic is concerned with giving his opinion. That's what he's paid for." Hal Burton, of *Newsday*, agrees, adding, "My readers expect it." Dwight Newton, television critic of the *San Francisco Examiner*, says emphatically, "The foundation of criticism is 'What do I think of this?'" Clara Hieronymus, drama critic of the *Nashville Tennessean*, concludes, "What else is a review but a subjective analysis as seen by one critic at a given time and place, a production evaluated by a given mind and set of individual responses?"

Those who agree that the critic's relation to an art work is more important than his evaluation of it were a much less vocal minority. The former *National Observer*'s Clifford A. Ridley said of the issues, "A little simplistic, but true; it properly identifies criticism as a subjective enterprise that consists of more than the passing out of stars."

Nearly as many critics as favored "What do I think of this?" said both questions were essential to one's task. The most common statements supporting both parts of the statement are: "Cannot separate" and "both are necessary." *St. Petersburg Times* critic Dorothy Smiljanich says of the ties between the two parts, "I don't see how anyone could hope to define their relationship to something without first describing what you think of it." James Doussard, of the *Louisville Courier-Journal*, says the two positions were interdependent, "To do the first, you must understand the second." Roger Ebert, film critic of the *Chicago Sun-Times*, concludes, "In practice, the two statements are the same. They could, however, lead to a theoretical quagmire."

Ron Butler wants to avoid such a scene. The *Tulsa World* critic says of the statement, "Sounds like something Vincent Canby, Pauline Kael and Rex Reed could argue boringly for hours but it is of no particular interest to me in getting the job done." Others who believe that neither question should be of primary interest to critics have other concerns. Wolf von Eckardt, architecture critic of the *Washington Post*, believes another question is more important: "What does it mean to the reader, community and society?" John Ardoin, of the *Dallas Morning News*, thinks critics ought to be concerned with "What makes this experience what it is and unlike another?" Digby Diehl of *The Los Angeles Times* prefers "What kind of experience was this for me?"

Joseph Gelmis of *Newsday* offers more insight into the perception and analytical process:

> Both are equally valid secondary responses to the emotional experience—the fact of the feelings—of art. Both are already at the rationalization phase where the mind seeks reasons or references for its visceral reactions and intuitive insights on the non-verbal level.

A handful of critics respond to the issue with divergent points. For example, Robert C. Marsh, of the *Chicago Sun-Times*, posits, "Good criticism is about the object discussed, not the critic's internal responses to it." Robert Evett, of the *Washington Star-News*, adds, "A critic should be as objective as possible and make it clear that his personal reaction is only one of those within the range of tolerable variation."

William A. Payne, of the *Dallas Morning News*, believes that critics should give their opinions of a work and consider the intent of the performer or producer. Sara S. Morrow, of the *Nashville Banner*, goes even further, "I put myself in the position of performers, the audience, the readers and make every effort to be fair, helpful and kindly in my criticism."

Two New York critics cite a conflict between the two views. "I prefer to review based on the first statement," admitted *Cosmopolitan* film critic Liz Smith, "but I must work according to the second." Richard Natale, of *Women's Wear Daily*, said the difference was that reviewers relied on opinion and critics preferred to discuss their relationship to art.

Michael Feingold, of the *Village Voice*, reacted positively to the dilemma:

> This sort of silly word game bugs me. Critics are like other intelligent folk; they don't stop thinking or evaluating simply because they relate or respond. James Agee said, "A man watched a movie and the critic must admit that he is that man." I would add: A man knows he has a mind and doesn't stop having it just because he is watching a movie. The persistent problem of criticism (and of modern life, in general) is balancing consciousness with feeling, objectivity with empathy.

Film critic Mary Knoblauch, of the *Chicago Tribune*, says,

> You *do* ask what the thing is trying to do, but sometimes you question the value of that purpose. Harold Clurman would take the persona of the critic out of the process, which is as impossible as taking the emotions out of the audience and still expecting

them to value what they see. The artist is not always the bright-est person involved in this process, nor is what he is trying to say the ultimate value against which all other participants in the process (interpreters and audience) must judge themselves. Art is a process of communication and the communicator is not necessarily the most important person in this process. As Clur-man asks the question, the artist is the arbiter. If the first ques-tion is restated to 'Why do I have this reaction?', it would cover the situation better.

Which may bring us back to Ron Butler's point!

• • • •

Critics inevitably face a philosophical dilemma, wails John Rockwell, who reviews rock and contemporary music for *The New York Times*.

The continuum between popular culture and high art is one that can be traced in purely sociological terms from 1800 to now. The audience now is a by-product of democratization. Everybody is into the game now. This is terrific on one level. On the other hand, you simply cannot have the kind of elitist expectations you did 200 years ago. That's what makes me so uptight about popular culture by definition. But presumably, if one has a vested interest in popular culture, it is something one welcomes. When you say that you judge an artist on his ability to please an audience and be true to himself, what you're really saying is that you're hung delicately between popularism and elitism. But that's an awful place to be. . . . And the only place to be.

• • • •

Critical Note: The critic leaves at curtain fall
To find, in starting to review it
He scarcely saw the play at all
For watching his reaction to it.
                              —E. B. White

• • • •

In addition to an aesthetic standard, do critics use audience reaction to assess a work?

Stage actors and actresses are often quite aware of the influ-ence of live audiences on their performances after they work in films or television. "I like to have an audience as a sounding board for what kind of job I'm doing," said Broadway actress Marcia Rodd, after making her first film "Little Murders." "I can instantly tell whether I'm getting through or not and learn timing of lines and subtle effects that work effectively."

Critics of the performing arts also recognize the influence of audience feedback on a production and nearly two out of three prefer to review a performance with a live audience rather than a dress rehearsal. Some critics acknowledge that the audience is part of the performance and that actors react differently, as Miss Rodd suggests, without an audience. These critics are also interested in how the audience responds to the performance, mostly as a point of comparison for their own response. A few critics detest opening night audiences, which they consider atypical and often packed with media people whose reactions they deem mediated and dishonest.

Film and television critics are more likely to prefer private showings for review purposes, sometimes because they dislike boorish audiences and sometimes merely for the convenience and additional time to write a review before its public appearance. Chicago critic Knoblauch explains her preference as practical: "Contrary to the wishes of distributors, I like to see only comedies without an audience, because, if they're good, too much of the dialogue is drowned out by laughter." *New York Times* music critic Schonberg says he reviews the performance of the work with an audience but that if a difficult, modern work is being performed, he'll often go to rehearsals as well in order to become more familiar with the work.

Of those who prefer to review works with audiences, more than two to one say they will include comments about audiences and their reactions in their reviews, especially if the audience response is unusual or different from their own or if it makes a provocative point. One example comes from drama critic Clive Barnes' review of the Broadway musical "Good News":

> I took the precaution of seeing the production at last Saturday's matinee, wanting to see this particular show with a live, paying, unbiased audience. That audience loved "Good News." It applauded every oldie as it came up, it gushed over Alice Faye, it laughed at jokes obvious enough to give banana skins a bad name, and it just had a lovely experience. With certain exceptions, I did not.[14]

Barnes then describes his objections to the play, seemingly bending over backwards to be fair.

Martin Bernheimer, music critic of *The Los Angeles Times*, not only notes audience reaction in his reviews but also scolds unacceptable behavior. In one instance, he berated an over-enthusiastic opera crowd heralding the return of Beverly Sills:

> Introductory busymusic was obliterated by waves of applause, stamping of feet, cries of greeting. The zealots who care less for

good grammar than for good cheerleading roared a contrapuntal chorus of bravos. The sports fans, oblivious of theatrical superstition, whistled.[15]

On another occasion, he ended a review that reviled a tacky opera production with this note: "Our opera-starved audience cheered as if the sets were by Zeffirelli, as if the principals were Birgit Nilsson and Franco Corelli and the conductor Toscanini. Humbug."[16]

Certainly not all comments on audiences are negative. Bernheimer's colleague, Dan Sullivan, heaped praise on playgoers struggling with O'Neill's "Moon for the Misbegotten":

> It's encouraging to see this happen at a time when theatre audiences are supposed to have been made so lazy by films and TV that they won't even listen to live actors, let alone help them wrestle down a serious and admittedly difficult play. It's encouraging to watch an audience experience the fact that fine theatre, like many fine things, takes time.[17]

• • • •

Critical Note: "The only critic I respect is the public," said Irving Wallace, Mark Twain and others.

• • • •

Do critics have a role as consumer guides?

More than half of the critics said they write their reviews to serve as a consumer guide for readers. Film and television critics were slightly more inclined toward this practice than others and live music critics were less inclined.

Critics who like to recommend events or advise their readers to avoid them favor this approach. Others said that while they didn't write reviews with this purpose in mind—or that it was certainly a low priority of consideration—readers often consulted their reviews as guides. "Inescapable" and "inevitable result" were their phrases.

Some media, concerned with consumer journalism, have reduced a critic's judgment to a code, frequently using such tags as dull or interesting, avoid or don't miss this. Symbols denoting judgment are sometimes employed as graphic representation of a critic's verdict. The *New York Daily News* uses four stars to denote its highest rating for films and theatre. *Village Voice* pop critic Robert Christgau gives record albums he reviews letter grades: A for excellent, B for good, C for so-so, and so on. *Los Angeles Times* rock music critic Robert Hilburn applies an incredibly simplistic Yes/No test to records, tacking his final judgment onto the two or three short paragraphs he writes about the album. He occasionally hedges with a MAYBE.

And, the *St. Petersburg Times* uses symbols denoting sex, nudity, profanity, and violence to visually alert readers of a film's explicit content, along with a capsulized mini-review following the critic's full comments.

Taking a cue from Brooks Atkinson, *The New York Times* man about Broadway from 1926 to 1946, *Philadelphia Daily News* drama reviewer Stuart D. Bykofsky appends an italicized "Audience Note" to each review stating how long after the "announced" time the opening night performance actually began. Delays have ranged from a few minutes (Bykofsky believes less than five is excusable) to as many as 20.

Should critics suggest what type of audience a work might appeal to?

Most do. As the arts have differentiated, increasingly artists, the public and critics recognize that few works can appeal to every individual. More than 80 per cent of the critics surveyed indicate in their reviews the type of audience for which a particular work might be intended, best suited or most appealing. Film critics, because of the diversity of their medium and the Motion Picture Association code which restricts some pictures for younger audiences, are most in agreement on the necessity of specifying to whom each movie might appeal. Art and music critics less often do so. A few critics believe that prejudging an audience for a given work is too presumptive or just impossible. "I can't possibly know what my readers are interested in," moans *Time* critic Kalem. "It's a good play or a bad one with me."

Village Voice critic Feingold believes that the failure to define a work's intended audience is actually detrimental:

> Directing large audiences to modish works that they are not yet ready to respond to has been one of the chief faults of the new breed of journalistic critics. Media pressure has been destructive to a great many experimental artists.

Los Angeles Times critic Sullivan shares Feingold's concern for new work. He recently wrote that Tom Stoppard's "Jumpers" was "not for all markets. Certainly it's not for those who go to the theatre for a kind of illustrated daydream."[18] He explained that one had to listen intently to catch its linguistic and philosophical richness.

For extreme fare, advice can become warnings. *Los Angeles*

Times cultural staff writer Kevin Thomas wrote of the X-rated film, "Pink Flamingos: An Exercise in Poor Taste," "strictly for the very openminded and is best left to those who've been able to go along to the outermost limits of film-makers like Andy Warhol and Robert Downey." Underscoring this point, he said "Blazing Saddles" was in comparison to "Pink Flamingos," "a proverbial Sunday school picnic." He concluded his review with a repeated warning that the film contained "all manner of shenanigans that can't even be hinted at, let alone described, in a family paper."[19] *Caveat emptor.*

While wavering somewhat because of his personal attraction for an Off-Off Broadway play, "Our Late Night," which he called the "sickest of sick jokes," then-*New York Times* critic Clive Barnes was equally explicit: "This is the most obscene show in town, so please don't imagine that you have not been warned." Barnes even reiterated in the final tag line of his review: "Not, definitely not, a play to take your aunt to."[20]

Should critics be concerned with the social relevance (or lack of it) of some cultural work and question why it was produced?

With music critics being an exception, most critics say they attempt to determine the social relevance of art works. Though instrumental music and abstract visual arts generally lack social messages for audiences, most popular arts do have educational content and critics generally write about that aspect of the artist's intention. "You talk about what the work says. If what it says is 'socially relevant,' then you talk about that, among other things," says ex-*National Observer* critic Ridley.

Writers about the arts should put a work's message in a timely sociological context, believed the late music critic Ralph J. Gleason, because it's vital to the arts. "It's important because art doesn't exist in a vacuum, but is part of the sociology and ambience of the times. It is impossible to write about blues music, for instance, without writing about the sociological problem of race," he said.

"I look at films, especially the way audiences react to them, as social barometers," adds Chicago film critic Knoblauch. The *Nashville Banner*'s Sara S. Morrow also ties art to society in reviewing, "I believe that, since the Greeks, theatre evolves from the society producing it."

While critics generally believe that it depends on the message whether they attempt to write about that aspect of the work, others, led by the television critics, argue that it is highly important to include comments on it.

Few think it's not important or are not concerned. Hobe Morrison, a *Variety* critic, is among the skeptical, "Most work is produced to make money and for an artistic purpose." *Time*'s T. E. Kalen also offers, "I simply don't believe that so-called socially significant works have much to offer aesthetically."

Yet, nearly three times as many critics write about why works are produced—even though they have little relevance—than don't. Recent examples offered as evidence of their attempts to discuss why works are produced include: major TV documentaries and specials such as "The Autobiography of Miss Jane Pittman," the controversial political films of Costa-Gavras, phenomena such as "Walking Tall," "Billy Jack," and "Harold & Maude," revivals and works produced to exploit genre or fads, vanity works, art works primarily produced for experimentation and cheap promotional campaigns.

Is investigative reporting part of the critic's role?

Nearly two-thirds of the critics polled do investigative reporting in the arts, in addition to criticism. One film critic, for example, wrote about a film that was X-rated in the newspaper advertisement but that had had all the scenes showing explicit sex trimmed out and was now carrying an "R" rating without informing customers at the box office. Hard-core fans were being duped, the critic reported.

St. Petersburg Times music critic Mary Nic Shenk went to a local nightclub to hear pianist Jan August, who was billed there. When she heard the wretched performance, she suspected the pianist was an impostor and threatened to expose him. The nightclub owner changed the name of the performer in the following day's ad.

Newsday film critic Gelmis recently wrote about tricks exhibitors and distributors played on each other and the public. Al Rudis of the *Chicago Sun-Times* has written about ticket swindles and promotional frauds. Emerson Batdorff of the *Cleveland Plain Dealer* monitors how movies are merchandised. Chicago film critic Mary Knoblauch has written about why some prints in theatres are in such bad condition.

Television critic Bettelou Peterson of the *Detroit Free Press* examines the background on station changes in her area. Dwight Newton of the *San Francisco Examiner* writes about cable and pay TV service, effects of energy cutbacks and locations of new

TV towers. The *Washington Post* is concerned with attempts to break up public television and appointments to the Federal Communications Commission.

Other types of investigative stories reported deal with government's role in the arts, institutions' policies and changes, financial and artistic problems of local arts groups, labor issues, sales practices of art dealers, and trends in publishing.

Do critics have a responsibility to report on the economics of the arts?

While nearly four-fifths of the critics surveyed said they wrote stories on the economics of the arts—articles about financial problems, success stories and the like—few believe critics should play active roles in fund-raising propagandizing or in advocating subsidies.

"Critics are not meant to help or hinder financial subsidy questions, deficits, even though some influence can be felt by groups concerned through recognition of merit or lack of it," says Lawrence DeVine, of the *Detroit Free Press*.

"Economics is independent of critical response," says Glenn Giffin, of the *Denver Post*. "Fund raising is not our business," adds Ann Guarino of the *New York Daily News*. William Glover of the Associated Press explains, "If critics become fund-raising activists, they warp their responsibility."

Other critics admit they are powerless in the area of finances, even though some assume they know what's best, mostly it's a self-serving exercise. Jim Shertzer, of the *Winston-Salem (N.C.) Journal*, notes, "People will go to what *they* want to go to—not what a critic *tells* them to go to."

Some critics say they should only support quality work and let the fittest survive. "Write well about what is good in a way that excites people and makes art important to them," says Paul D. Zimmerman of *Newsweek*. The *Cleveland Plain Dealer*'s Batdorff is more blunt: "If the arts can't make it on their own, maybe the answer is TV and bowling."

Time's Kalem sees another problem: "A few critics have felt they could help by simply praising every show that opens. This is disastrous since critics then lose whatever credence they have."

Other critics say they should report financial crises in the arts so the public will be informed. "Exposing the crisis is some help," says Charles Champlin, entertainment editor of *The Los Angeles Times*. Bernie Harrison, of the *Washington Star-News*, also wants limits of this function: "Report the problem but not to the extent of deep involvement which may affect judgment." James M. Auer, of the *Milwaukee Journal*, worries about Kalem's point: "The most a reviewer can contribute is simply to do his job energetically and well. The moment he becomes a promoter he loses his credibility."

Almost as many critics believe they should help educate readers on financial matters in the arts. This group wants to increase public awareness and help build intelligent consumers, who will support the arts. "I try to show the real need for the art in our lives," says John Ardoin, of the *Dallas Morning News*. "The arts should be treated as part of the social mainstream and not as an isolated commodity," adds Mike Steele, of the *Minneapolis Tribune*. Bill Donaldson, of the *Tulsa Tribune*, says by reporting and explaining the needs of the arts, he encourages individual and corporate participation.

A sizable minority calls for activism. "Rabble rouse," insists Martin Bernheimer of *The Los Angeles Times*. "Urge greater government and private support," goes along Paul Hume of the *Washington Post*. "Lean on the politicians" advises John Huddy of the *Miami Herald*.

"Press for artistic subsidies and propagandize for same," says *Cosmopolitan*'s Liz Smith. "I write articles supporting subsidies and other possible solutions," says *Cue*'s Marilyn Stasio. "I try to persuade the government to give moviemakers tax breaks like other countries do," pleads *Newsday*'s Gelmis.

Should critics be concerned about cultural physical facilities?

Yes. Critics almost unanimously agree that their role encompasses concern for and writing about local cultural facilities—concert halls, theatres, museums, libraries. The few exceptions either worked for national publications without a local community or were book reviewers.

One example will suffice: In 1971 when New York City decided to purchase and modernize Yankee Stadium in order to keep its baseball and football tenants, *The New York Times* music critic Harold C. Schonberg railed against the move in light of other priorities. He cited the needs of Lincoln Center and compared statistics: sporting events in the stadium attracted two million fans in 1970 while Lincoln Center accommodated nearly 3.5 million. Yankee Stadium's box office take was about $7 million while patrons of Lincoln Center spent more than $25 million. He concluded that "In every respect Lincoln Center is more valuable property than Yankee Stadium" and finally asked, "If the city is prepared to spend $24 million to make a baseball team and a football team happy, how much is it prepared to spend to help the much more important (by any standards) Lincoln Center?"[21]

What other professional activities are part of critics' roles?

Only imagination and energy limit the purview of most critics. Many routinely exercise their arts expertise by reviewing new books in their field for their publication's book section.

The New York Times' critics contribute to that newspaper's reputation for thoroughness. They regularly write news analysis and appraisal articles related to news events. For example, when a major art museum issued a report on its controversial transactions, art critic John Canaday said, in his analysis, the museum's policy of openness reflected a major change in the relationship between all American museums and their publics. And, when the world's oldest song was deciphered in 1974, music critic Schonberg said in his appraisal of the history of music that the frontier of notated music had been pushed back well over a thousand years.

The *Times'* critics always write appraisals of major artists' work to accompany obituaries. These articles dwell on the artists' contribution to their field and their significance.

When major arts facilities are opened, the *Times* not only has its architectural critic report on it and assess its design but also has another critic—an art critic for a museum, music critic for an orchestra hall or drama critic for a new theatre—write about its suitability for its function.

Another effective idea that *The New York Times* experimented with was publishing an edited transcript of a year-end critics' roundtable discussion. Each critic offered a succinct assessment of the past year's main events as well as comments on the state of the art. The discussion also offered a multi-perspective or pluralistic overview of the entire spectrum of the cultural arts.

Occasionally, critics review works out of their own field. For example, music critics will review films on musicians. Or film critics will acknowledge made-for-television movies. Former *National Observer* television critic John H. Corcoran, Jr., once reviewed, somewhat tongue-in-cheek, the spate of pulp magazines devoted to gossipy tales of TV personalities.

Critics can also apply their aesthetic perspective to other

fields with delightful results. *Washington Post* art critic Paul Richard, for example, recently wrote about the visual experience of looking at the modern art of football and its open, all-at-onceness image, which he characterized as "conceptual, kinetic, popular and funky." Linda Winer, the *Chicago Tribune* dance critic, has written about the aesthetic athletics of professional basketball. Covering a Bulls game, she found fascinating kinesthetic parallels between making a basket and executing a *pas de deux.*

Once they established public recognition and credibility, critics have numerous opportunities to earn both additional exposure and income. Given celebrity status by their media position, they become sought-after commodities representing authority and prestige.

Publicity notices for the *Britannica Encyclopedia of American Art* were quick to state that more than 30 art critics had been consulted in compiling its 400,000-word volume.

Several film critics, including *Newsweek*'s Charles Michener and *Saturday Review*'s Arthur Knight, have been witnesses paid to defend X-rated movies in pornography trials. Michener even admitted on a Boston court record that he received $500 plus expenses for his "expert testimony" on the socially redeeming value of "The Devil in Miss Jones."

And the lecture circuit, mostly centered on college and university campuses, is a receptive outlet for exposure and source of lucrative fees for some superstar critics. Film critic Judith Crist, who teaches a criticism workshop once a year at the Columbia University Graduate School of Journalism, commands a fee of $1700 for a single speaking appearance on some other campus. A few other critics receive higher fees for such speeches, though most get considerably less.

• • • •

Critical Dictum à la Woody Allen: What is the function of the (film) critic? Precisely to interpret the audio-visual electronic image and fragmentize individual coercive response against a background of selective subjectivity. He can do this either standing up or sitting and some of the better ones spend a lot of time in hotel rooms with women they're not married to. Also to alert the public to new dimensions in art and of course, whenever possible, to point where the fire exits are.[22]

• • • •

NOTES FOR CHAPTER 2

[1] "Year-End Roundtable on the Arts," *The New York Times*, December 27, 1972.

[2] "The Role of the Critic in Mass Communications," by Robert S. Albert, *The Journal of Social Psychology*, 1958, 48, page 268.

[3] *Ibid.*, page 272.

[4] "To the Critics: How Would *You* Improve Things?" by John J. O'Connor, *The New York Times*, October 10, 1971, page 33.

[5] "Once More Unto the Breach," by John Simon, *New York*, July 30, 1973, page 60.

[6] "Do You Know *Why* You Like a Particular Novel, Painting, or Symphony?" with Nikki Giovanni, *Today's Health*, May, 1974, page 32.

[7] "Critics and Creators," by Ivor Brown, *Saturday Review*, August 10, 1963, page 11.

[8] "The Role of the Critic in Mass Communication: The Critic Speaks," by Robert S. Albert and Peter Whitelam, *The Journal of Social Psychology*, 1963, page 153.

[9] Saturday Review, *op. cit.*, page 11.

[10] "So You Think Being a Critic Is a Picnic?" by Vincent Canby, *The New York Times*, Jan. 26, 1975, page 19.

[11] "Is Springsteen Worth the Hype?" by Paul Nelson, *Village Voice*, August 25, 1975, page 94.

[12] "How Does One Do A Serious Play," by Martin Gottfried, *The New York Times*, October 18, 1970, page 13.

[13] "The Pop Life," by John Rockwell *The New York Times*, June 11, 1976, page 71.

[14] " 'Good News' of 1927 Is for Lovers of the Obvious," by Clive Barnes, *The New York Times*, Dec. 25, 1974, page 53.

[15] "The Return of Beverly Sills," by Martin Bernheimer, *The Los Angeles Times*, Dec. 6, 1974, page 1, Part IV.

[16] "L.A. Gives N.Y. Tacky 'Turandot'," by Martin Bernheimer, *The Los Angeles Times*, Nov. 18, 1974, Part IV.

[17] "Helping Jamie Make It Through the Night," by Dan Sullivan, *The Los Angeles Times*, December 15, 1974, page 66, Calendar.

[18] "Jumpers' Keep ACT Hopping," by Dan Sullivan, *The Los Angeles Times*, Dec. 19, 1974, page 1, Part IV.

[19] " 'Pink Flamingos' Strictly for the Very Open-Minded," by Kevin Thomas, *The Los Angeles Times*, Dec. 13, 1974, page 21, Part IV.

[20] "Our Late Night," by Clive Barnes, *The New York Times*, Jan. 4, 1975, page 16.

[21] "The Year the Yankees Beat Lincoln Center," by Harold C. Schonberg, *The New York Times*, March 14, 1971, page 13.

[22] "Woody, the Would-Be Critic," by Woody Allen, *The New York Times*, May 2, 1971, page 11.

3

THE CRITIC'S NETWORK

Who do critics write for? What type of readers do they have in mind while preparing reviews?

"As many as possible," responds Paul Richard of the *Washington Post*.

"None," says John Ardoin, of the *Dallas Morning News*. "I write what I must and hope it finds an audience."

"That *Cosmopolitan* girl," quips *Cosmo* film critic Liz Smith.

"Mostly those who may want to share," says Charles Champlin of *The Los Angeles Times*."

"Bright high school and college kids," says rock critic Robert Christgau of the *Village Voice*. "Most rock critics write for other critics," admits Wayne Robins, *Newsday* and *Creem* critic.

"Myself"—Lawrence DeVine of the *Detroit Free Press*. "Selective TV viewers"—John J. O'Connor, *The New York Times*. "Dummies," blurts Marilyn Stasio, of *Cue Magazine*.

"Typical middle-aged executives," says Joy Boyum, of the *Wall Street Journal*. "It's very nice to say that you write only for yourself, but this is nonsense. I write to be understood. Sometimes your audience is a terrifying burden to you but quite clearly if you're not talking to anybody then why are you writing?

Your concept of your audience becomes a guidepost for the kind of remarks that you make."

"The best reader is one who is already about as discriminating as the critic," John Simon confessed in *The New Leader*, "in other words, as much of an elitist."[1]

In addition to these and other specific audiences, critics generally have a range of readers in mind when they approach their typewriters. Their preferences fall into two groups—primary readers and secondary ones, though all are subgroups of general newspaper audiences. Most critics write for those members of the arts public who did not share this particular event but want to know about it because of their on-going interest in the arts. A complete description of the event will be important for this type of reader, as well as an analysis and assessment. The other most often cited reader is also a member of the regular arts public who did share this event and who may want to read the critic's review for its evaluation and interpretation. Some readers evidently want to check their own views with the critics and to see if he saw something they didn't. And the experience of reading about an event in which you have first-hand experience tells you something about yourself as well as the critic and criticism.

The third category of primary readers are those who rarely attend arts events but are interested and want to stay informed. Their requirements are similar to those in the first category.

Secondary readers include the artists involved, peers which include editors, other critics and journalists, casual readers with little arts interest, and producers and others in the entertainment or arts industry. Critics who said they wrote for artists as well as general readers usually covered art, theatre and film.

Other critics offered socio-metric indices probably gathered in readership surveys done for advertisers. "Youngish, college-educated and middle class," said a *Newsday* critic. "Women over 40" are theatre goers and review readers to a Nashville drama critic. "Most quite conservative" a Tulsa critic said of his audience.

Specialized publications have a more definite sense of their readership. *Women's Wear Daily* critics say their readers have high incomes and are superficially trendy. *SoHo Weekly News* critics write mainly for artists who live in their community.

Arts audiences, too, are a clue about who will be interested in reading about new works in the field. Movie-goers tend to be under 30; classical music connoisseurs are older; and book review readers are better educated than average newspaper readers, critics report.

To debate whether the critic serves the theatre or the reading public misses the point, insists Elliott Norton, theatre critic for the *Boston Herald American.*

> His primary obligation is to the readers who buy the paper. Before all else, he is a reporter, getting and writing the news about what Brooks Atkinson once called "last night's disturbance in the theatre."
>
> If he does this fairly and adequately, it seems to me, he serves not only the reader who buys his report but the theatre which produced the play and beyond that The Theatre itself, the larger entity which encompasses all productions and which depends for its existence and for the ultimate quality of its work, even in this age of television, on such written transmission of information.[2]

Stanley Kauffmann is even more blunt on this subject: "The critic would not exist if the public did not want him to exist. Not one newspaper or magazine, however high-minded, would carry criticism one day after the editor became convinced that the public had stopped reading it."[3]

Aside from critics' intuitive responses, what else is known about the arts audience—readers of criticism?

The arts public, which presumably includes the audience for criticism, has been variously described in several recent studies. In a 1974 survey conducted for Associated Councils of the Arts, almost 9 of 10 American adults said they thought the arts "are important to the quality of life in their communities." Attendance at cultural events, the survey showed, did not vary as much by sex or race as by such other socio-economic factors as age, income and education. More than 49 per cent of the American population attend such visual arts activities as art shows, museums and craft shows and 48 per cent go to theatre, movies, ballet or modern dance performances, opera, the circus and other pageants. About 37 per cent reportedly attend musical performances such as rock, jazz, folk, symphony or chamber music concerts.[4]

Of the 3,000 Americans interviewed in the ACA survey, about 71 per cent of the adult public, or more than 103 million people, had attended at least one live performing arts event during the past year.

Frequent attenders were most often young (20s to 40s), upper middle class (white collar types and professionals), and educated (college graduates).

A pioneering 1973 survey of New York State residents, also conducted by Louis Harris & Associates, had statistically shattered the myth that the general public has little use or respect for the arts.[5]

"Not only the rich or the highly educated value and esteem the arts," said Joseph Farrell, of the National Research Center of the Arts. "The survey shows that these feelings are shared by many among the butchers and bakers, the plumbers and policemen, by many people up and down the economic scale and in every region of the state. What this means is the existence of a 'culturally inclined coalition' far broader and different than the traditionally conceived audience for the arts."

The "culturally inclined coalition" was estimated to be about 47 per cent of the state population—22 per cent who are active in the arts and 25 per cent who have fairly frequent involvement with the arts.

Another myth laid to rest by the survey is the notion that people who like the arts are not well-rounded individuals. The report concluded:

> Far from being stoop-shouldered aesthetes, the active culture buff appears to be more active generally and something of a Renaissance man, engaging in outdoor activities, attending or participating in sports and social events somewhat more frequently than the average man.

Both the ACA national survey and the New York State sample found that respondents ranked their sources of arts information in similar order: About three-fourths of the public cited local newspapers as their primary source of news and views about cultural events in their community. The non-urban, affluent-educated and culture-prone groups most often rely on newspapers while a majority of city residents, nonwhites and teenagers use word-of-mouth—recommendations from friends and relatives—to keep abreast of events. Comments from radio and TV are a source of information for about one-third of the public and about one-fourth are reached by posters, handbills and sidewalk advertising. Magazine stories and reviews, direct mail ads and subscription solicitations are the minor methods people use to stay up-to-date on cultural and entertainment possibilities.

• • • •

Critical Note: "There are three classes of people: those who do not see, those who see when they are shown and those who see by themselves," Leonardo da Vinci said.

• • • •

Can critics help educate readers about criticism?

Yes, but the majority don't attempt it.

If patrons of the arts and readers of criticism all consider themselves informal critics, as *Variety*'s Hobe Morrison and others speculate, then occasional articles explaining the subtleties of the critical process could help audiences improve their skill. Yet slightly less than half the critics ever write about their craft. A few critics cite examples they've written to help educate readers. Roger Ebert, *Chicago Sun-Times* critic, for instance, did a Sunday magazine piece on the meaning of various visual compositions, camera movements and cinemagraphic strategies for film-buff readers. *Newsday* film critic Joseph Gelmis detailed the behind-the-scenes techniques employed in the selling of "Last Tango in Paris," so his readers would better understand the industry. Others who write on criticism occasionally say they try to explain their biases or tell why or how they reached a particular viewpoint about a work. John Simon, for example, regularly writes about criticism and his perspective and problems during the August doldrums.

"Critics who write about criticism are unemployed," jibes Alfred Frankenstein, *San Francisco Chronicle* art critic. "Navel gazing is an indulgent luxury," adds Martin Bernheimer of *The L. A. Times.* Other reasons listed for not writing about criticism include: "too self-serving," "too parochial," "incestuous," "irrelevant," "dull," "process is too complex," "done too much already," and "editors frown on it."

Many who refuse believe readers aren't interested or they already know as much about criticism as they want. Yet there's some evidence to doubt critics' low estimate of public interest. Several critics said they've had to explain the critical process to readers who wrote irate letters to them. Others confessed that they were often asked questions about their work when they spoke in public forums. And, a *Milwaukee Journal* critic said the paper's ombudsman had written about criticism, though he hadn't because "it wasn't in his sphere."

• • • •

Critical Note: "All first rate critics are, in some measure, banded in one army, fighting in the same everlasting war, and substantially agreed in distinguishing the uniforms of trash, the immemorial enemy, and of sound work, the friend."—C. E. Montague of *The Manchester Guardian*

• • • •

Why does the public periodically malign critics as a group?

The anti-critic and anti-criticism sentiment in America is large and often vocal in its attacks. Its adherents—those who blame critics for failures—seem to increase during hard times, such as cultural lulls or recessions. In this school, critics are all considered negativistic, hostile and even irresponsible. Obviously, the arts and society would be better off without such doomsayers, they'd argue.

The Wall Street Journal, one of the best newspapers in the country and one that has critics on its staff, railed against television critics in an editorial several years ago on the following grounds:

> Most people who criticize mass communications media cannot bring themselves to accept the fact that when the public is free to choose among various products, it chooses, time after time, those which intellectuals abhor. They seem unable to reconcile themselves to the fact that their hunger for more news, better plays, more serious debate, is not a hunger characteristic of man.[6]

The editorial concluded with more damnation:

> It is important that America's intellectual and cultural elite, which so frequently is out of touch with the political and social concerns of the majority of Americans, refrain from portraying its particular esthetic values as the only ones worth holding.

The editorial implies that critics are intellectual and pits them against "man," as if the two categories were exclusive. Nevertheless, the result, considering America's tradition of anti-intellectualism, is anti-critic and pro-non-intellectual reader.

Faubion Bowers, himself a critic of music, books and Oriental art and theatre, penned a fiercely anti-critic Letter to the Editor of *The New York Times* aimed mainly at attacking Clive Barnes. Bowers wrote:

> Critics are the only people who don't have a right to their own opinion. . . . Years ago I learned that the critic must describe, not opine, must evaluate the performance on its own terms, not his. Performance is where a reviewer reports an event in fair representation. It must be that failure inheres within any newspaper critic's job. Flaubert once said that 'the only way not to be unhappy is to shut yourself up in art, and count everything else as nothing.' Relevant as this sounds, it does not apply to the critic. Habitual passive presence before a practicing and practiced art leads not to expanded experience but to staleness. You begin to look without seeing, listen without hearing, react with-

out feeling. A critic's visits are more or less compulsory, choice-less, commercial. He attends for a livelihood, not a life. The basic anomaly is that he, perforce, takes or denies pleasure with-out ever completing the traffic by giving. The critic is a non-creative, unoriginal person perpetually exposed to inventive and innovative personalities, and this likens him to a magistrate who neither commits a crime nor is victimized, only an administrator of arbitrary law as presumed protection against a supposed soci-ety.[7]

In one of his annual August reflective articles in *New York*, John Simon admitted that he gets nearly five times as much hate mail as fan letters. "Who is the complainer?" he asked and an-swered:

> He or she may be a literate, theatre-loving outsider; or, more often, a vociferously self-satisfied pretender, whose lack of cul-ture and discrimination is reflected in his or her inability to cope with the English of mere letter writing, never mind the vastly more complex and subtle language of art. Sometimes the corre-spondent is a practicing theatre person; but, in that case, there is usually a personal axe to be ground.[8]

Simon went on to generalize about anti-critics:

> It is a curious, rampant if not endemic, symptom of an ar-rogantly, unthinkingly pseudo-liberated society, this assumption that everyone's opinion about theatre is equally good as anyone else's—and if it happens to be that of an indignant corre-spondent, not merely equal but better. I wonder: do these su-periorly enlightened consumers write similarly insolent letters to engineers, physicists, biochemists, twelve-tone composers, structural anthropologists, to name but a few? Of course not, because even they realize that they know little or nothing about engineering, dodecaphony or enzymes. And yet (to take engineer-ing) have they not crossed innumerable bridges?

Hitting back with this final punch, Simon concluded:

> What is especially quaint is the assumption of these gab-gifted amateurs that, because of their presumed numerousness or ac-tual vociferousness, the dissenting critic should be fired. If criti-cism were merely a business (as, alas, it is for some), the cus-tomer might be 'always right.' But serious criticism is an art, a mode of perception and expression, an ability to evaluate based on multiplicity of experience and—less definably—taste. And here mass opinion has, historically, more often proven wrong than right. The critic, like any other artist, would be suspect if he did not—by not being only of his time—antagonize the multi-tude.

Citing further dangers of the anti-criticism phenomenon, Grace and Fred M. Hechinger wrote in *The New York Times Magazine:*

> When press-agentry wins out over criticism, the inevitable result is the kind of smug self-satisfaction that makes national standards increasingly less demanding and the national product, artistic as well as commercial, more shabby. It leads to pleas by television producers to judge their serious efforts more kindly, on a sliding scale of criticism, with the sights of comparison trained on the valleys of mediocrity rather than the peaks of excellence.
>
> Whether in the field of drama, art, music or literature, this anti-critical atmosphere increasingly demands that critics be held to the practice of 'topical reporting' without the bite of comparison or opinion. Inevitably, such 'objective reporting' without value judgments, gives limitless license to those who lack talent, or even honesty. While it may protect an artist's feelings and a collector's investment, it makes the public easy prey of fads, cliques and coteries.[9]

The Hechingers, like many others, insist that any self-improvement in achievement, effort and taste requires high standards, tough comparisons and honest evaluations. Critics, who dedicate themselves to this task, must remain outside the domain of vested interests for their comments to be valued.

"In an age when shoddiness is often condoned in the interest of harmony or to protect financial investments, the critical voice is needed more than ever to praise or condemn on the basis of independent judgment and integrity," wrote the Hechingers. "Unpleasant as it may be, we must be ready to face our personal, professional, institutional and national image in the critic's mirror."

• • • •

Critical Note: "The trade of critic in literature, music and the drama is most degraded of all trades," Mark Twain once said.

• • • •

What do artists think of critics?

While no systematic attempt was made to poll artists about their views of critics, a sampling of feedback exists from interviews and letters to the editor:

Lyricist-composer Earl Wilson, Jr. refused to have an "official opening" for his Off Broadway musical review, "Let My People Come." In explaining his position, he said,

When you take in $10,000 in the first week, and now $30,000 a week, why should you let critics determine what happens to your show? I knew that a few critics could destroy us if they happened not to understand the show. The critics don't know anything about young people and what they have to say about their bodies or their feelings about sex. Critics live on another planet. So we took a gamble.[10]

• • • •

Playwright Arthur Miller: "For the most part our critics are more reportorial than analytical or critical. I don't see how it can be much different when you have to write a review in 20 minutes . . . you are bound to be driven back to retelling the story and saying whether or not you were affected by it . . . the bulk of the audience is not interested in any more than that."

• • • •

English actor Nicol Williamson: "I think they're more terrified than actors, in a way; they want to be liked, they want to have an impact, too."

• • • •

Broadway director Tom O'Horgan: "I don't read reviews very much. Critics never seem to review plays any more. They're busy reviewing subject matter."

• • • •

Screenwriter Stirling Silliphant said of the *L.A. Times'* Charles Champlin: "He's never criticized a film I've done on which I haven't felt his criticism was absolutely correct and I only wished I called Chuck before I wrote it and asked him about it."

• • • •

Actor Dustin Hoffman: "I'd rather have a critic jump on me than praise me. When a critic says a movie is great, he's just building up the importance of his job. Critics do to movies what plant lovers do to plants. They water them until they die. It's called assassination by adoration. Why we take these people seriously I can't imagine."

• • • •

Playwright Ed Bullins: "A dichotomy between the Black artists and the reactionary Black pseudo-intellectual elements that exploit the community is most evident today in the 'Destroy Black Theatre' propaganda of the so-called Black critics who have access to national publications. These untalented few attempt to hold forth as the arbiters of the values that they want infused within the Black theatre artist's work.

"These parasites, sucking a living off the energies and talents of Black playwrights, actors, directors, designers, musicians, and technicians, feel so above their prey, the artists, that they are very seldom seen in their company, feeling threatened by the strong, positive presences of the artists—surely, but smugly thinking that they cannot learn anything by the association.

"Nor are these so-called Black critics found in the Black community, except when they are on assignment for their publications. Picture the group, if one can: almost without exception they wear glasses, and are never out of their uniform of suit and tie, resembling unsuccessful colored insurance men; as they stand around the lobbies of Black theatres before curtain, among clusters of grass-roots Black people which cause them nervous perspiration, they grin insincerely like morticians' apprentices and talk out of the sides of their mouths to each other.

"When they leave, to write of how far the Black production was from their preconceived models, this cadre of mediocrity returns to little pockets of integrated Black bourgeois/dom and carried on what passes for intellectual conversation with other Black pseudo-intelligences and their white cronies."[11]

• • • •

Director Stanley Kramer: "My critics are severe, but that only makes it more exciting. I read their stuff, all their pat bourgeois intellectuality. I love approval as much as anyone, but I've also been around a while. When I was younger what I wanted to do was give a negative critic a cement overcoat. But I've sublimated that, so sometimes I just don't read them anymore. Too much self-analysis is dangerous. I've survived failure. I'm always pursuing the next dream, hunting for the next truth."

• • • •

Filmmaker Paul Morrissey: "We'd rather make films that, hopefully, critics would be forced *not* to review."

• • • •

Filmmaker William Friedkin ("The French Connection" and "The Exorcist"): "I have a theory of criticism: If a film is liked by the critics and the audience, it's probably a great film. If a film is liked by the audience, but not by the critics, it's still probably a great film. If a film is liked only by the critics, it is a piece of s——t!" [12]

• • • •

Film director, producer and distributor Roger Corman charges that syndicated critic Rex Reed is "more interested in his own image than the film he is reviewing."

• • • •

Screenwriter Lonnie Elder III, attacking *New York Times* film critic Vincent Canby:

"He is widely read, accepted and classified as a leader (by virtue of the *Times* imprimatur) among the select group of contemporary critics who continuously mount paeans of praise for the works of so-called director-auteurs. His meat is the personal statement film, those which rarely reach or fascinate mass audiences because they are obtuse, overly symbolic, intellectualized beyond belief.

"But these are films that demand and require column after column of copy from critics like Canby who explain, interpret, relate, re-evaluate, re-review, etc., ad nauseam. These are films and fodder to make the critic feel most important. From his comments on "Sounder," I can only get the impression that Canby, in wanting to be important, simply cannot be so with the likes of a 'Sounder.'

"He can only do it with films rooted in enigmas and inpenetrable profundities. It follows that he can only maintain his importance by the deception of chopping away at a 'Sounder' or any other film that reaches quickly and directly into the hearts and minds of the public." [13]

• • • •

Opera composer Gian Carlo Menotti: "Why is it that so many critics continually repeat the same old boring clichés about me. I am, of course, aware that most music critics are unimaginative and undiscerning people—that they are people who read each other's reviews, and keep repeating themselves endlessly. But what is really discouraging is that the younger critics do not have the courage to express a different opinion. They all follow the opinions of their chief critics—their bosses—and don't care to strike out on their own. . . .When you know that any new opera of yours will be damned and panned by the chief music critic of *The New York Times* even *before* it's put on, then, naturally, you (want to) go somewhere else. After all, I make my living as a composer."[14]

• • • •

Writer-artist Gertrude Stein: "No artist needs criticism, he needs only appreciation. If he needs criticism, he is no artist."

• • • •

Television personality Dick Cavett, responding to a review by critic John J. O'Connor: "I often ask, and am asked, when should you respond to a critic? The answer is: virtually never. For several reasons. It makes you look like a poor sport, thin-skinned, and one who can't take it. It also calls attention to something that people have either misused or forgotten. . . .

"I think you *should* respond to a critic when you have done something that you know is good and he doesn't agree. . . . Something I would hope for from a critic: recognition when you have done something important . . . . It is so bloody hard to get anything newsworthy on TV, with the constant pressure to be escapist and show-biz, that it seems part of a critic's contribution might be to give credit when it is done. Or at least indicate that he is aware of it. It would help.

"A final danger in answering a critic is the tendency to say something nasty about him to get even. I will not. Suppose for a moment that I think his prose has all the sparkle of a second mortgage. I would be foolish to say so here, because it would not be relevant. Besides, we performers are vulnerable and sensitive creatures, wanting affection. I want O'Connor to like me. In hopes that he will, I am going to send him a list of what I plan to wear in the upcoming weeks (O'Connor complained about Cavett's dress); so he can continue his fashion reporting without actually tuning in and risking depression."[15]

• • • •

Artist James Rosenquist, replying to *New York Times* art critic John Canaday's "personal attack on my character": "Long live artists, long live art collectors, long live art dealers, long live art critics, but damn a person like Mr. Canaday."

• • • •

Drama critic Richard Gilman, after directing his first major production: "Theatre people are forever pointing out that critics ought to know a great deal more than most of them do about the sheer logistics and subtle complex actualities of putting on plays. However often such an argument is used as an excuse for ineptitude or stupidity or inferior vision, it isn't *always* used that way, and it was a valuable and humbling experience for me to find out that it's not."[16]

• • • •

Critical Note: "A critic at whom artists throw palettes and blowtorches is likely to have merits because who would bother to throw things at a fool?" said psychologist Rudolf Arnheim.

• • • •

How do critics view their relationship with artists?

Most critics don't believe they are in business to help artists stay in business, yet they recognize that their fortunes entwine. A few critics have had so much to say about the work of artists they like, they have become identified together. Pauline Kael has certainly advanced the careers of Bernardo Bertolucci and Robert Altman; Clement Greenberg and Jackson Pollock, Harold Rosenberg and William de Kooning are some such duos.

Michael Feingold, drama critic of the *Village Voice*, said of the relationship:

> The critic and the artist are engaged in a long and complicated dance, and it's dangerous when the dance turns into mutual seduction, and the critic starts getting dependent on the artist, all the while thinking that the artist is dependent on him.
>
> A critic has to believe that criticism is an art in its own right, that what gives his work value is what he writes, not what he writes about; otherwise criticism becomes flattery and apology for one's friends, and the critic turns into the artist's valet, skittering after him with whiskbroom and a notebook full of friendly phrases.

Art critic John Canaday, of *The New York Times*, acknowledged the tenuous link this way:

> Artists are mercurial spirits, easily pleased and easily cast down. They respond to a kind word with the spontaneity of a child unexpectedly proffered an ice cream cone, and like the child's, their response is unaffected by the identity of the giver, who may be a critic, a colleague, or the village idiot. It is all the same to them. Their pleasure is simple, direct, and unanalytical—a joy to see. But drop a hint that their work leaves something to be desired, that something more than an extended generation gap accounts for the aesthetic lag between their latest effort and Michelangelo's Sistine Ceiling, and you are in for it. They become boiling amalgams of fury, contempt, and despair.[17]

"Ultimately, the relationship between a creative performer and an open-minded critic will always hang in delicate balance," agrees John Ardoin, music critic of the *Dallas Morning News*. "No matter how strong an artist's belief in his reviewer's competence and honesty, this will be of little comfort to him when faced with a reaction that is less than enthusiastic."[18]

Francois Truffaut sees the two as mismatched adversaries and he knows both professions since he began his career as a film critic and then turned to directing and acting. "In the relations between artist and critic, the critic never forgets that in the power relationship he is the weaker, even if he tries to hide the fact by an aggressive tone, while the artist constantly loses sight of his ontological supremacy," Truffaut observes.[19]

John Simon prefers Old Testament criticism (an eye for an eye) to the New Testament type (turn the other cheek). Simon says theatrical experiences are both happy and unhappy,

> especially when one is obliged to excoriate a performance. Its perpetrator has—with deficiencies of voice, body or deportment; of face, gesture or timing—made you acutely miserable for three hours and very much longer if you count the time an ugly image can linger in your consciousness. One must repay injury with injury . . . . The critic writes for posterity. And posterity will not care whose feelings were hurt.[20]

In assaying critics' attitudes toward new artists, Clive Barnes observes that critics are generally among the most intelligent of the artist's audience:

> Years ago critics were very confident and very concerned that they should not be made fools of. They hated the idea of being hostage to someone else's originality and, as a result, would damn anything that had a dangerous sense of the new to it. There are a few conventional critics that are still like that. But

mostly critics are too generous to the new. We care very much for the art we are working with, love the form, and want to give every new artistic sucker a break. This works well for the audience—which gets shaken up once in a while—and it works well for the artist, who is, at least, generously handled in his embryonic stage.[21]

● ● ● ●

Critical Note: "The one chief and damning disability of the young critic is that he always has some pet author and pet work for whose supremacy he is mortally jealous," wrote George Bernard Shaw in *Advice to a Young Critic.*

● ● ● ●

What about the critic's relationship with a work of art?

This relationship must be considered on several levels. First, in a general sense, the selected major critics interviewed in the Louis Harris study said they didn't believe the arts are "high brow," but an integral part of American life and that public interest in the arts can best be promoted by enthusiasm, honesty, good writing, and critical leadership.

At a different level, the issue of defining what a work of art is must be dealt with, since it seems to differ in the performing arts from the visual arts. In the visual arts, an object exists and it can be observed, described, analyzed, compared and so forth. In the performing arts, the work is trickier to pin down: generally it is a performance by a specific group of people at a certain time in a specific place. The artist's creation and his intentions in the work must be translated or interpreted from a play script or musical score, which are the written representation of the work, but not it itself.

Dance critic Deborah Jowitt, attempting to puzzle out what a dance work is or was, wondered if the first performance was definitive or whether the consensus "best" version was the standard of the work. She concluded that

> most people, consciously or unconsciously, accept each performance of a dance they're watching as The Work itself; if they see it again, they may adjust their mental picture. It's only in discussion or critical writing that you become aware of the ephemeral nature of even a frequently performed work.[22]

Some critics' estimation of their field, based on their whole body of experience, seems to affect their perception of specific works. Film critic Andrew Sarris complains that few new movies hold his interest. Art critic Barbara Rose, writing in *New York*, observed that art criticism was

> in such bad shape because criticism cannot be separated from the art it examines, and the art currently filling the museums and galleries is of such low quality generally that no real critical intelligence could possibly feel challenged to analyze it. . . . Critics endlessly complain that modern art has become increasingly hermetic, complex, specialized. When Roy Lichtenstein says, 'the great public for art is about as large as the great public for chemistry', he is pointing to a serious difficulty for the artist in terms of reaching viewers.[23]

Finally, a critic's verdict—or final judgment—about a work indicates his/her willingness to distinguish between a critical judgment of the work—an intellectual assessment of its quality—and one's personal taste or intuitive preference for the work. These two decisions might be related, but not necessarily so.

The variety of verdicts rendered by the critic specifies both his attitude toward art and his own values. David K. Kirby, of Florida State University,[24] has devised eight verdicts that critics might use: it's a work of art and I like it; art and I don't like it; art and I don't like it now, but I could learn to like it; art and I'm indifferent to it; it's trash and I like it; trash and I don't like it; trash and I don't like it now, but I could learn to like it; and trash and I'm indifferent to it.

Kirby's delineation of a critic's personal preference for the work is useful, but his lumping of all critical judgment into either art or trash omits the mixed category. An expansion of verdicts to 12 would include all possible distinctions.

Yet, critics rarely make such subtle judgments. Too often, reviews are simply "It's art and I like it" such as Howard Thompson's rave in *The New York Times*:

> Don Quixote's 'impossible dream' in 'Man of La Mancha' looked and sounded splendid last night in a stunning revival of Dale Wasserman's musical at the Vivian Beaumont Theater. How it could have been better, we cannot imagine.

Or they are "it's trash and I don't like it," as Terrence O'Flaherty illustrated when he panned a new television show in the *San Francisco Chronicle*:

> If there had been a shred of inventiveness or craft or inspiration or performing talent in this new dramatic entry, it might have passed without comment as just another polyester production from NBC, but its barrenness deserves a critical raspberry of major proportions.

Occasionally a few critics acknowledge that "the work is art but I don't like it" as John Rockwell once noted in a *New York Times* review of Grand Funk Railroad: "Grand Funk is solidly, crunchingly effective in what it does: steady, inexorable, heavy metal rock 'n roll." But he apparently sided with other rock critics who called the band "loud" and "crude" and not really deserving of the adulatory success it has enjoyed. John Simon, in an *Esquire* review, was more direct: "Some films are merely bad, others actually loathesome, still others loathesome without being literally bad. In this last category belongs 'Going Places'."

When critics have a mixed reaction to a work, they often hesitate to tag it either Art or trash. Rex Reed, in the *New York Daily News*, for example, began one review with the equivocation:

> First the good news: 'The Great Gatsby' is a most impressive film indeed. Now for the bad news: with so much going for it, it's a shame that it isn't better, but it is my sad duty to report that the end result is a disappointment.

However, Reed showed an affinity for the film throughout his review and ended with: "Whatever nitpicking one cares to indulge in, 'The Great Gatsby' is still true to the book's reverent nastiness."

Bruce Cook, in the now-defunct *The National Observer*, began one review noting the limitations of films ("More than in other arts, there is in film a kind of tyranny of style over content") and genre films in particular:

> Style is the standard by which we must judge 'Murder on the Orient Express'. That makes it seem, I'm sure, as though I intend to come down hard on 'Murder on the Orient Express', and I have no such intention. It is, as they say, fun, the kind of movie you can't really dislike. But don't be misled. With all those names above the title, you may expect a grander movie than this one, something on an epic scale at least. Actually, this is nothing more nor less than an Agatha Christie mystery done perfectly in period.[25]

New Yorker drama critic Brendan Gill's review of "Lorelei," a remake of the 1949 musical "Gentlemen Prefer Blondes," was mixed another way. He admired its star, Carol Channing as "an impressive national resource," but said the show was "a botch of a particularly unpleasant sort."

Sometimes, the sheer amount of space critics devote to commenting on a controversial work is the only clue the audience can glean about its value and interest. For example, films such as "A Clockwork Orange" or "Last Tango in Paris" evoked reams of copy from critics. Virtually no one dismissed these works as minor achievements, regardless of their attitude toward the issues raised by the filmmakers. Such controversial works best illustrate the difficulty critics have with the so-called "critical objectivity." While they afford critics ample opportunity to express personal tastes, readers often learn less about the work than the critic.

Some critics appear to be cultural snobs, insisting art is for the few. Art critic John Russell of *The New York Times* took this posture when he wrote a certain exhibition lacked "the kind of pictures which even very dull people can recognize as 'important'."

• • • •

Critical Note: To herald the release of "Family Plot," Alfred Hitchcock threw a press party stylishly based on a cemetery theme. Decorations included tombstones boldly emblazoned with various critics' names.

• • • •

How do critics view their peers?

Clive Barnes, not long ago, said he thought criticism was getting better, that it was both better conceived and written. The critics interviewed by Louis Harris in 1970 agreed; more specifically, they thought that criticism in newspapers and magazines had improved in quality during the previous 10 years but that criticism on television and radio—what little there is of it—had remained about the same. Critics in the poll said the highest quality criticism appears in magazines with criticism in newspapers in second place and that on television a poor third. Criticism on radio was considered lowest of all.

About two-thirds of the critics in the survey also said that their peers tended to emphasize their style too much and their content too little, though about half of the prominent critics interviewed disagreed with that point.

When critics from across the country were surveyed in 1974 about the other critics they read, almost half cited critics of *The New York Times*. New York critics dominated the list, generally. The other most often mentioned critics represented the *New Yorker, New York, Newsweek, Time, Los Angeles Times, Washington Post* and the *Village Voice*.

A significant number of critics said they never looked at the work of their peers or just omitted responding to the question.

The earlier Harris poll also showed that the most critics read *The New York Times* critics (five of the eight critics most frequently mentioned represented the *Times;* Barnes led the pack; others were Judith Crist, Pauline Kael and Irving Kolodin).

Ms. Kael says she avoids her colleagues to insure her professional purity. On a PBS show, she reported that she preferred to write her immediate response right after she saw the work. "If I had time for reflection, I might pick up the consensus opinion of other critics and might not be so true to what I felt," she reasoned.[26]

The critic most often criticized by critics is John Simon. When Brooks Atkinson called Simon "the worst natured" New York drama critic, Simon countered with "Goodness of nature, as Mae West might have said, has nothing to do with it." Simon, who sees himself as a policeman of his fellow watchdogs ("alas, to no avail"), has often stirred public feuds with other critics. Once he told his readers that if they didn't like reading his views, they could "read instead Clive Barnes's home-on-the-range kind of criticism, where seldom is heard a discouraging word." He has also reviled unprofessional film critics who "cannot distinguish between competence and incompetence."

While some rivalry among New York's highly competitive clique of film critics reaches the public—the Simon-Sarris flap of 1971, Kael's slams at Sarris, Canby's swipes at Kael, Crist's snubbing of Reed—their alliances rarely do. *Village Voice* critics Andrew Sarris and Molly Haskell are married and friends of the *Times'* Vincent Canby. Younger generation critics—such as David Denby, Frank Rich, of the *New York Post*, and Jay Cocks, of *Time*—are also friendly with one another. Responsible critics acknowledge they share vested interests with others and know they can learn from one another if they'll only stay in touch.

How do critics' salaries compare with peers' covering business or politics?

While nearly a third of the critics asked said they didn't know how their salaries compared with their colleagues, close to half said their paychecks were in the same range as peers. The remainder tended to be on the higher side of average rather than lower. Some of the equity is surely attributed to those under Newspaper Guild contracts and to those with long periods of service. In any case, journalists employed as critics are paid as well as other professionals.

Do critics view criticism as a profession?

Most of the full-time critics (those who spend more than half their time writing criticism) believe criticism is a separate profession, while about half of the part-time critics surveyed by Harris thought so. Film, drama and music critics, more often than others, see their roles as a profession in itself.

Do critics usually join professional associations?

For whatever reasons, some critics are joiners and others aren't.

"I am not now and I never have been a member of any organization of critics," stated the late *San Francisco Chronicle* jazz critic and *Rolling Stone* columnist Ralph J. Gleason. "And what is more, I never will be. I don't believe in organizations of critics."

Gleason's adamant opposition is shared by some of the more than two-thirds of the critics recently surveyed who do not belong to some type of critics' association and some of those who are basically non-joiners.

After joining, Michael Feingold, *Village Voice* critic, blasts the New York Drama Desk: "I never go to their meetings, as the topics and most of the people involved tend to bore me." Alan Rich, *New York* critic, describes the Music Critics Association as "a pretty dreary bunch." And *L.A. Times* music critic Martin Bernheimer says he belongs, "but it is a waste of time."

Others refuse to join critics' groups for various reasons. Drama critic Stewart Klein bluntly confesses: "I'd rather not be seen with them." Wade Mosby, television critic of the *Milwaukee Journal*, opines, "I think being a member of a group would imperil my own objectivity." Robert C. Marsh, music critic of the *Chicago Sun-Times*, adds, "Criticism is not an organizable activity."

However, some critics, because of their specialization, have been pushing for recognition of criticism as a separate profession. Critics of emerging popular arts, often led by those in provincial locations, apparently feel the need for fraternization, and in recent times at least three national groups of critics have sprung up, which initially attracted sizable memberships: The Rock Writers of the World held its organizing meeting (and only) in Memphis in June, 1973. The Dance Critics Association was formed in June, 1974, and the American Theatre Critics Association followed in August, 1974.

Network models: real and ideal

These five models of critics' relationships with art and artists and with the arts public are an attempt to conceptualize visually examples of interaction suggested in the preceding text. The aim here is to describe networks and to generalize about states of attunedness, not to infer causality. The connecting lines specify the intensity of interest—solid lines indicate stronger interaction than dotted ones. One further purpose of this model-building is to suggest some areas requiring additional study.

MODEL 1: Here the role of the critic is negligible and critical input is largely disregarded by the public. The public is attracted to art and artists mostly through word-of-mouth sources, advertising, publicity and other non-judgmental factors. The critic is definitely out-of-touch with his audience. Perhaps he has mocked work that will be popularly successful for non-aesthetic reasons: a star is involved, timely with current fad, etc. Or the critic may be becoming jaded because he's seen too much of the same kind of art.

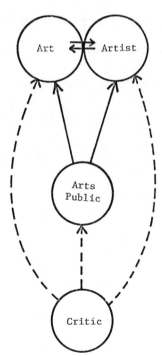

MODEL 2: Here the critic also has an insignificant role in encouraging people to embrace art. Although the critic regards the work highly, he is not capable of delivering the public to share it. Perhaps the work is difficult (such as a literary film in a foreign language with subtitles) or strange (such as non-narrative experimental drama or conceptual art or serial music), but, for whatever reason, the critic can't connect with the public about it.

If the critic pays more attention to the artist than the work of art, he may be an *auteur*. Again the public probably doesn't care about this interaction.

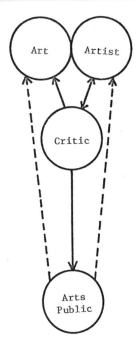

MODEL 3: Here the critic serves effectively as a consumer guide. In fact, the public relinquishes too much self-determination to the critic and lets him mitigate its choices. The public tends to look at art more through the critic's eyes and theories than its own.

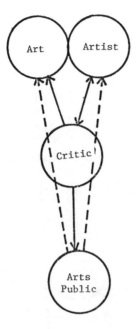

MODEL 4: Here the critic fails to connect to his readers because of other factors. He may prefer to write to impress other critics or those in the arts industry or his editor. Nonetheless, the critic's link to his readers is weak or non-existent and the public's ties with art are weak.

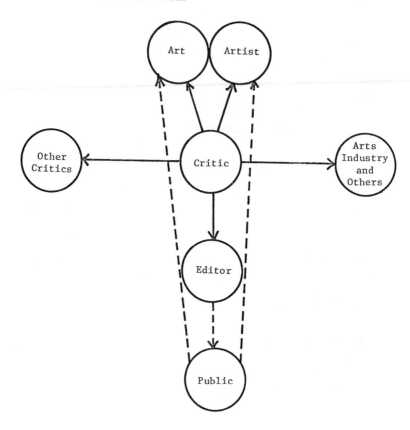

MODEL 5: Here the relationship between the critic, art and artist and the public is nearly equal. The flow among all parts is strong. The critic's role is to initiate dialogue with the public about art and mostly help explain new work. The public is discriminating in taking critical output and embracing art and artists.

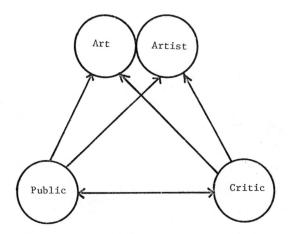

CHAPTER 3

[1] "On Being an Elitist Critic," by John Simon, *The New Leader*, October 27, 1975, page 23.

[2] "How to be a theatre critic? The answer is 'you try.' ", by Elliot Norton, *Boston Herald American Magazine*, June 18, 1978, page 19.

[3] Stanley Kauffmann, *Persons of the Drama* (New York: Harper & Row, 1976), page 373.

[4] *Americans and the Arts*, a survey of public opinion conducted by National Research Center of the Arts, New York: Associated Councils of the Arts, 1975, page 123.

[5] *Arts and the People*, A survey of Public Attitudes and Participation in the Arts and Culture in New York State, conducted by the National Research Center of the Arts, New York: American Councils for the Arts in Education, 1973, pp. 99.

[6] "TV and Its Critics," *Wall Street Journal*, Apr. 25, 1972, page 28.

[7] Letter to the Editor by Faubion Bowers, *The New York Times*, Feb. 21, 1971, page 12.

[8] "Who Pens the Poison," by John Simon, *New York*, August 21, 1972, page 39.

[9] "In Criticism of Anti-Criticism," by Grace and Fred Hechinger, *The New York Times Magazine*, March 11, 1962, pages 28–29.

[10] "How to Succeed in Show Business Without Really Opening," interview with Earl Wilson Jr. by Judy Klemesrud, *The New York Times*, Sept. 15, 1974, page 3, Section II.

[11] "Black Theatre, Bourgeois Critics," by Ed Bullins, *The New York Times*, August 27, 1972, page 10, Section II.

[12] "Rough Riding," by John Simon, *New York*, Aug. 1, 1977, page 65, quoting *The Story Behind The Exorcist* by Travers and Reiff.

[13] Letter to the Editor by Lonne Elder, *The New York Times*, November 26, 1972, page 10, Section II.

[14] "When the New York Critics Damn You . . . ," interview with Gian Carlo Menotti by John Gruen, *The New York Times*, April 14, 1974, page 1, Section II.

[15] Letter to the Editor by Dick Cavett, *The New York Times*, Feb. 11, 1973, page 24, Section II.

[16] "A Critic Crosses Over," by Richard Gilman, *The New York Times*, Sept. 22, 1970, page 1, Section II.

[17] "So What's Wrong With a Clothesline," by John Canaday, *The New York Times*, August 29, 1971, page 35, Section II.

[18] "A Critic Looks at Criticism," by John Ardoin, *Catalyst*, Spring 1976, page 9.

[19] "A Kind Word for Critics," by Francois Truffaut, *Harpers*, October 1977, page 98.

[20] "Once More Unto the Breach," by John Simon, *New York*, July 30, 1973, page 60.

[21] "Three Who May Be the Future," by Clive Barnes, *The New York Times*, December 23, 1973, page 10, Section II.

[22] "Detective Story: Find the Work," by Deborah Jowitt, *The New York Times*, August 20, 1972, page 14, Section II.

[23] "How to Know More Than What You Like," by Barbara Rose, *New York*, August 13, 1973, page 53.

[24] "Art and the Eight Verdicts," paper by David K. Kirby, Florida State University, presented at the Popular Culture Association in the South regional meeting in Atlanta, Ga., October 11, 1973.

[25] "Dreamstyle, Bondstyle, Turnstyle: Surface is All in the Genre Films," by Bruce Cook, *The National Observer*, Dec. 21, 1974, page 18.

[26] "Critics on Criticism," *Behind the Lines* show from WNET, New York, aired February 26, 1975.

4

THE ETHICAL TRAP

In recent years, some journalists have fretted over their "crisis in credibility," or the lack of public confidence in the press as an institution. Exact figures may vary from survey to survey, but less than one-third of the public often expresses high confidence in the print media and less than one-half of the public puts faith in broadcast journalism.

While reporters have traditionally been astute in questioning the ethics of public officials or spotting conflicts of interest or illegal practices of others, they have rarely focused their consciences on their own system. In the early 1970s, a noticeable change occurred and press criticism became increasingly available to the interested public. Some of this criticism certainly came from the scores of local journalism reviews that emerged around the nation, each devoted to monitoring the local press on its performance. Journalists, like others in society, were being held accountable, in large part by their peers. In the process, the public learned of major press weaknesses and of innumerable local problems, all of which no doubt contributed to a weakened credibility.

Surprisingly, though, the critics and reviewers rarely were the target of critical scrutiny, probably because they were generally considered "different." In one "Behind the Lines" show (a

97

Public Broadcasting Service journalism review) devoted to press ethics, however, rock music critic Richard Goldstein, of the *Village Voice*, confessed that he had turned down a $25,000 bribe offered by one music publisher in exchange for giving a series of lectures favoring that firm at a convention. Certainly Goldstein's revelation was shocking, but the $2 billion record industry was rife with scandal—payola, Clive Davis' expense account excesses and cocaine trafficking. An attempt to buy a critic was trivial in comparison.

Other questionable practices of critics surfaced elsewhere. In *The Art Crowd*, Sophy Burnham detailed the wheeling and dealing of critic Clement Greenberg, who reportedly accepted paintings as gifts from artist-"friends" and later resold them at peak market prices. His praising reviews of these same artists' work was said to enhance the value of his own art collection. Greenberg denies he profited from such activities.

Burnham insists the practice is still widespread: "The matter of giving pictures to critics hasn't changed in twenty years—a critic still accepts a picture but now it's wrong, whereas then it wasn't. Twenty years ago the picture was valueless and it was just a gift from one person to another. Today it's a gift of money. Critics have no standards; they aren't corrupt, but they haven't thought. A critic of twenty years recently called me and said after he'd read my book, he realized that accepting pictures was wrong, so he wanted me to know that he'd called up all the artists who had given him pictures and asked them to take them back."

Ralph Ortwell, managing editor of the *Chicago Sun-Times*, reported another probable conflict of interest in an *Editor & Publisher* story, "A radio-TV critic for a Chicago newspaper took a leave of absence recently to work as a consultant to a committee which was pushing a controversial transit district; one of his jobs was to help seek support of radio and TV stations in winning a referendum battle, the very same radio and TV stations he normally covers on his beat."

And, on "60 Minutes," Mike Wallace lambasted the inconsistency of his own network: "Ironically, while employees of CBS News are forbidden to go on junkets, the public relations people in another CBS division are busy setting up such junkets for television critics."

When the Associated Press Managing Editors' Professional Standards Committee surveyed 229 newspapers in 1972,[1] they found that 70 per cent said they allowed reporters and editors to accept free trips (junkets) provided by business and industry to "events of some significance." About 40 per cent said it was okay to accept all-expense-paid trips overseas. Only 21 per cent said that their staff were not allowed to accept gifts.

(Although some examples of the old lavish Hollywood fun-and-games junket days remain, a typical junket today is "briskly businesslike," reports Aljean Harmetz, in *The New York Times*. "It lasts two days, costs between $25,000 and $50,000 and consists of flying from 28 to 40 print and television journalists to Los Angeles for a screening, a relatively modest buffet dinner afterwards, and a day of interviews with the stars, director and producers.")

In a detailed section on Amusements, the APME study showed that 56 per cent of the newspapers regularly accepted a number of complimentary tickets to theatres and movie houses. Although most quality newspapers have adopted the policy of paying their own way in—and refusing all freebies—many middle-sized and small newspapers not only still accept complimentary passes but also request or solicit them. Few critics were said to disagree with the newspaper's policy on the matter.

Entertainment editors and writers from more than 100 medium-sized markets were the "key press" courted by a $1 million public relations program undertaken in mid-1975 by United Artists. UA Vice President Gabe Sumner said five major junkets were held for the "key press" because they worked for newspapers where "a good part of our business, grosses and interests lie."

Of his hard-sell publicity program, Sumner told *Variety:*

> We feel the activities are the kind most entertainment writers want to report on. We're meeting their needs. If we've heard any complaints from the press, overwhelmingly it has been 'Where is exciting story material? What has happened to the flow of publicity photos and feature stuff? Send us more. Send us suggestions and angles.' That's what we've heard.[2]

Sumner also accuses the major press which refuses junkets of ignoring their audience, which he says has the same fantasy and escape needs as everyone else.

Public relations publicists representing clients in the popular arts work at cross purposes with critics. The activities of the publicist all center on getting favorable mention of the client in the press, though some say they would rather have an unfavorable notice than no mention on the theory that the public will not remember the critic's viewpoint as much as the client's name.

Publicists, then, generally work on getting critics to be aware of their clients and on corrupting the critic's evaluation or natural reactions. The ploy most PR staffers use is arranging personal meetings or interviews between artists and critics, so that the "personal relationship" will somehow induce critics to make favorable comments about work that might have been ignored or criticized severely. The presumption is that critics are less likely to knock an artist they have met (and like) than someone they don't know.

"The ideal critic knows no artists personally," the late Ralph J. Gleason wrote in *Rolling Stone*, "is in contact only by mail with promo and publicity people and deals with the task of reviewing a record or performance as objectively as humanly possible even while giving a subjective reaction."[3]

Gleason believed critics should shun interviews with artists and leave such assignments to feature writers. Yet many critics do conduct interviews and write features of celebrities sent to major markets to promote their work—a film, book or record album. Whether it's the irresistible charisma of a star, just curiousity or an assignment, more than a third of the critics surveyed say they often write about celebrities visiting their area. Film, TV, book and art critics are slightly more likely to follow this practice than other types of critics.

"I couldn't do interviews with stars or directors unless they came through town, so I guess publicity activities affect me," confesses film critic Mary Knoblauch, of the *Chicago Tribune*. *Newsday*'s Joseph Gelmis admits public relations activities of arts interests affect his work, "mostly to the extent that movie companies determine when the cast and filmmakers will be available and indirectly control scheduling of interviews to coincide with movie openings." Others, including James Doussard of the *Louisville Courier-Journal*, insist that PR activities may affect what they write about—"If a mountain appears, I look at it"—but not what they say about it.

Others, striving for Gleason's ideal, say they sometimes write about PR activities themselves. *L.A. Times* critic Martin Bernheimer says he usually treats PR ploys with derision. *New York's* Alan Rich says he generally ignores publicity activities "unless they're so stupid they should be written about and stepped on." *Village Voice* drama critic Michael Feingold says he writes about them "only if they influence the event itself, or the audience's response to it, or if they get on my nerves."

"Press parties and junkets are an abomination, a device to substitute money for intelligence and to buy the press' cooperation with jet flights, free booze and the rest," Gleason raged on, in *Rolling Stone*. "Were I in charge of any rock paper I would forbid the staff to attend press parties and insist that any interview which has to include a flight to Vegas and one or two days at the Century Plaza is no interview at all."[4]

Critics are rarely taken in by staged publicity stunts or other PR pseudo-events. Only 10 per cent of the critics said they ever wrote about such activities, although one critic said he did in an attempt to "puncture their balloon."

Nearly 40 per cent of the critics surveyed in 1974 say they write about "information" contained in press releases or stimulated from direct personal contacts with publicists, agents, distributors or others in the arts industry. One critic said PR people had occasionally contributed facts, ideas and opinions that were the starting point of a story. Art, book and television critics were more likely to utilize press agentry of this type than others.

More than a third of the critics said that stories in other media had on occasion exerted pressure on them to cover a particular story they might have otherwise ignored. A Chicago critic said that her editors may mention a story they read in *The New York Times* or a newsweekly but they left the decision to write about it up to her. Another reported that if an editor saw a story similar to one he had in mind in another medium it might prevent him from writing about it. A Los Angeles critic said he might write about a story that others had done if they had done it badly.

Massive advertising campaigns, while they may enhance the value of a review or feature in the mind of an editor, affect fewer critics. TV critics are slightly more susceptible to this practice than others. Roger Ebert, film critic of the *Chicago Sun-Times*, says his editor sometimes tries to sway him to write about some film because of its advertising, but says "I can usually prevail with reasoning."

Film critic Pauline Kael, on a "Behind the Lines" show, lashed out at industry influences on critics,

> Movie advertising is a very, very big factor in the economic health of a number of newspapers, and a critic who pans an important picture that has a big advertising budget generally doesn't hold his job very long. And so, he learns how to read the signals and tailors his opinions to that. That's also true in some of the largest magazines; I'd say it's true in almost all of the big women's magazines.[5]

Other corporate attempts to corrupt critical journalism surface occasionally, especially when companies hope to use critics to help stimulate slow business. While record companies, for example, routinely send music critics in major markets as many as 30 free albums a week, they sometimes resort to more insidious practices to insure favorable reviews. Recording executives have been known to offer editors of rock music publications a simple trade-out: a healthy schedule of advertising in exchange for favorable reviews. Editors comply by soliciting reviews from rock writers whose personal taste they know will support the company's demands. (The critic may be unaware of the reason for his selection to review a certain product, but if he pans what's he's *supposed* to like, he will soon learn to write what the editor wants—a favorable review—or get his articles rejected and never be asked again.)

In the same way that Washington political correspondents lose some of their credibility when they take government jobs and then return to journalism, music critics who work for record companies are also suspect of conflicts of interest. Even though these critics, such as *Rolling Stone* reviewers Bud Scoppa and Stephen Holden who work for A & M and RCA Records respectively, never review their companies' acts, the motivation for panning a competitor's acts becomes questionable. Rave reviews might also bolster another firm's products and jeopardize one's jobs. So, while some publications condone having industry employees pose as independent critical voices, it is the public that may be misled by the practice.

A traditional way that film companies and producers attempt to bribe ambitious film critics is to offer to buy their screenplay or film rights to their novel and then string them along indefinitely.

Director Francis Ford Coppola, during an interview in the July 1975 *Playboy,* said that some critics have intimated "the implied threat of a bad review" if filmmakers didn't "participate in certain things that accrue to the critic's advantage." Coppola refused to be specific and name names but warned that "extortion and blackmail could blow up into the biggest scandal the field of criticism has known. It's corruption right down to the bottom."

Most critics adamantly deny Coppola's charges, although concede that small-scale corruption exists in any field. Yet few ever write about their under-the-table perquisites. One exception is Alan Rich, of *New York*, who not only wrote about a London junket he went on with 18 other members of the rock music press, but also admitted he accepted "payola" in the form of free show tickets and expense account lunches. "A certain amount of corruption exists in the industry," Rich wrote in his "Lively Arts" column.

> But I am too old and cynical to think that show-business processes could be run in any other way. Naturally, I have to regard a paid family vacation to the Caribbean as more corrupt than lunch *a deux* at The Forum, but that's only a matter of degree. The only problem comes when people on either side of the table

start taking the process seriously, and forget that it's just an artificial and intricately choreographed *pas de deux.*[6]

The most threatening conflict of interest that critics must deal with is reviewing works of "friends" in the arts. Although critic John Simon once stated in the lead of a review that a friend of his had written the play under consideration and he wanted to say so because "it is likely to make me more severe with his work," less candor from critics is more often the case.

Film critic Judith Crist draws sharp comments for her sponsorship of a series of Film Weekends at the Tarrytown (N.Y.) Conference Center. Her two-day "seminars" with film directors such as Frank Perry, Sidney Lumet, Arthur Penn, Peter Bogdanovich and actors/actresses such as Warren Beatty, Robert Redford, Paul Newman and Joanne Woodward and Bette Davis, certainly stir ethical questions of "cashing in on friendships" and reflect on Crist's continued ability to review with credibility the work of her Weekend "guests."

Two examples fuel one's suspicions about Mrs. Crist's friendships and her critical independence. In June 1975, after Director Arthur Penn previewed his film "Night Moves" at a Tarrytown conference in December 1974, Mrs. Crist called the work a "meaningful entertainment" in a warm review in *New York.* After John Schlesinger's Weekend appearance of April 25, 1975, she was ecstatic over "The Day of the Locust": "To call it the finest film of the past several years is to belittle it. It stands beyond comparison."

Another public friendship that seemed to indicate ethical compromise occurred when Rex Reed introduced director John Schlesinger at a meeting in New York. Reed admitted to his audience that Schlesinger's "The Day of the Locust" was one film he'd be able to rave about without having to see it.

Reed, who reportedly earns up to $150,000 a year from his critic-as-celebrity status, compromised his integrity in an even more outrageous manner: he made a television commercial for the Warner Brother's film *Billy Jack,* a practice that obviously doesn't permit him any freedom for critical comments on the film.

But Reed was out-crassed by five television critics who in early 1978 agreed to read excerpts of their previously published and favorable reviews of the "Lou Grant" show on 30-second network promos. The five who answered the CBS call for help— Bill Mandel of the *San Francisco Examiner,* Steve Hoffman, of the *Cincinnati Enquirer,* Bud Wilkinson, of the *Columbus Dispatch,* Jerry Krupnick, of the *Newark Star-Ledger,* and Newbern Jones, of the *Baltimore News American*—were not paid for their performances. Yet despite everyone's good intentions of aiding a show about newspapering, the commercials raised a lot of eyebrows. The notoriety stirred up by such an open ethical compromise undoubtedly had deleterious effects on the public credibility of critics charged with watchdogging the airwaves. Even Lou Grant would have been appalled.

A model of incorruptability, former *New York Times* drama critic Brooks Atkinson had a personal policy of never even meeting with actors or theatre directors socially. He maintained this standard until he retired.

"I never go to lunch with anyone," *Time's* film critic Frank Rich says, obviously referring to the ecological postulate that "There are no *free* lunches," when dealing with influence peddlers. *Variety* critic Carroll Carroll also observes a simple proposition: "Anything that requires a junket or freebie to promote probably isn't worth writing about. A good work of art inspires people to write about it."

Do critics select the quotes used in advertisements?

No. Producers, distributors and their advertising representatives do that. Critics have nothing to do with the practice. In fact, many openly dislike the idea of having reviews ransacked for blurbs. In New York, where quote ads are frequently used, using single words or phrases from reviews that distort the overall opinion is prohibited by a 1971 law enacted through the insistence of the city's Department of Consumer Affairs. This restraint has cut down on much of the misrepresentation, but not all.

Vincent Canby, in lambasting the excerpting of adjectives and exaggerating them with exclamation marks, said he usually felt foolish and depressed after seeing his words and name quoted in such ads, but that they did serve as "a constant incentive to write cleaner, leaner prose."[7]

Recently even bad reviews have been used to hype a work. Distributor Joseph E. Levine used negative remarks to promote "The Night Porter." Mulberry Square, which distributed "Hawmps," also took on the New York critics when they published four favorable reviews from Los Angeles and Dallas for their film along with two downbeat reviews from New York. The ad implied that New York audiences would like the picture even if their critics didn't.

● ● ● ●

Marquee quotes you'll never see:
"a mess of a film" . . . Canby, *Times*
"pathetic garbage" . . . Eder, *Times*

• • • •

When critics appear in advertisements for consumer goods, do they violate ethical codes?

Technically, no. But two examples can best illustrate the repercussions. In 1970, when Judith Crist was reviewing for the "Today" show and *TV Guide* reaching an estimated audience of 30 million, she cashed in on her "instant recognition" by appearing in a two-page testimonial ad that ran in national women's magazines. Mrs. Crist commented on women's changing roles in the movies in a commissioned "interview" headlined "woman's new freedom." The ad stated explicitly that the product involved—Pristeen feminine hygiene deodorant spray—had "something to do" with women "getting more beautiful, more womanly all the time."

A few years later, Rex Reed by-lined a "critique" for Teacher's Scotch whisky, which was also published in major magazines. Reed attempted to parody a review under the witty headline: "Half the fun of writing his critique was becoming totally immersed in the subject matter." One paragraph of copy even appeared anti-critic: "There I was, drinking alone. Critics do that a lot, you know."

Both cases evoked harsh responses from critics and others. The irony of Mrs. Crist talking about women's gains and Pristeen in the same breath irked feminists and stirred her peers to question the whole business of such endorsements. Reed's unbridled self-promotion and his slur on the critical community also drew caustic remarks. Both instances were said to hurt journalistic credibility with the public and to help usher in the age of critic-as-superstar. But all either could be accused of was greed, irresponsibility and bad taste.

None of the critics' organizations has spelled out specific codes of ethics for their members, preferring to let personal integrity and institutional policy be the guidelines. Thus, a hodgepodge of ethical standards exists.

The model code of ethics, adopted by the Society of Professional Journalists, Sigma Delta Chi, at its 1973 convention, has been adopted by many publications and individuals. "Journalists must be free of obligation to any interest other than the public's right to know the truth," the code says. Its ethical guidelines are uncompromising:

Gifts, favors, free travel, special treatment or privileges can compromise the integrity of journalists and their employers. Nothing of value should be accepted.

Secondary employment, political involvement, holding public office and service in community organizations should be avoided if it compromises the integrity of journalists and their employers. Journalists and their employers should conduct their personal lives in a manner which protects them from conflict of interest, real or apparent. Their responsibilities to the public are paramount. That is the nature of their profession.

The National News Council, in its Statement on General Ethics, also believes journalists, including critics, are fully accountable. The NCC urges all media communicators to recognize that they "are under the obvious obligation to live under the same standards they demand of those who hold public office."

Critics, then, must decide for themselves to what extent they'll go to to remain "pure." For some it means returning the bottle of Scotch that M-G-M sent at Christmas. One wonders what the line is for the 125 critics who accepted the all-expenses-paid weekend at Gotham's Warwick Hotel and a chance to attend Woody Allen's press conference hyping his "Love and Death." Or for those who flaunt briefcases and cassette tape recorders monogrammed "C.E.T.K.", mementoes of a junket for "Close Encounters of the Third Kind."?

One final note about the incorruptability of some critics: When this researcher sent out questionnaires to about 250 selected critics across the country, he included 25 cents and a note offering to treat respondents to a cup of coffee while they filled in the survey. One surprising aspect of the study was that nearly a third of the respondents returned the quarter, often with the comment that it was company policy for them not to accept *any* gifts for their services.

Do critics adhere to the professional standards of other journalists?

Most critics perform their professional role responsibly though a few demonstrate poor judgment, bad manners and deplorable habits of personal style. Broadway gossips always tattle when a critic shows up at the theatre drunk and sleeps through most of the second act; his credibility is destroyed forever when he then writes a favorable review of a performance he barely witnessed. But that happens.

A few critics are so concerned over their public deportment

that they fret over laughing out loud at a comedy or applauding a work they appreciated. Others steadfastly refuse to talk about a work—be it a movie or art show—until after they have written their review and will even get rude when a curious spectator broaches such a discussion. While these quirks may seem trivial, to the critic they may serve as his device to retain his critical distance from both his subject and his audience.

Generally, the public must remember that when they approach an arts event they are seeking pleasure and recreation, while a critic is primarily on the job and hoping for pleasure second. Yet he must not forget that how he conducts himself while working in some small measure affects how his readers judge his work.

NOTES FOR CHAPTER 4

[1] *APME Professional Standards*, George Gill, Ed., Nov. 1972, p. 71.

[2] "UA Bally High on Junkets; $1-Mil Spread For Five Films to Romance Grass Roots Press," by Harlan Jacobson, *Variety*, May 7, 1975, p. 3.

[3] "Pitfalls for the Critics," by Ralph J. Gleason, *Rolling Stone*, March 29, 1972, p. 26.

[4] Ibid.

[5] "Critics on Criticism," a *Behind the Lines* show from WNET, Aired on February 26, 1973.

[6] "Critics Can't Be Bought, Just Rented," by Alan Rich, *New York*, December 6, 1971, p. 74.

[7] "Dazzling! Hilarious! Once-in-a-Lifetime! Says Who," by Vincent Canby, *The New York Times*, July 20, 1975, p. 11, Section II.

THE EFFECTS OF
CRITICISM

What is the most influential arts periodical?

The "Arts and Leisure" section of the Sunday *New York Times* is certainly the largest arts publication in the country—it averages 40 pages each week—and has a national circulation of nearly 1.5 million. Daily critics of the *Times* and a host of free lance writers produce long, reflective articles on the entire spectrum of the arts. Such *Times'* luminaries as drama critic Walter Kerr and architecture critic Ada Louise Huxtable plus art critic Hilton Kramer and photography critic Gene Thornton appear exclusively in the Sunday Arts section. Not only do the *Times'* regulars cover the major arts issues, but also the columns are frequently thrown open for divergent views on controversial subjects. Occasional forums solicit comments from a number of arts figures on a single topic—such as black exploitation films. A lively letters-to-the-editor page generates some fascinating dialogue between writers and readers. Though one often hears complaints that the *Times'* Section Two, as it's called, is dull and poorly edited or written, the section is still the most widely read of any arts journal and without question the most influential.

What do the critics themselves have to say about the effect of their work?

In the Louis Harris poll, nearly all critics thought the arts-oriented public not only paid attention to criticism but also were informed and educated by it. More specifically, critics agreed that reviews gave audiences something to compare their own reactions with and often pointed out things the audience should be aware of. The overwhelming majority also said criticism should make some contribution to scholarship or the body of thought in the area.

Two-thirds of the critics surveyed said that critics had an economic impact on works reviewed. Television critics were the exception, no doubt because of the nature of the medium. Most critics also believed that serious criticism, when well done, had some effect on the public's social and political attitudes.

Nearly three-fourths of the critics said criticism, in the long run, affected the field criticized, but they were evenly divided over whether they had stimulated an improvement in the quality of the arts in the previous decade. Nearly half of the critics said criticism had the effect of encouraging innovation in the arts, while nearly one-fourth believed it stifled innovation.

Many critics stressed the effect their work had on audiences, insisting they had helped upgrade the public's taste, sophistication and demands for superior art. Nonetheless, slightly more than half were also concerned that many critics were writing for an "in-group" and not spending enough time evaluating the importance of the work in broad terms for the general public. About 60 per cent of the critics fretted over the dilution of the impact of criticism by their peers who are too intellectual in their approach and thus are out of touch with the public. Less than 30 per cent believed critics were so *avant garde* they were not able to communicate with their audiences.

A majority of critics expressed concern that a few powerful critics had excessive influence, especially on other critics in other areas who only echoed what they pronounced.

Overall, critics see criticism as having just about the right amount of influence on public attitudes and preferences. The few who thought critics had too much influence said the public was lazy in not thinking for themselves and "thus, allowing criticism to have an unhealthy, overly powerful economic influence on the sale of tickets and books." Those who believed critics had too little influence cited the success of expensive advertising and promotion campaigns for inferior work and the public's gullibility for novelty and fads.

In sum, the Harris study concluded that "the critical profession believes they have considerable impact in our society, and although some have mixed feelings about it (particularly their economic impact), they generally feel the effect is for the good and are in favor of increased influence."

How do critics assess their critical power?

While critics almost unanimously agree that their reviews can have a significant influence in helping a good, though obscure work or artist gain recognition, they are nearly divided on whether they can thwart the success of other work. Drama critics tend to be slightly more positive about their influence than others and music critics a bit more often pessimistic.

"The public is much more ready for various kinds of 'new' art than most critics," offers Michael Feingold, which may needle critics more than praise the public. Yet few critics believe reviews can do much to stop people from going to see work that's destined to be popular. "Important work will succeed in spite of a bad press," says Robert G. Marsh, of the *Chicago Sun-Times*. "I know of few instances where critics have thwarted really good work," adds James M. Auer, of the *Milwaukee Journal*.

"Movies are now conceived as kinky, gory, decadent circus spectacle," writes free lance film critic Stephen Farber. "When the public is in the market for carnival thrills, criticism is virtually irrelevant. Bad reviews couldn't keep people away from 'The Exorcist.' At the same time, critics have not been able to persuade people to see subtler, quieter films like 'Badlands,' 'Thieves Like Us,' or 'The Conversation.' "[1]

Critics can have the greatest impact by ignoring work, believes Roger Ebert, of the *Chicago Sun-Times*.

A critic's influence depends on his publication, insists *Newsday*'s drama critic George Oppenheimer. "The (*New York*) *Times* can thwart the success of some work. Others have a tougher job of it," he says. "No, impossible," succinctly counters the *Times'* Harold Schonberg.

While critics insist they have only a "moderate" effect on public opinion, they also acknowledged to researchers Albert and Whitelam that their reviews did influence an artist's prestige regardless of who the artist is.

Reviews rarely have an immediate, measurable effect, said Ralph Gleason. "But they do have a cumulative effect upon the public consciousness of an artist and, if the critic can establish a clear profile of responsibility, they can have a direct effect."[2]

Some critics fret that negative reviews have a deleterious effect on artists. "Unfortunately, a cruel review can damage an artist's confidence and the ego that makes him an artist," worries *Variety*'s Hobe Morrison. T. E. Kalem, of *Time*, refutes that concern: "No, not if the guy really has it."

"Criticism should not be written to influence opinions but to stimulate others into *having* opinions," agrees John Ardoin, music critic of the *Dallas Morning News*. "It is pure fiction that a critic can literally make or break a career. If a performer can be finished off with a single review, then the sooner he is off the stage the better. If an artist has something valid to say, it will be heard through even the heaviest flak."[3]

"I don't know what bearing a critic's responses can have on anybody else's," cracks *Village Voice* drama critic Michael Smith. "You have to postulate a well-organized life, and who has time for that."

Joe Pollock, critic for the *St. Louis Post-Dispatch*, is also downbeat: "A critic has only as much influence as people give him. The question is why the reader gives it, and I find that hard to answer."

New York Times film critic Vincent Canby also complains: "A lot of readers don't want to make up their own minds. They want to be told what to buy, as if we were rating air-conditioners."

"For some films, some critics may have some influence on some moviegoers in some cities—some times," is the conclusion *Los Angeles Times* writer David Shaw made after studying the power of film critics.[4] He also noted that critics were unlikely to dissuade moviegoers from seeing films with such pre-sold qualities as a best-selling book ("Once is Not Enough") or a hit Broadway play ("Grease") or a star (Robert Redford) or character (Inspector Clouseau) or studio imprimatur (Disney) or gimmick (Sensurround) or subject matter (sex or the occult).

Francois Truffaut also believes the effect of criticism is mitigated by related factors: "Criticism is only one element among others: advertising, the atmosphere, competition, timing. When a film achieves a certain success, it becomes a sociological event, and the question of its quality becomes secondary."[5]

Stephen Koch, writing in *Saturday Review*, noted a major irony of whom critics reach: "The most and the least self-aware branches of the film audience are unaffected by reviews; neither the highbrows nor the lowbrows could care less. It is only with the slightly perplexed middlebrow that the critics have what they call their clout."[6]

Two other areas of influence concern critics: peer persuasion and the effect of reviews on funding groups.

"I've found in motion picture criticism, unfortunately, that a very small group of critics in New York can influence all the criticism in the rest of the country," continues Canby. "And it's really kind of sad, when you get maybe 18 or 20 people in New York not who decide the fate of a film but who decide the way a lot of other people will write criticism."[7]

Another sphere of the critic's influence is on funding. Many artists and a few critics believe that it is not the critic's role to comment on subsidy issues.

Clive Barnes insists that any artist who accepts public funds—either from federal, state, city or foundation sources—should be accountable for that work, both to the funding agency and to the public which supports them. "The press has a duty to raise its voice when it feels that this money is being squandered," Barnes wrote after being attacked for complaining that the work of a small dance company did not deserve the grant given it.

"The people who control public funds should take enormous care where they deliver public money," Barnes went on. "No one who believes in an artist enough to provide him with some kind of help should remove that help merely on the say-so of one critic."[8]

What evidence do critics cite that reviews affect artists or producers?

Reactions have ranged from "pleased to pissed off," blurted Chicago critic Norman Mark. Generally, critics are divided on whether reviews even ought to try to influence artists or producers. "Financial considerations are much greater than critical ones," opined film critic Roger Ebert. "Art-making is too complex for direct results like that," the *Voice*'s Michael Feingold said, "though sometimes artists will discuss their work with me afterwards."

Skeptical critics are more adamant. "That's not what I write for," Alan Rich stated. "A critic who wants power of that sort should be fired on the spot," insisted Mary Knoblauch. "Artists or producers may write you nice or nasty letters, but that's it." James M. Auer also urged creative types to maintain their independence: "I rather hope they're tough enough not to let themselves be molded by outside writers."

Architecture critics are convinced that their reviews do have some effect on building designers. "Critiques are often cited by architects as leverage for new commissions," observed Rob Cuscaden, of the *Chicago Sun-Time.*

Paul Goldberger, of *The New York Times*, has doubts that architectural critics have any real power. "They don't tear down a building on Saturday night if you don't like it. It might be nice if it happened, but the fact that it doesn't gives you a little more honesty in a field where you have no great weight."

Music and drama critics tend to believe their reviews have greater effect than those of other critics. John Huddy believes that his comments have affected live variety concerts in Miami, even altering subsequent bookings. The *Washington Post*'s Richard L. Coe said that changes have been made in productions after he wrote his play review citing major flaws.

Film critics are extremely doubtful that reviews have any effect on production, although Peter Davis Dibble of *Women's Wear Daily* said "2001 was re-cut after reviews made the same complaints." Paul Zimmerman of *Newsweek* added that occasionally a review of a film he's liked will be used to push its second distribution. *Newsday*'s Gelmis was also reserved, "Only as part of the accumulated effect that critics individually and collectively exert on producers, studios and Oscar-awarders to recognize talent whether it does well at the box office or not."

TV critic Peter V. Rahn of the *St. Louis Globe-Democrat* also thinks a consensus viewpoint on a work has its impact, "Overall rejection of a TV show by the main body of reviewers can harm its chances for survival."

Aside from phone calls and letters, perhaps the most direct feedback from a producer was reported by Stewart Klein, drama critic for WNEW-TV in New York: "David Merrick has personally threatened assault many times."

"The industry doesn't have an ear so it doesn't hear or care what critics are saying," says Carroll Carroll, TV advertising critic of *Variety*. "It only has a pocketbook."

What feedback do producers and artists give critics?

Very little, really. Producers on occasion withdraw complimentary tickets from critics they believe hostile to their work. Yet such gestures of defiance are usually invoked against critics of smaller media and rarely against the most important publication of the community. For example, the San Francisco Opera rashly dropped press privileges for a music critic reviewing for *The Pacific Sun, San Francisco* magazine and the New York-based *Opera News* after she called a guest conductor's performance "amateurish ineptitude." In New York, press agent, producer and director Arthur Cantor has steadfastly refused "comps" to Martin

Gottfried of *Women's Wear Daily* and John Simon of *New York*, presumably because he doesn't like their style. No critic, however, can be legally barred from attending a show open to the public if he buys a ticket like everyone else. So the practice is generally ineffectual and probably acerbates the ill will.

Another tactic is direct confrontation. Two private instances have been widely reported. Actress Sylvia Miles once dumped a plate of food on John Simon's head at a New York party as reprisal for a negative review he gave her. And, producer Joseph Papp's nasty phone call to Clive Barnes after a scoring of "Boom Boom Boom" was chronicled in detail. A recent public display of critical disapproval appeared in the *Los Angeles Times* in May, 1976, when producer Stephen Papich bought a full-page ad "to apologize" to his cast on behalf of drama critic Dan Sullivan who called his show a "disaster."

Occasionally artists will take swipes at critics during interviews. "I wish I could say that reviews don't bother me," filmmaker Sydney Pollack told the *SoHo Weekly News*. "The fact is they do. I always try to understand what, if anything, is instructive in a review because you are always learning." Actress Ruth Gordon told an interviewer of her subtle measure of critics' effects: "I never read reviews, but I can tell if they're bad. The day after you open, there are no flowers, no telephone calls. Oh, it's easy to tell." Film director Stanley Kubrick told *Take One* that critics only influence the box office when they reinforce word-of-mouth advertising: "Critics only appear to have any importance when their views coincide with those of the audience."

Rumors abound that the avant garde is dead. What effects do critics believe their work has on innovation in the arts?

About 20 per cent of the critics responding to the 1974 survey said critics had no influence on arts innovation, while another 20 per cent admitted that whatever small effect their reviews had, it was occasional, faint, remote and even temporary. Three critics represent the disbelievers' viewpoint: Harold Schonberg—"Creators create, critics criticize and that is the way it always has been. No adverse review ever stopped a major work." Clara Hieronymus—"The arts develop in response to and as a mirror of the times." Joseph Gelmis—"Criticism doesn't start fires. It feeds the flames."

The majority of critics was united in their belief that criticism affected innovation, but differed on the impact of reviews and whether the avant garde was thriving or dormant. Several critics thought reviews brought new, experimental work to the public's attention, aroused its curiosity about that work and educated people to accept it. Mike Steele also observed, "Criticism is one of many things—public philanthropy, colleges, traditions, etc.—which create climates for innovation."

John Pastier was among those critics who worry about undesired effects: "It can both validate and cripple innovation, which is a fragile quality." Paul Zimmerman felt critics could have positive effects "only to the extent that they can locate and celebrate real talent." Ron Butler was concerned that critics could also "boost trash that is merely chic." Charles Benbow said criticism had "promoted novelty in the visual arts, to the detriment of that art." James Auer decried journalistic overkill: "Often the problem is not that critics kill innovation, but that they leap on and publicize it too eagerly."

"Critical acceptance precedes popular in most cases," adds Lawrence DeVine. "The reverse is not always true, regarding condemnation." DeVine and a number of others don't believe the avant garde is dead. Bernie Harrison of the *Washington Star-News* says, "The real problem is most critics are unfamiliar with it." Bettelou Peterson of the *Detroit Free Press* takes the same side: "Who said it's dead? In TV, there has never been an avant garde. In the other arts, it's still around."

Two critics from New York's Greenwich Village, the country's center of arts innovation, assume a more pessimistic stance than the others. Art critic of the *SoHo Weekly News* Peter Frank: "The avant garde spirit died with the onset of an overwhelming self-consciousness in art and in art criticism. History looks over our shoulder at every step."

Village Voice drama critic Michael Feingold:

> I think the word avant garde is dead. It is true that the mass audience has absorbed modern innovations—without understanding them, however. Mostly nowadays "avant garde" refers to a social subgroup made up of a few artists and a few critic/artists who are their friends. Naturally, the people in each of these many subgroups have an effect on each other (there are often sexual entanglements as well) and occasionally these little effects have larger effects on the outside world. But there is no single avant garde, because there is no unified culture for it to be ahead of; we are an unassembled jigsaw puzzle of a world.

What evidence do critics cite that their reviews have any effect—positive or negative—on local audiences?

More than two-thirds of the critics polled by this writer in 1974 believed they did have some effect on their readers or viewers. Evaluations of the critic's power ranged from "very strong influence on the box office" (*Miami Herald*'s John Huddy) to "one large drop in the bucket" (*Newsweek*'s Paul Zimmerman).

"Extreme reviews—good and bad—have an effect, I've heard," says the *St. Petersburg Times'* Dorothy Smiljanich. "Evidence supports both theories," agrees the *L.A. Times'* Martin Bernheimer.

Many critics are confident that positive reviews encourage the public to witness the event. "I think I can send people to see things I write about," states Paul Richard of the *Washington Post*. Harold Haydon, of the *Chicago Sun-Times*, insists that a good review aids art show attendance, while Norman Mark, also of Chicago, thinks a favorable television review boosts its ratings. *New York*'s Alan Rich is a bit less certain about the direct power of his reviews, but says he tries "to make people curious about everything."

Some critics deny any personal influence, giving the credit of effect to their medium. "A *Times'* review does carry some weight, I am told," modestly states Harold Schonberg. Milwaukee art critic James M. Auer shares the view: "Naturally, a paper as large as the *Journal* has impact in all cultural fields."

While many critics admit that the evidence of effects of their reviews is often inconsistent and indirect, most assume they hold significant impact on local or specialized interest art. "There's considerable effect on local stage plays," says Emerson Batdorff of the *Cleveland Plain Dealer*. Tulsa's Ron Butler agrees: "Borderline products may benefit or suffer most from reviews." Chicago theatre critic Richard Christianson also believes reviews aid small arts groups struggling to find an audience.

Chicago film critic Mary Knoblauch and Detroit drama critic Lawrence DeVine believe their influence depends on what's being criticized. "I can sometimes help an obscure work, but have no effect on a major production like 'Good News'," says DeVine. Knoblauch adds, "When all Chicago daily critics get together for or against an unknown art film, it has some effect because art filmgoers tend to put more reliance on critics than others."

San Francisco music critic Ralph Gleason often ran experiments to check on the impact of his reviews. He reported that an enthusiastic record review always resulted in direct sales increases. However, he also noted that it wasn't possible to stop the sale of an album or the success of a concern in advance with negative criticism.

Most of the feedback on critics' effects comes to them as letters, phone calls or meetings with artists or producers. Little concrete evidence actually exists on effects.

"Theatres have run movies I've liked which otherwise would not have been shown on Long Island," boasts *Newsday*'s Joseph Gelmis.

Television critics, again, are an exception. They are evenly divided on whether reviews have any effect on the audience or television. "Although we may guide a few people to watch a particular show," Bettelou Peterson of the *Detroit Free Press* states, "TV critics have little power."

William Glover, drama critic of the Associated Press, is constantly aware that his reviews are not the only ones available to readers. "Anyone interested in art or any field is probably not going to be guided by only one critic alone. They read him because they become interested in what he says, his viewpoint, his provocative qualities as a writer. But they're not going to read him exclusively. In the theatre, certainly, a consensus feeling develops after a production opens. That's what most of the theatre-going public absorbs by some process like osmosis. The atmosphere that develops around any production is a collective composite of voices."

How much influence does the public say critics have on its decision to go to particular arts events?

Very little research has probed this area with the public, but one 1975 report showed that critics' opinions were a relatively unimportant factor in people's decisions to go to a play or film.

The study, a massive survey called "Americans and the Arts" conducted by Louis Harris and Associates for the Associated Councils of the Arts, indicated that about 60 per cent of the more than 3,000 people interviewed said critics' reviews were of minor importance in affecting their choice of entertainment fare.[9]

Of the 40 per cent who said previews were an influence, the majority were frequent attenders at arts events, young, affluent and well educated. Critical influence was most significant for the 16- to 20-year olds and steadily diminished for older groups. As education level and income of respondents increased, however, they were also more likely to regard critical opinion more highly.

A similar study, conducted in 1973 for the American Council for the Arts in Education, also found that only 13 per cent of those polled rated critics as a very important factor affecting movie attendance, while about 30 per cent said they were somewhat important. The public's use of critics is related to life style, Louis Harris analysts concluded. "By 50 to 34 per cent, a majority would prefer waiting to hear what friends or critics say about a new play or movie, to going themselves as soon as it opens," the report noted. "When offered a choice, then, it can be said that more people prefer informal entertainment to serious culture, and that they like to have some advance assurance of its quality from other sources before risking their own money on a show."[10]

Can reviewers help educate the public to become attuned to the arts? Can they elevate the standards of arts?

Three-fourths of the critics polled believe the answer to both questions is affirmative. Only TV critics doubt they can do much to improve the medium.

Of their educative role, the majority of respondents expressed cautious reserve. Qualifiers such as "marginally," "somewhat," "part of an audience, part of the time," "ever so slowly," were often used. Of the dissenters, Clara Hieronymus of the *Nashville Tennessean* thinks critics can only increase public awareness of the arts, while veteran book critic Robert Evett, of the *Washington Star-News*, pooh-poohs the whole notion: "Reviewers write for an audience that has already been educated."

On elevating the standards of art, many critics are again quite tentative. Mike Steele, of the *Minneapolis Tribune*, notes, "Yes, over a period of time. Single reviews are less influential." Tulsan Ron Butler is optimistic, but wary: "Yes, only by making the public want something better. The box office is still the regulator." Lawrence DeVine of the *Detroit Free Press* assumes more responsibility: "The more clear art is made, the more accessible it becomes—and once it's understood, the higher quality is demanded." *Newsday*'s Allan Wallach also thinks criticism can elevate standards "primarily through the negative function of discouraging inferior work."

A few critics assume that effectiveness depends on the individual. "Powerful critics can affect artistic choices by exercising economic clout on producers," says *Cue*'s Marilyn Stasio. *Newsday* veteran George Oppenheimer believes "really good ones like Walter Kerr or Harold Clurman" can improve theatre. Michael Feingold also notes: "All can try. G. B. Shaw and William Archer nearly succeeded." James Auer shares the objective but says excesses may impede it, "This pursuit often becomes an excuse for a critical ego trip."

Of the nay-sayers, John Ardoin of the *Dallas Morning News* wishes it were possible. Joe Meade of the *San Diego Union* also wants to elevate standards, but believes nothing affects "middlebrow audience tastes." Charles Benbow, of the *St. Petersburg*

Times is also frustrated: "Try as we may, the factors in the vitality of the art are too diverse to be 'controlled' by free agents like critics." Music critic F. W. Woolsey of the *Louisville Times* is terse: "Artists do this, not critics." And, New York dance critic Robb Baker is dubious for another reason: "Most critics can't even elevate the standards of criticism." The final word of wisdom goes to the *Cleveland Plain Dealer*'s Emerson Batdorff: "Who's to say what's elevated? This is simply do-gooder talk."

Isn't critical influence mitigated by media effects in general?

Of course. Pioneer communications researcher Joseph T. Klapper wrote in 1949 that the mass media catered to existing tastes—high for elite audiences and low for low-brows—and reinforced rather than altered patterns. Neither group was likely to change its taste because of selective exposure habits.

Today, as director of CBS's research division, Klapper still insists the media make little or no attempt to educate or guide audiences to develop tastes. He believes the "instant analysis" critics give a play or movie or concert simply lacks pedagogical approach.[11]

Perhaps the worst than can be said about attention to repetitive, banal and sentimental fare is that it wastes one's time, time that might be spent with fare offering more pleasure and value for the mind. Complete submersion into escapist fare might even distort one's "sense of reality" over a long period of time.

On the other side, the boom in arts attendance and participation lends support to the theory that new and untutored audiences gradually become bored with light material and low forms and entertainment and slowly advance to the next highest level. Serious critics who advocate "good taste" no doubt play a small part in this development process, although interpersonal influence of one's cultural peer group is also strong.

The development of audience sophistication and its growth in arts knowledge and experience has a profound and healthy effect on all culture. Audiences have begun to express their reactions to productions openly: if they are bored, angered or offended, they not only get up and walk out with increasing frequency but also boo and catcall what they disfavor. They also applaud enthusiastically and cheer and encourage work that pleases them. In this way, then, artists receive direct feedback that subtly affects their future output.

Critics are probably most influential on high media users, the referential group tagged "opinion leaders" in the two-step flow of communications. The theory posits that critics guide certain influential members of the audience who in turn affect others in their peer group. It's a common experience for those attuned to the media to have a strong viewpoint about a cultural event or artifact they haven't yet experienced themselves.

Despite critical focus on the content of the popular arts, the most important effects may reside elsewhere, as Marshall McLuhan has theorized. For example, one certain result of television drama has been to create a firm notion among viewers on what an actor is and does as well as create a standard of dramatic performance. Similarly, readers of criticism may develop a rich appreciation of good writing long before they absorb the critic's value judgments.

• • • •

"Some critics repeat themselves,
some repeat other critics,
and some repeat their own repetitions of
other critics self-repetitions. Repeatedly."
–Dan Carlinsky

• • • •

What about readers' evaluation of reviews?

There have virtually been no studies in this area. Until now.

Communications researchers have avoided studying critical writing because of its highly subjective nature. Readability studies, mainly using Cloze-based formulae to predict readers' comprehension difficulty, have concentrated on objective news stories. Only one project dealt with any form of subjective writing; when researchers Moznette and Harick found editorials more readable than news, they challenged conventional professional thought.

In an effort to explore this subject of how readers perceive cultural criticism, this writer, with the assistance of quantitative research specialist Dr. Charles H. Martin, designed and executed a massive study. The goal was to find out if readers thought critics shared any stylistic traits or common linguistic attributes.

A seven-point, self-administered questionnaire using a semantic differential was devised to measure the response of individual readers to specific reviews. The questionnaire used polar adjective pairs (see Appendix) drawn from Osgood's evaluative, potency and activity factors, Bales' leadership variables, Cattell's personality variable, Tobolski's persuasive message variables as well as others chosen for their rational links to critical writing.

The subjects used were 300 University of Georgia undergraduates in the fields of art, drama, music, dance, English and journalism.

Thirty reviews from critics working for metropolitan newspapers and national magazines were selected for analysis. An East Coast bias was intentional, since most criticism is known to be produced in the Northeast area. Of the 30 critics studied (Clive Barnes, then of *The New York Times*, now with the *New York Post*) was included in both the drama and dance categories), six were film critics, four art critics, five music critics, six drama critics, four dance critics and five television critics. (For a complete list, see Appendix.) Their reviews all dealt with major works by well-known artists; in short, subject matter that a general reader with an interest in the arts would recognize. No attempt was made to balance reviews by verdict: some were clearly raves, many were mixed and a few were pans. The unit of analysis was the whole review and readers were asked to rate each review on the scales provided.

RESULTS

Fifteen high-scoring variables were identified through factor analysis (Varimax rotation). Three factors accounted for nearly 90 per cent of the variance of stylistic effect. Table 1 reports the factors and loading on each variable.

The essential characteristic of Factor I is the socio-evaluative aspect of meaning. As shown in Table II, reviews of art critics were rated highest on all social evaluative variables. Dance and drama reviews were judged less meaningful and less enriching than other types of criticism.

Factor II's essential attribute is understandability. The focus is on form and the message variables themselves. Television criticism scored the highest on Factor II variables, becoming the model of readability. Art reviews were also considered clear and highly understandable, while dance and drama criticism ranked again lowest on all variables.

Empathy between the critic and his popular arts subject is the central aspect of Factor III. Art and music reviews exhibited the highest level of interaction between critic and art, readers said. Film and drama reviews were judged more pragmatic than others, but generally were ranked lowest on other variables in Factor III.

The data also showed that readers thought dance reviews were less succinct, less persuasive and less satisfying than all others; nonetheless, dance critics were rated involved with their subject.

TABLE I
MAJOR STYLISTIC EFFECTS FACTORS

Factor I: Social Evaluative Affect on the Reader (58.5% of variance)

Variable	Loading
Meaningful	.80
Enriching	.80
Important	.77
Valuable	.74
Intelligent	.73

Factor II: Attributes of Critical Writing Style (Readability) (18.1% of variance)

Variable	Loading
Understandable	.82
Clear	.77
Concrete	.62
Consistent	.51
Simple	.45

Factor III: Readers estimate of critic/art interaction (12.7% of variance)

Variable	Loading
Soft	.75
Lenient	.74
Positive	.71
Pragmatic	.59
Popular	.44

The data also indicate that, contrary to popular belief, critical writing is not all that subjective, idiosyncratic and diffuse. Rather, it suggests that arts criticism can be parsimoniously described in terms of conceptually clean factors. Further, this characteristic lends support to the notion that such writing may follow almost formulaic lines, which readers can apparently perceive and respond to.

In line with this thinking, it seems possible to even select specific writers as representative of their specific craft. For example, readers said of all the critics, *Newsweek's* Arthur Cooper (film) and *The New York Times'* John S. Wilson (music) were the most predictable, inasmuch as their ratings were consistently typical of the stylistic attributes of their fellow craftsmen. Thus, Cooper appropriately scored rather low on meaningfulness, appropriately high on readability, and way down there on love of topic.

TABLE II
CRITICS RANKS ON STYLISTIC FACTORS

	Factor I	Factor II	Factor III
Film	4	2	5
Art	1	3	1
Music	3	4	2
Drama	5	5	6
Dance	6	6	3
TV	2	1	3

Wilson, as would be "proper," did middling well on evaluative and readability factors, but scored neatly on a loving affiliation with the subject.

Not all critics were so typical of their group. *Time's* Robert Hughes (art) displayed attributes that traditionally were associated with dance and music reviews, which would infer a broader style than that possessed by his compadres.

So, while one may say that some display of singular attributes may be fine, the assertive power of good critical writing resides within talents that provide meaning to the reader, understandability, and positive rapture with the topic.

READABILITY OF REVIEWS DEFINES THE CRITIC

A second phase of this study—running a hierarchal discriminant regression analysis on the top-loading variables—produced four other insights.

1. Two major canonical functions were established and labeled "content evaluation" and "reader interaction." The data suggested that clarity and value are the most powerful organizing concepts of critical writing, followed by positiveness and intensity.

2. Content evaluative qualities such as clarity, positiveness, understandability, lenience, softness and simplicity were more often linked to art, dance and music critics than with TV, film or drama critics.

Reader interactive characteristics such as value, intensity, popularity, interest, involvement and goodness were most often associated with drama, dance and art critics than with TV, film and music critics.

Curiously, though drama reviews ranked lowest on content evaluation, they rated highest on reader interaction. Clearly drama reviews, on the whole, were rated more often unfavorable in relation to the art being considered than others. If respondents perceive negative reviews as valuable, intense, interesting and involving, they reinforce the public attitude of criticism as negative comments on art.

3. Review readers are able to discern the shared attributes that groups of critics exhibit in their writing. For instance, the similarities between dance and art critics and between drama and film critics were apparent. Television critics have the least distinct attributes, generally resembling a combination of the other five types. Drama critics have least in common with music critics.

4. Readers were also able to predict group membership by reading reviews and determining the shared attributes each type of critic possessed. Drama and film critics were said to be the most predictable; dance, art and music critics were moderately predictable in group membership, while television critics had the lowest level of predictability.

This study then establishes a basis for a readability index of subjective writing. Attributes highly regarded by readers, such as value, clarity, positiveness and intensity, are not unlike those found applicable to objective journalism.

TABLE III
CRITIC GROUPS PLOTTED ON MAP OF REDUCED SPACE
(Function I Horizontal; Function II Vertical)

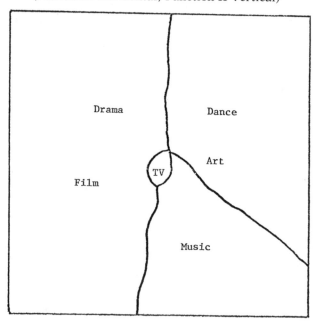

Readers also reported that critics of all stripes do share attributes as well as hold some distinctive to their type. Such common characteristics can be used to identify as well as predict which type of critic writes a particular review.

Finally, this study posits an important second dimension of critical writing: the reader-perceived interaction between the critic and his arts subject. The data on drama criticism are especially revealing since drama reviews—mostly unfavorable in their verdict in this sample—were rated lowest on content evaluation but highest in reader interaction. This confirms the public impression that criticism is generally regarded as negative comment on art.

Is there a relation between critical and popular successes?

No, would say TV critic John J. O'Connor. "Audience ratings can measure popularity. The reviewer should be measuring quality. No correlation has yet been convincingly established between popularity and quality."

Some critics divide artistic experience into "serious," which is worthy of critical acclaim, and "popular," which isn't. Others eschew such a division. *New York Times'* music critic John Rockwell writes simply: "All music is part of the same experience, ranging from the largest audience and the broadest, most vital gestures to refined pleasures for the few." Critics, like Rockwell, approach each work in an egalitarian attitude, ready to judge it on the basis of his personal reaction to it and his assessment of its quality, rather than audience appeal.

"There was a long period in which commercial success indicated excellence," rock critic Robert Christgau, of the *Village Voice*, says of the music scene. "But not now. It started changing in 1968 and has been getting worse since. One of the reasons it changed is that money separates the artist from his audience. It makes it impossible for him to do any work that is anything more than repeats of what he has already done, basing it on memory rather than experience. Memory becomes more and more faulty as the years go on."

A few critics seem to make a career out of putting down popular work. John Simon began a review of "Equus" by observing that the play had earned good reviews from critics and that audiences loved the play, but that to him the play was "a bundle of anathemas." Similarly, *New York Times* art critic John Russell acknowledged the "great commercial success" of Richard Estes' paintings while assailing their "rat-trap compositional formulas."

The split between critical and popular acclaim was probably nowhere more obvious than in late 1973 when film critics examined two new releases, both destined to soar in the all-time box office standings. "The Exorcist," pre-sold as a best-selling occult novel and hyped by phenomenal press coverage, garnered unfavorable notices from about 50 per cent of the 40 critics examined in a random survey. About one-third wrote favorably of the film and the rest turned out mixed reviews. While "The Exorcist" was criticized as "bad entertainment," another successful release, "The Sting" was tagged "good entertainment" after racking up nearly two-thirds favorable comments from 33 critics. Why the public supported both pictures with nearly equal enthusiasm is inexplicable. If reviews have any effect on attendance, then perhaps crowds flocked to "The Exorcist" just to see how bad it was. Clearly both films were popular cultural phenomena, critical opinion notwithstanding.

"Critical remarks about film don't seem to have anything, or very little, to do with its success or failure," says Joy Boyum, of the *Wall Street Journal.* "In fact, it is an illusion to believe that critics have any kind of real weight in the market. I think the critic is talking to an awfully small audience. That great mass of audience does not read the critics. They are still looking at the four stars in *The Daily News.* How else would you explain the fact that we all hate a certain film and it makes $40 million and we all love one and it only makes a quarter of a million."

While few critics attempt to predict the popularity of a new work, hence judge its economic success, some can't resist the practice. West Coast film critic Arthur Knight, for example, recently predicted in the *SoHo Weekly News:* "I happen to think that 'All the President's Men' might make it." Vincent Canby's review in the *Times* also called the film "an unequivocal smash-hit—the thinking man's 'Jaws.' "

Yet O'Connor insists: "A critic is not, or at least shouldn't be, in the game of picking hits and flops." [12]

One research project measured popular taste and critical opinion of the same films and found that in 53 per cent of the 5,644 movies considered that the critics rated the film the same as the audience members. Jules J. Wanderer of the University of Colorado also learned that 28 per cent of the time the critics were tougher on films than the public and in 19 per cent of the cases they were more lenient. Prof. Wanderer further concluded that critics shared upper-middle tastes with that sector of the audience and that the case for critical snobbism just didn't exist. [13]

• • • •

"The public is supposed to understand a critics's position without being told," quipped George Bernard Shaw.

• • • •

What about ideological criticism?

Ideological criticism is written and published mostly in specialized periodicals. For example, Ben Levine, who writes television criticism for the *New York Daily World*, the successor to the *Daily Worker*, is open about his politics and critical perspective:

> The paper I write for is committed to the politics and philosophy of Marxism as reflected in the Communist Party, U.S.A. The "parameter" of my criticism, therefore, is the policy of the Communist Party, but the interpretation of it is left completely up to me.

In film criticism, *Jump Cut*, a bi-monthly tabloid published in Berkeley (Calif.), is committed to developing "Marxist cultural and aesthetic theory and criticism." Structuralism and semiology are the critical methodologies employed by their critics. Similarly, feminist film criticism, as espoused by *Women & Film* seeks to aid feminist political activity and to fight sexism and women's oppression by "collective action against those institutions which are built on class, racial and sexual oppression: namely, the institutions of capitalism." (Feminist Betty Friedan has even proposed a code that would rate films according to their treatment of women. A W+ would be excellent and W−− would be terrible, for example.)

A "black aesthetic" applicable to black music, poetry, plays and films is evident in some black publications. Even religious ("the Jewish perspective," for example) and regional bias surfaces among some critics.

In the early 1970s, Pauline Kael initiated an attack on fascism in the arts with her diatribe against Sam Peckinpah's "Straw Dogs." Other critics quickly picked up the banner and began seeing fascist references everywhere.

Critics who write under the rubric of ideology are apparently willing to abandon artistic freedom in order to serve the *idee fixe* of the moment. Such pseudo-intellectual faddishness makes little contribution to criticism or art. Adhering to a "party line" also produces notoriously dull and monotonous criticism. Pluralist critics recognize that there is no such thing as women's art, black art, homosexual art, Jewish art, Marxist or Fascist art. Art deals with all aspects of human experience. To screen it through a narrow bias is to ignore its complex milieu and relationship to every interested witness.

Do critics ever change their mind about works they've reviewed?

Yes. Both ways. For example, John Simon, writing about the 1972 film "The Ruling Class," revised his opinion upward after a second viewing: "That second time, as the lights went up, I looked everywhere for my objections—under my seat and all the neighboring ones—but I could not find them."

On the other side of the ledger, Clive Barnes apologized to his readers for overpraising Stravinsky's "Pulcinella," staged by George Balanchine and Jerome Robbins, with the confession: "No one likes to admit that he has overpraised something."

What do ten best lists reveal?

Picking Ten Best Lists has become an institutionalized year-end activity of critics of all types, though many still refuse to do it and others offer a host of caveats on why the practice is so silly and unsatisfying. Vincent Canby, who does publish his list, noted in 1975 that the annual game was misleading, because it asked readers to take seriously the results of compromise in which the deciding factor was often personal or irrelevant. Charles Champlin, who had to round out his 1975 list (a "nonvintage" year) with five foreign films, snidely observed of the practice:"The annual critic's rites of picking a Top 10 creates some ad copy and a document against which the film faithful can vent their spleen without tearing the larger society apart." [14]

John Simon, who used to devise a list and now refuses to do so, was, as usual, the most acerbic: "There is something antithetical to the very notion of criticism in the concept of a Ten Best list; it is almost as deplorable as reviewing a movie by meting out to it one to four stars." Simon insists critics need space to expound their opinions, to compare and contrast works, to apply aesthetic and moral judgments, to illustrate their points with examples and to put the whole matter in a broad perspective. [15]

While film critics may excel in list making, other critics have begun imitating them. At the *New York Times*, John J. O'Connor taps the "sparklers and clinkers" of the TV season, John Rockwell ranks new albums of the year according to the number of times he played them, how much he enjoyed each as well as how important he considered them, and even restaurant critic John Canaday records retrospective bests-worsts from his dining-out forays.

Rock critic Robert Hilburn ranks major concerts in Los Angeles in his *Times'* column, while at the *Village Voice* Robert Christgau ambitiously polled 38 other rock writers in 1975 and constructed a consensus Top Ten List of albums of the year. (Only one of the top finishers appeared on the *Billboard* list of 100 best-selling albums for the year.)

Some critics push the idea to excess by publishing their Ten Worst List, too. Canby called his loser's list: "Bad movies that ask to be rapped in the mouth." Theatre critic Dan Sullivan reserves his Humbug Awards more for those who market theatre than those who create it.

At least one newspaper—*The New York Times*—has decided to stop the "worst list" nonsense. In early 1978, executive editor A. M. Rosenthal issued an editorial policy memo which said in part: "It is not our function to be needlessly wounding or destructive. . . . What the critic does when he selects a list of the worst is simply to review his own opinions. Nothing new is added except a little more blood." That dictum spiked two such listings that had already been prepared.

About the best that can be said about Ten Best Lists is that they give a critic an opportunity to reflect on and reassess the year's creativity in his field. Generally, preceding each list is a short evaluation of the year, which attempts to put some order on the chaos. Aside from serving as light cocktail party chatter, the Ten Best Lists add little to criticism's stature or to our appreciation of the popular arts.

NOTES FOR CHAPTER 5

1 "Hollywood's New Sensationalism: The Power and the Glory," by Stephen Farber, *The New York Times*, July 7, 1974, page 17, Section II.
2 "Pitfalls for the Critics," by Ralph J. Gleason, *Rolling Stone*, March 29, 1972, page 26.
3 "A Critic Looks At Criticism," by John Ardoin, *Catalyst*, Spring 1976, page 8.
4 "Movie Critics: Power of Pen Has Sharp Limits," by David Shaw, *The Los Angeles Times*, July 6, 1976, pages 3 and 16.
5 "A Kind Word for Critics," by Francois Truffaut, *Harpers*, October 1977, page 100.
6 "The Cruel, Cruel Critics," by Stephen Koch, *Saturday Review*, Dec. 26, 1970, page 13.

[7] "Year-End Roundtable on the Arts," *The New York Times*, Dec. 27, 1972.

[8] "May Critics Say, 'Stop the Money?' " by Clive Barnes, *The New York Times*, April 15, 1973, page 23, Section II.

[9] *Op. cit.*, page 42.

[10] *Ibid.*, pp. 56–57 and 66.

[11] "The Effects of Mass Media," by Joseph T. Klapper, unpublished manuscript, August 1949, and interview with author.

[12] "Should the Reviewer Pick the Hits and Flops?" by John J. O'Connor, *The New York Times*, January 23, 1972, page 25, Section II.

[13] "In Defense of Popular Taste: Film Ratings among Professionals and Lay Audiences," by Jules J. Wanderer, *American Journal of Sociology*,, 1970, 2, pp. 262–272.

[14] "Picking the Best Films in a Nonvintage Year," by Charles Champlin, *Los Angeles Times*, Jan. 4, 1976, page 1, Calendar.

[15] "List, List, O List," by John Simon, *New York*, December 22, 1975, page 68.

6

RANDOM NOTES ON
THE STATE OF THE ART

FILM

Is film criticism better than the movies?

Followup on a "news" story:

In April 1975, Tom Laughlin, the actor-writer-director of "Billy Jack," launched an assault on movie critics as part of a promotion campaign for the release of the sequel, "The Trial of Billy Jack." In two full-page ads headlined "Billy Jack vs. the Critics," which appeared in 18 newspapers including the *Los Angeles Times, New York Times* and *Variety,*[1] Laughlin exhumed the myth that some discrepancy exists between a movie's quality and its popularity.

In his first "open letter" to the public, Laughlin asked three questions: "Why is it that editors continue to employ critics who are totally out of touch with the audiences they are paid to review for? Why is it that critics almost consistently condemn the very pictures that their readers want to see the most? Why is it that critics invariably look down their noses at the 'mediocrity' of certain films when their readers have overwhelmingly voted them the most popular by buying tickets at the box office with their hard-earned cash?" To "prove" the disproven point that what critics and audiences like are drastically different, Laughlin contrasted the top 20 grossing films with nine critics' Ten Best lists of 1974, with the sophistic conclusion that "the facts" showed that critics had no effect whatsoever on what audiences preferred to see.

In the second ad, a 5,000-word tome, Laughlin elaborated on his popular vs. great theory of art (the classics always emerge from what was popular) and unleashed more invective on the critics, especially the New York bunch, saying most critics were unqualified for their roles, peer-oriented and elitist in outlook, and contemptuous of mediocre films as well as their audiences. While opposing all critical evaluation of art, Laughlin piously reminded readers that reviews were nothing more than "unverifiable, unsubstantiated opinion" which often revealed more about the critic than the work being considered. By citing reviews of "The Trial of Billy Jack," he noted that critics who thought the picture was too long wrote long reviews and those who found it simple-minded wrote simple-mindedly about it. He also lamented that critics had entirely missed the film's intentions—to report some historically true events and to discuss some powerful social issues of the day. Laughlin said he wouldn't bother with critics at all if those in the film industry—producers, directors, distributors and exhibitors—didn't pay undue attention to critics and make decisions based on their reviews.

In true evangelical fashion, Laughlin offered two solutions to improve the state of film criticism: critics shouldn't write about works they don't like and negative opinions should always be balanced by a positive review, so readers can make up their own minds.

Additionally, the ads announced a writing contest in which essays of 300 words or less were sought to answer the question: "Why are movie critics out of touch with the audiences?" Open only to Southern Californians, the contest offered the allure of 917 prizes totaling $100,000, yet it elicited only 5,000 responses and was openly called a "flop" by Laughlin himself. When the prizes were doled out in August, Laughlin didn't even show up at the Burbank shindig and only a one paragraph excerpt of Brant Cortright's $25,000-winning essay was released to the press. (The whole episode sank out of public view after *Variety* ran an 8-inch story on the awards ceremony.)

Cortright observed (to Laughlin's delight no doubt) that art and criticism were paradoxically incompatible since art was an everchanging process and criticism had to latch onto the static institution of publishing to survive; hence critics were virtually incapable of ever analyzing anything new and creative. The filmgoing audience, obviously, was not saddled with an institutional perspective and therefore free to appreciate new works.

Although Billy Jack Enterprises insisted on retaining publication rights to the other top essays, this researcher extracted the following ideas from them:

Surprisingly, the second-place winner, Mary E. Dunn, demurred from the Laughlin line and took a pro-critic tack when she suggested that by virtue of their training, critics use rigorous standards to judge art, while audiences are capricious and only seek fulfilling recreation-level experience from movies. Miss Dunn also said critics gave artists reliable feedback, warnings that shouldn't be ignored.

Robert Joseph opined that critics differed from audiences because they are more print-oriented and believe their reviews are of more value than most films they consider.

Robert T. Solton berated critics for being obsessed with power over their readers, elitist in judgment and cliquish conspirators. He also believed that critics betrayed their readers by currying friendships and seeking privileges from those in the entertainment industry.

Robert Reveal honed in on other critical problems: distortions that stem from saturation exposure and from accepting freebies from exhibitors. He also harped on critics' biases and their lack of creativity.

While these public responses to critics may not have turned out to be of much interest to Laughlin, the campaign can be considered a success in one way—it generated gobs of publicity for Laughlin and his views. In rapid succession, he was featured in major articles in *Rolling Stone, Los Angeles Times'* "Calendar" section, *New York, True,* and *People.* Although none of the New York film critics responded to his challenges in print, Alan Rich castigated him for "double talk" and his "culture-for-everyone" mentality which produces pseudo-cultural artifacts (like "greatest hits" records). Only Stephen Farber challenged his thesis: "Most critics seem to be closer to the commercial mainstream than either Tom Laughlin or the critics themselves would like to admit."[2]

Judith Crist is probably America's best known film critic, having worked for the *New York Herald Tribune, New York,* NBC "Today" Show, *Playgirl, Saturday Review, Vogue,* the *New York Post* and *TV Guide.* As a self-described "populist critic," she says her judgment more closely reflects the tastes of average moviegoers than those of her peers. But a comparison between her list of the 10 greatest movies of all time with *Variety's* top mon-

eymakers would challenge her position. Back to you, Tom
Laughlin.

Crist's Favorites	Variety's Money-Makers
1. City Lights	1. Star Wars
2. Rules of the Game	2. Jaws
3. Citizen Kane	3. The Godfather
4. Grand Illusion	4. The Exorcist
5. 8½	5. The Sound of Music
6. La Guerre Est Fini	6. The Sting
7. Tokyo Story	7. Gone With the Wind
8. Cries and Whispers	8. One Flew Over the Cuckoo's
9. War and Peace	Nest
10. The Maltese Falcon	9. Rocky
	10. (tie) The Towering Inferno
	Love Story

Whither auteurism?

Of all the methodological approaches critics advocate—
humanistic, sociological, psychological, moral, historical, impres-
sionistic and literary—the auteur theory has become the most
pervasive and perhaps influential since its importation from
France in the early 1960s. Simply stated, the auteur critics believe that the director is the main "author" (auteur) of a film. An
auteur director exhibits an easily recognizable cinematic style
stemming from his personality. The personal films produced (as
opposed to the formulaic works that rolled off the Hollywood as-
sembly lines during the old studio days) reflect not only a style
consistent from film to film but also a re-statement of familiar
themes—ideas and emotions.

In favoring film form over content, auteurist critics laud
strong directors with readily apparent visual style because their
work is easiest to catalog, analyze and write about. Critics
quickly establish their own pantheons of favorite directors and
routinely review each new offering as infallible.

"The distinguishable personality of the director as a criterion
of value" was the way Andrew Sarris stated the theory's major
principle. Nonsense, insists anti-auteurist Stephen Farber:
"Identifying and defining a filmmaker's personality may well be
interesting in its own right, but it has nothing to do with evaluating his work."[3]

Other anti-auteurists cite other weaknesses with the theory.
Some say auteurists consider "B" action pictures by stylish Hol-

lywood "hacks" with the same concern as work by film artists exhibiting truly original style and content.

The question of authorship is obviously more complex than auteurists acknowledge. Since filmmaking is a collaborative effort involving screenwriter, actors, cameraman, sound technicians, editors and others, the singling out of the director who may rule his set with an iron fist is a distortion of the creative process involved.

Still others mock the auteurist's practice of dividing a film into form and content components, a technique further developed by new theoreticians called structuralists, who probe deep-structure myths using Marxist tenets, and semiologists, who study cinematic signs using linguistic analysis.

One benefit of auteur criticism by Sarris, Canby, Roger Greenspun and others has been some scholarly writing about obscure films of interest. While auteurism's greatest value may come from its reevaluation of the past, Sarris himself noted at a recent conference: "Methodology is no substitute for history."

More confessions of cultist Sarris.

"The rigidity and tyranny that's been set up around auteurism has been set up by people who profess to hate it," Sarris told interviewer Maurice Peterson in the *Metropolitan Review.*[4]

"If you like something you can find all sorts of rationalizations for things directors do," he later admitted publicly. "If you don't like them, you can explain away their excesses.

"Evaluating films is like evaluating a great sensational or sexual experience and at the same time evaluating a painting or a book: it draws from both types, things close to reality and things close to art," he has said. "When we say 'greatness' I think it's very often a personal statement, something that's excited us very much in a period in our lives."

"Criticism can be an art in the sense of *belles lettres*," he said at the same time, slightly backing off from his film buff-auteur stance. "It's essay writing as much as it is criticizing; it isn't entirely responsible to film, it reflects the critic's tastes and relates a film to the rest of the cultural, political and natural world.

"In auteurism, elucidation not only precedes evaluation; it very often transcends it," he reminds detractors.

At a colloquium at Columbia University, where he teaches, Sarris said succinctly: "A critic's job is to define choices and let the public decide what they want."

On another reflective instance, Sarris told his following in the

Village Voice: "The critic must somehow seduce the reader with his enthusiasm and erudition. The young, particularly, fall asleep at solemn sermons. Some are so zonked out that they would fall asleep during strip tease, a few are so awake and so alive that they make the most dedicated critic and teacher feel inadequate. In between the zonks and the zings are the great silent majority with whom the critic and teacher must establish some communication. A certain degree of vulgarization becomes inevitable."[5]

On another public occasion, he reminded a New York audience that "critics are rather trivial people in the celebrity stage, but any critic who doesn't say he wants the whole world to love him is lying."

Almost sadly, he bemoans: "Being a film critic isn't the ultimate in life."

Beyond genreism.

Despite enlightened critics' insistence on pluralism in both the arts and criticism, the notion of categories or genre remains, along with hierarchical, status relationships. For example, filmed dramas have more prestige than monster movies, or surrealistic films are ranked higher than westerns. While clearly different types of work are discernible—genre exist—the lines separating them rarely are, and the numerous combinations and inter-relationships of types are ignored. One strength of the auteur approach to film criticism is that it follows a particular director's production across genre in order to examine his total career in perspective.

Congenital high-brow criticism: I know what I like—art!

Fearlessly fighting America's twin cultural problems—antiintellectualism and rampaging pop culture—is John Simon, a self-described elitist critic. Harvard-educated (a doctorate in comparative literature) and suavely European in demeanor, the Yugoslav-born Simon detailed his critical philosophy in *The New Leader:*

> Criticism is, by definition, one of the most elitist activities extant. It is highly presumptuous to sit in judgment on other people's work and talent; to pronounce, in a democratic society, on what is superior and inferior, and know, even while doing this, that masses of people will not comprehend such discrimination, feel threatened by it, and resent it bitterly. The only kind

SCHEMATIC VIEW OF A FILMMAKER'S WORK
THROUGH HISTORY AND GENRE ANALYSIS

Overall Assessment
  Of All Current
    Film Types

———————— Comedy

———————— Historical spectacle

———————— Adventure

———————— Melodrama

———————— Horror

———————— Science Fiction

———————— Crime & Detective

———————— Western

———————— War

———————— Legend & Fairy Tale

———————— Documentary

———————— Love Story

———————— Animation

———————— Filmed Theatre

———————— Surrealism

———————— Satire

———————— Suspense

———————— And Others . . .

Present   Past

Assessment by genre through history of each type

of critic not considered an elitist at all is one who likes most things, but he is not a critic at all. To be choosey, to be stern, is to be elitist; yet what is discrimination and tough-mindedness except strong conviction based on intense comparative evaluation.[6]

Since he strives to be a cultural Renaissance man, he quite rightly believes that all critics should be more than buffs and should explore other fields of art and write about them in addition to their speciality.

Yet he waffles on concern for readers. At one point, he writes: "It is not for the critic to do the reader's thinking for him; it is for the critic merely to do his own thinking for the reader's benefit."

Further, he says he writes for the ages, that readers fifty years hence will recognize the accuracy of his reviews: his ideal critic is one who prefigures the judgment of time, anticipates the voice of posterity.

He also believes that readers can benefit just as much from disagreeing with a critic's views as agreeing: "The test of valid criticism is that instead of eliciting rote consent or hysterical opposition, it stimulates thought."

By applying the formalist, literary standards of art to popular culture, not surpisingly, Simon finds mostly grist for scathing dismissals. His negativism has become legendary. The adjective "acerbic" has become linked to his name. Unquestionably, he is the most detested critic around and is proud of it. In a *More* interview, he told Philip Nobile:

> If you carry truthfulness to the nth degree, it becomes offensive to some. Untalented people don't like being told in no uncertain terms how untalented you consider them to be. . . . I don't believe in merely reprimanding pseudo-artists and other fakes. I believe in trying to stop them from defrauding the public. I consider this a legitimate function of criticism.[7]

His preoccupation with perfection causes Simon to elevate trivial concerns into canon. For example, a grammatical error can become the basis for condemning an entire work. Or the physical appearance of a performer that displeases him draws harsh personal insults that weaken his credibility.

But his main pitfall is that his method doesn't suit his subject. Popular culture offerings are entertainment vehicles by design; so few films (or plays) ever achieve the status of art. Hence, Simon and other elitists have almost nothing new to say about most works except that they aren't art. Such criticism, like the media they seek to scrutinize, is, by nature, quite impure.

• • • •

The gospel of Pauline Kael: eclectic pluralism (with hyper-enthusiasm).

As the critic that filmmakers, buffs and other critics most often read, Pauline Kael's approach to criticism has special interest. Working in the tradition of Gilbert Seldes, Otis Ferguson, James Agee and Robert Warshow—that the best film critics use everything they know—Kael has already spawned her own proteges: Gary Arnold of the *Washington Post*, Paul Zimmerman of *Newsweek*, Roger Ebert of the *Chicgo Tribune*, David Denby, Stephen Farber and others.

Her method eschews simple theories formulas: "Those who ask for objective standards seem to want a theory of criticism which makes the critic unnecessary. And he is expendable if categories replace experience," she writes in "I Lost It at the Movies."[8] Kael insists that film criticism not only draws from film history but also other fields of culture and that critics must judge films by how they extend experience and deliver pleasure. "You must use everything you are and everything you know that is relevant," she says succinctly.

Kael defines the role of the critic as messianic:

> to help see what is in the work, what is in it that shouldn't be, what is not in it that could be. He is a good critic if he helps people understand more about the work than they could see for themselves; he is a great critic, if by his understanding and feeling for the work, by his passion, he can excite people so that they want to experience more of the art than is there, waiting to be seized.[9]

She also believes that critics must rely on their own genuine, emotional responses to work and not aesthetic yardsticks or standards. For her, criticism is mostly comparative and one works from the good taste of the past. "I don't trust critics who care only for the highest and the best; it's an inhuman position, and I don't believe them. I think it's simply their method of exalting themselves," she once wrote in her *New Yorker* column[10] (perhaps subtly chiding the High Browism of Simon).

Kael readily admits that "good-bad movies" offer both "minimal entertainment for a relaxed evening's pleasure" as well as satisfy her appetite for trash. But she also recognizes her responsibility to guide readers selectively:

> It's part of the function of a movie critic to know and indicate the difference between a bad movie that doesn't much matter because it's so much like other bad movies and a bad movie that matters . . . because it affects people strongly in new, different ways.[11]

To accomplish this objective, Kael enlivens reviews with her knack for amateur sociology and occasionally gives almost as much space to the audience reaction as to the movie itself. In reviewing "Billy Jack," for example, she combined an insight on the audience with another forte, a bit of autobiography:

> Though the audience I saw "Billy Jack" with was almost all male, it responded happily to the independent, tough-talking girls. It is a curious fact of movie history (and one that may be lost sight of) that, in general, the men always did like the independent women. It was the women who like the sobbing and

suffering ladies. (My father's favorite actresses were Joan Blondell and Barbara Stanwyck; my mother's were Helen Hayes and Ruth Chatterton.)[12]

Along with being in tune with film audiences, Kael exhibits a fierce loyalty to her medium though certainly not to its present system of production and distribution. Perhaps the most anti-Hollywood of film critics, Kael has boldly hypothesized that the size of a picture's budget appears inversely related to its quality, enraging producers. She further proposed that innovative filmmakers begin distributing their work themselves as a way to subvert the system run by movie moguls and their bookkeepers.

Kael's popular appeal stems in part from her high involvement with films and their audiences but also from her readability. In a *Village Voice* review of her sixth book,[13] "Reeling," Richard Gilman noted her increased use of fashionable diction—"film" became "movies," and hip words such as "dig," "downer," and "macho" mixed with 1930s perjoratives such as "crummy" and "klutzy"—became part of her new voice. More than anything, though, Gilman accuses her of gush, unabashed enthusiasm for American movies, a charge which she admits to even in the book's title.

Yet her hyperenthusiasm has earned other critical comments. Some have said that her overuse of absolute superlatives is what one might expect from a critic unable to convince a reader by argument, allusion or example; in short, her insensate praise reduces her reviews to meaninglessness. *Time*'s Jay Cocks complained that film companies were frequently reprinting her entire reviews in advertisements, converting her criticism into promotional material and press agentry and making her part of the very marketing process of the system she so much despises.

Kael earns criticism in one other area. Perhaps more than any other critic, she has gained a reputation for having criticized her peers in print.[14] Dwight Macdonald, former *Esquire* film critic, who endured numerous Kael tongue-lashings, retaliated in a review of her first book: "She is obsessed with other critics, using their opinions as a springboard for her own performance and almost always quoting them adversely, and often unfairly." Macdonald also observed that Kael considered other critics as "rivals or butts," neither of which could be allowed to impede her success. True, Kael has repeatedly blasted Bosley Crowther, Judith Crist, Stanley Kauffmann, Andrew Sarris, and even her *New Yorker* colleagues Penelope Gilliat and Brendan Gill, yet she defends her tactics with a single-minded purpose: "In order to try for a fresh approach to certain movies, I tried to clear away the Eastern view, my aim being for people to look at movies somewhat differently from the delivered dicta."

• • • •

"Over the last few years there's been a change in status in this field—movies have evolved into film" notes Joy Boyum of the *Wall Street Journal.* "Film was implied to be more important than movies and possibly an art. Movie reviewing evolved into something called criticism. Yet these labels seemed to change without the objects themselves changing very much. So there also was a confused set of demands and questions. Reviewing has never traditionally been confused with criticism. You wouldn't confuse the remarks of a book reviewer in *The New York Times* with remarks of Lionel Trilling, who wrote criticism. But in the case of film, there's no real body of criticism, the only criticism there is is reviewing, which confuses the issue. When the reviews of James Agee were published in 1957, they were published as *James Agee's Reviews and Comments.* Ten years later, Otis Ferguson's reviews were collected under the title of *The Film Criticism of Otis Ferguson.* Both wrote reviews. But what had happened was a change in our perception of them rather than a change in the content."

• • • •

In a war to have "the first word," as they say, New York film critics have increasingly been rushing their reviews into print even before the film premieres. (Pauline Kael set the record in 1975 when she reviewed a rough cut of "Nashville" four months before it was released.) In an effort to formalize the oft-violated ground rules (which said reviews were to run *the day after* the film opened) the three New York daily papers revamped their policies in mid-1978 to publish reviews on *the same day* that films opened, necessitating advance private screenings for critics.

• • • •

Today's film critics are the fourth generation of their kind. Their writing considers film in an entirely different way than did the earliest critics who raved with fascination over their infant medium or even those second and third generation critics who wrote about a mass medium and powerful cultural force in its heyday. Today, critics are aware that film is a diminishing medium and it faces stiff competition for public attention in an era of multi-media.

• • • •

A *Public Interest* listing of the nation's leading intellectuals cited only two critics: Pauline Kael and John Simon.

• • • •

Because the public sees more films than it reads books, it places enormous pressures on critics to deal with a staggering volume of material, grouses Andrew Sarris: "Film critics are expected to see between 400 and 500 films a year and be knowledgeable about them, while book reviewers can be selective and aren't expected to have read everything. Film reviewers are expected to be conversant with all movies past, present and future."

• • • •

Although her published reviews often run up to 5,000 words, *New Yorker* film critic Pauline Kael is paid only for the first 800.

• • • •

Time critic Richard Schickel, speaking at a Columbia University colloquium, advised, "Practicing journalists are first to give a response to a new work and get a discussion going. Our initial response is sometimes subject to change. Critics should be very modest about what they say because anything they say isn't the last word on it. There's also something advantageous about shooting from the hip, offering a true response that's fresh, direct and unpretentious. There's often such wonderful accuracy in instant reviewing."

• • • •

As was his style, Robert Warshow, *Commentary* critic until 1955, said simply: "A man watches a movie, and the critic must acknowledge that he is that man."

• • • •

Among those who believe critics should primarily write about their proprioceptive responses to film—those physiological feelings of surprise, joy, terror, sadness, anger, etc.—is Bruce Cook, of the now extinct *National Observer:*

You don't go to the movies to be instructed. You go to the movies to be hit between the eyes—splat!—with action, energy, emotion, most of all with that grand sense of style that you get from no other form. The very nature of film limits intellectual con-

SCHEMATIC VIEW OF CRITIC/REVIEWER DICHOTOMY

	Reviewer
Gene Shalit	—————
Archer Winston, Rex Reed	—————
Joseph Gelmis, Judith Crist	—————
John Simon, Paul Zimmerman, Richard Schickel	—————
Arthur Knight, Vincent Canby	—————
Charles Champlin	—————
Penelope Gilliat, Stanley Kauffmann	—————
Stephen Farber, Pauline Kael	—————
Richard Roud	—————
Penelope Houston, Robin Wood, Parker Tyler	—————
Andrew Sarris	—————
James Agee, Robert Warshow, Otis Ferguson	—————
Siegfried Kracauer, Rudolf Arnheim	—————
Andre Bazin, Sergei Eisenstein	—————

Critic

tent. Film is something you do in the dark, a dream run before your eyes, a fantasy.[15]

• • • •

"Movies are one product you buy sight unseen, unpretested. If you buy a ticket, you've voted for it," Judith Crist told a Hunter College audience. She also urged moviegoers to get over their awe of critics·and openly react to pictures: demand one's money back from the box office if one gets outraged and compliment the theatre manager if one is truly pleased by what one sees.

• • • •

Advocating a film reviewing system Hollywood could live with, Don Carle Gillette wrote in the *Journal of the Producers Guild of America:*

> Since movies are made for the entertainment of the general public, the fairest way for a reviewer to judge whether or not they fulfill that objective is to see each picture in a theatre where the reactions of the paying customers can be noted. Any good and honest reporter can cover these showings. He merely has to report impartially the regular audience response. That, plus the

film credits and a brief synopsis of the story, will give prospective ticket buyers the information they want.[16]

• • • •

Mario Puzo, author of "The Godfather," analyzed how critics apportioned credit for the movie's success:

           30% for director Francis Ford Coppola
           20% for Marlon Brando
           15% for Al Pacino
            5% for set director, costumes, etc.
            5% for editing
            0% for the best-selling novel from which the film's characters and incidents were taken.
           10% for the movie critics themselves.

Total: 85% Critics never give any artist 100% credit for his work, Puzo insisted in *New York* magazine.[17]

• • • •

Auteurist Vincent Canby defined one handicap critics have: not being able to erase from their memories the anticipations and even the prejudices they have stored up through their experience with the films of any filmmaker.

• • • •

"A film critic not knowing production technique is like a literary critic not knowing grammar," critic Frank Rich told an N.Y.U. class.

Critics should not write about technique, however, insists Pauline Kael, unless it's used for something worth doing.

• • • •

Clifford A. Ridley believes critics should serve readers a full table of delights:

> Simply telling the critic, "Quit talking around and just tell me what you think," is doing yourself no service, because knowing a conclusion without knowing the reasoning and point of view that underlie it is equivalent to knowing almost nothing at all. The critic who delivers only "opinions" is like the chef who cooks nothing but hamburgers. He's squandering not only his talent (assuming he has any), but also the potential of his materials. The diner—and reader—deserves more."[18]

• • • •

Among those who abhor the trend toward thumbs up-thumbs down criticism is Stanley Kauffmann, who wrote in *The New Republic:*

> For many American decades, approximately since the heyday of Mencken, the chief hallmark of critics on "journals of opinion" and quarterlies has been nay-saying. For this, much of the time, we can be grateful. But out of it has grown a wretched rule of thumb: the critic who says "no" *must* be more perspective than the one who says "yes" or even "no, but," and the critic who says the flat "no" most frequently—and violently—is the best.
>
> Inarguably, most of what is produced in any art, particularly the audience arts of theatre and film, is junk; and obviously the nay-saying is a reaction against the most persistent yea-saying of the mass circulation press. Still, through the decades, the nay-saying has become almost as much of a reflex, in its way, as the mass yea-saying. What's worse, the nay-saying has sometimes been a cover for a lack of aesthetic sensibility as abysmal as that in most of the booster mass reviewers. The diction and the air differ; but on each side a gallery is being played to, by critics who are not much more than players to their respective galleries.
>
> I deplore both sides, and specially deplore the sort of mind which suspects that the critic who pans a work is, arbitrarily, sounder than the one who finds merit in it. I've done my share of panning and hope to do plenty more, but where an imperfect, even failed work has merits in it, I hope to exercise what discrimination I have (a modest cough here) to point them out, as pertinent to my own bona fides, the artists' due, and the reader's possible interest in coming along.[19]

● ● ● ●

From reading today's critics, one gets the impression that little had changed since Otis Ferguson, who reviewed films for *The New Republic* from 1934 to 1942, wrote: "Professional criticism, by and large, amounts to little more than parasitism and futility. . . . It is a little shameful to be always on the fringe and all the time talking, talking."[20]

● ● ● ●

Yet a few young critics still dream of better times. Writing in *The New York Times*, Stephen Farber said, "The quality of film criticism is of concern to anyone who cares about movies. Ideally there should be an intense, on-going dialogue between critics and filmmakers from which both can learn. But the critic's shortsightedness and fickleness inhibit that exchange of ideas. We are still a long way from achieving a serious film community in America."[21]

DRAMA

Why drama criticism isn't what it used to be.

" 'Criticism is, has been and eternally will be as bad as it possibly can be.' Thus spake George Bernard Shaw, the best theatre critic in the English language in at least the past hundred years," observed Harold Clurman, stage director and critic for *The Nation*, in his book, *The Divine Pastime*.

> What he meant was that critics will never satisfy everyone concerned, that they will always make horrendous "mistakes," that they are bound occasionally to cause damage, and that the degree of their benefactions will always fall under the shadow of serious doubt.[22]

This contempt of criticism partially stems from the uneasy state of theatre art today and the highly vocal nature of theatre people. Many observers contend that the fortunes of criticism and theatre are intertwined and that today's mediocre theatre scene naturally precipitates a similar kind of criticism.

Superstar novelist, journalist and playwright Norman Mailer believes criticism adds to the excitement of theatre. In *Existential Errands*, he writes:

> The opening-night review with all its inequities, yaws of judgment, its surrealistic surgeries upon aesthetic value, is nonetheless indispensable to the theatre. . . . An opening night before a full posse of critics is also part of the play . . . its dramatic edge. Those opening-night reviews, written to the demand of fever speed, are a ritual at the heart of the drama.[23]

Theatre's live and fleeting nature creates some special problems of coverage. The ephemerality of all performing arts places added responsibility on the critic to report thoroughly the performance, since reviews often become the only surviving documentation of an event in the historical record. If critics just dismiss a new work with a negative witticism and fail to describe its form and content, and the work is never performed again, it virtually ceases to exist. Theatre critics, then, must give a brief account of all they see, keeping in mind that future generations may one day re-discover this work and even find value in it.

The live interaction between performer and audience also demands special attention. Theatre people believe that the relationship among the play's characters is of no more significance than their relationships with the audience. Critics, then, are obliged to write not only about what is taking place on stage, but also how it connects with the audience.

While theatre is not a mass art form, its presentation takes the form of mass production, and this factor gives theatre reviewers more power over a play than a music critic might have over a series of concerts. Thus, a critic's remarks on the opening night version of a play would be applicable to each succeeding performance of it. Whereas, a music critic might pan a Brahms program of a symphony, the very next concert—a selection of Mozart—might be much better. In music, too, concert-goers often buy season tickets, while theatre audiences generally attend each show by its particular appeal.

Theatre reviewers vs. drama critics

"The theatre critic's job is in many ways more difficult than the drama critic's, and, in my prejudiced view, at least equally important," Stanley Kauffmann, theatre and film critic of the *New Republic*, writes in *Yale/Theatre*.[24]

> First, he is a journalist, therefore, what I call a front-line critic. He has the primary and important task of winnowing wheat from chaff—in effect, of selecting the materials that will eventually become the material for the drama critics. The best of theatre critics makes mistakes, but it is in the front lines that crucial decisions are made.
>
> The theatre critic spends most of his time with junk—junk of even a lower quality than most of the work in any other field except film. It is, objectively, a ridiculous mode of life. There seem to me only two real reasons to pursue it: first, the possession of a critical talent "which is death to hide," as true of critical talent as any other. Second, hope: hope for the arrival of good work, hope that one may help it to arrive and hope to connect it with its audience. This hope is, in some, an exponent of commitment.

Harold Clurman frets about the effect of theatre reviewers who author one-dimensional criticism, dealing exclusively with a particular performance of a play:

Theatre having become a luxury commodity with us, the person in quest of entertainment demands instantaneous guidance, and the daily critic is there to supply it with necessary dispatch. His columns tend to make the pronouncement of opinion a substitute for criticism, so that very few of his readers have any idea of what criticism really is.

Most daily reviewers are not critics because they are not richly enough endowed with sensibility, thoughtfulness, personality, knowledge of art and life or literary skill to hold our attention for much longer than it takes to read their reviews. . . . One of the authentic critic's main purposes is to enunciate or construct an attitude toward life—if you will, a "philosophy"—and to make it as cogently relevant as possible. This must necessarily scare a newspaper editor whose publication is designed to please "everybody," that is, from 40,000 to a million readers daily.

At best the critic is an artist whose point of departure is another artist's work. If he is truly a fine critic, he will make his reader something of an artist as well. It is not essential that he also make him a consumer.[25]

Women's Wear Daily reviewer Martin Gottfried attacks his peers on another score:

It is often said that first-night New York critics have too much power; that they can close a production before it has had a chance to win an audience. This is sometimes true but mainly, the critics have too little power. They cannot bring people to the plays they like and they do not lead or inspire those in the theatre (these are the most positive kinds of power), because they aren't respected. This is a power that must be earned if critics are to fill their roles in the theatre cycle and, conversely, it is this power that cannot be developed so long as the critics do not fill their roles.[26]

Gottfried says critics must decide whether professional stage work is "good" and he must understand and explain why, relating it to theatrical standards.

Other critics of critics charge that theatre reviewers don't appear to know how a play works and rarely consider production values in their reviews. Clurman believes few journalists know how theatre is put together much less what directors or actors do. Some say that critics are too "product oriented" and only interested in giving a play a grade instead of dealing with the process of theatre.

While most agree that theatre reviewing is a valuable public service, some envision critics as either consumer advocates or theatre boosters. Consumer-advocate critics are not particularly interested in art, but more concerned about producers attempting to market cheap entertainment at high prices and mislead the public into believing it's art. While scams are news, such reviewers neglect serious criticism of even popular works.

Critical boosterism is a problem related to the health of the theatre itself. Harold Clurman acknowledges that critics over-use superlatives largely as

> an implement of first aid to the box office. . . . The reviewer whose reaction to a play is contained in some such ejaculations of "electrifying," "inspired," "a mighty work," "a dismal bore," may in each instance be right, but his being right does not by itself make him a critic. For these epithets only indicate effects: pleasure and displeasure. The true critic is concerned with causes, with the composition of human, social, formal substances which have produced the effect. Strictly speaking, it is not even necessary that the critic name the effect; it is imperative that he take into account the sources from which it springs. In doing this the critic is faithful to the work he treats, while at the same time, he affords the reader some idea of what manner of man the critic himself is—which is a crucial consideration.[27]

Dan Sullivan, of the *Los Angeles Times*, takes an even tougher stance against boosterism:

> I suspect that theatre reviewers have already discouraged theatregoing to a certain extent by over-praising mediocrity. . . . Readers will, I have concluded, forgive a critic for being too critical. But God help the one they consider to be too lenient. Now if leniency becomes the name of the game—if critics start hyping up their praise-prose even further in a misguided effort to help the theatre—I am afraid the public is going to suspect that the fix is on, in which case theatre reviewing will become just another branch of theatrical advertising. And I don't believe many people are drawn to a show on the strength of how great the ads were.[28]

Sullivan steadfastly refuses to over-praise works:

> I cannot fake a reaction to a show. When you're faking it, you feel a little like a whore. Why? Ridiculous as it may seem to the creative people we write about, we parasitic critics are as jealous of the integrity of the work we turn out as they are of theirs. Ultimately, I don't think it helps. It seems to me that the tradition of the all-stops-out review, when at least a couple of stops should have been left in, has helped to decrease—not increase—the theatre's permanent congregation. It has led to the over-expectation on the part of the audience going to the show and disappointment on the way out, a sequence which repeated often leads people to conclude that the theatre just isn't for them. The theatre critic is trying to develop fans for the theatre, people

who really know and really care, because they can make their own distinctions. You don't do that by pretending the distinctions aren't there.

In an age of routine exaggeration, where "superstar" means someone who has appeared in two profitable movies in a row, anything less than an ecstatic review of a stage play will be taken by the public to mean that they can pass *that* one up, thank God. . . .[29]

I know it is depressing to be told that the theatre is as complicated as everything else these days, but, alas, dear reader, the opportunities for unmodified rapture or unalloyed disdain—each so energizing—are as rare in my profession as they are in yours. The conscientious critic crows when he can, and bellows when that seems right, but usually he is examining dark clouds for silver linings or counting flies in the ointment—in short, trying to get as exact a reading on a mixed dramatic experience as possible.[30]

Julius ("Jay") Novick, of the *Village Voice*, also opposes boosterism in criticism. In a *Yale/Theatre* interview, he said:

I do see myself trying to preserve the theatre, but not by boosting and propagandizing it. I don't go along with the school of thought that says we have to pretend it's better than it is, just to keep it alive, because I think that is lying. It is our function to help keep it alive by talking about it, by demonstrating our concern with it, by showing that it is possible for intelligent people to still care about it, and by denouncing evil and praising virtue to do what you can to create a theatre that deserves to live.

In describing his own reviewing philosophy, Novick says:

It's dangerous to come in with a rigid set of rules. . . . I try to stay as loose as I can. . . . A good critic does not depend upon the value of what he sees for the value of what he writes. . . . If a play is nothing as a play, what is its value, what is its interest as a symptom of one of our national sicknesses? In other words, the critic uses the play as an occasion for making some sense about the world outside the theatre. Shaw and Beerbohm often made small masterpieces of which bad plays were the raw material. As long as this is a possibility, then there will be some use in dramatic criticism.[31]

• • • •

The power of the New York Times theatre reviewer.

The increase in the power of the *Times'* critic is related to the demise of newspaper outlets for criticism in New York. Brooks

A Review For All Seasons

by Bob Edison

(If a critic you'd become
You must learn these rules of thumb:)

"The denouement's shattering, the lighting is flattering, the sets are serviceable (such lines make me nervousable), the score's inventive, the crowd's attentive, the plot line's tenuous, the ingenue's ingenuous, she's radiant, luminous, lights up the proceedings, she's shining, incandescent (sounds like meter readings), beloved star is unassailable, so she's never unavailable, her love for all is just outpouring, all of which gets pretty boring, British players have finesse, Americans are adequate, no more, no less, audience's attention is unflagging, second act's the one that's lagging, leading lady's face is sagging, orchestra is sometimes dragging, debut's auspicious, timing's propitious, motivation's murky, construction's jerky, leading lady's quirky and the play's a turkey."

(All together now, you're doing fine
Repeat the clichés, line by line:)

"The score's inventive, the theatre's attentive, the theme's compelling, some scenes need jelling, all eyes started welling, the plot bears retelling, new talent is soaring, her presence is scoring, her carriage is regal, her beauty illegal, first nighters wreathed in smiles, backers dancing in the aisles, will theatre wonders never cease? Ensemble style is of a piece, I still can hear the loud applauding, evening now's richly rewarding, insights penetrating, tedium enervating, laughs fast and furious, plot twists are spurious, loose ends abound, can't get off the ground, dancing contagious, star is upstageous, taste is appalling, soliloquy's enthralling, new find is endearing, leading lady's enduring, praise must be heaped, my heart fairly leaped, ideas are exciting, the wit is quite biting, audience entranced, author's reputation enhanced, performance provocative, staging evocative."

(These are the rules; be sure and get them
And once you do, friend—please FOR-
GET THEM!!)

Reprinted with the permission of <u>Playbill Magazine</u>, April 1975.

Atkinson, a former *Times'* Broadway reviewer, observed the change this way: "In 1925, when I first began, there were 13 critics, and I don't think anybody had the ability to sell a show. Now it's down to three."

The concentration of power in one reviewer understandably worries other critics. Stanley Kauffmann of the *New Republic,* writes in *Yale/Theatre:* "The *Times'* critic, now absolutely prime in power though attended by a covey of others to camouflage that fact, heads a Chamber of Commerce to keep the Broadway business alive." (Kauffman also says that while Broadway today is a "platinum-plated dwarf," it won't die as long as it serves audiences with popular fare such as musicals and comedies.) Richard Gilman, former critic with *Newsweek, Commonweal* and the *New Republic,* agrees: "The *Times* matters so much that a rave review of a play there can mean instant success, whatever the rest of the critics say, while a knock can close a production in two days."

While the *Times'* pre-eminence continually draws fire, so did reviewer Clive Barnes, who doubled as drama and dance critic for ten years. For example, Robert Brustein, head of the Yale School of Drama, blasts: "Barnes' writing for the *Times* combines a transparent lack of real interest in the American theatre with a manifest compulsion to save it from economic disaster."

Barnes often tried to belittle his importance, a ploy that also diminished his effectiveness. Speaking to the Dramatists Guild, he once told his critics:

> If the drama critic of the *Times* must stand on his head in public to stop people from taking him so seriously, then that's a valuable duty for him to do. Critics don't want power, they want influence, and there's a big difference. But it is really the producers who give the critics power. They are continually making the public aware of the critic's judgment in advertisements and other public statements. As soon as you have full-page advertisements shouting about "unanimous raves," you immediately put yourself in a vulnerable position when you have unanimous pans. Remember, the real box office power is word of mouth.[32]

After Barnes was replaced by Richard Eder in the spring of 1977, Ross Wetzsteon complained about the *Times'* excessive influence—"the unhealthy, even destructive concentration of power in the hands of whomever happens to be the *Times'* chief drama critic"—in a *Village Voice* article. Wetzsteon even proposed a number of ways in which the *Times* could dilute its power without weakening its status:

> Two first string critics instead of one first-string and one second-string critic. A series of rotating guest critics to complement the regulars. A box accompanying each review giving capsule summaries from other media. More reflective essays and fewer boffo-or-bomb notices. . . .
>
> The Times could have far more constructive power over American theatre if it relinquished its power to make or break specific plays and used its influence, instead, to help create a dialogue of sensibilities. Its power, then, would lie less in its judgments about individual plays than in its stimulation of theatre as a cultural necessity.[33]

For his part, Richard Eder believes that the power of the *Times'* critic is largely a myth: "I don't believe any single critic can break a play, not even the one who works for this newspaper. . . . The use of television spots and of advertising campaigns stressing and sometimes misusing favorable quotes has blurred the power of any single unfavorable review. . . . A single enthusiastic review, on the other hand, may have more weight. If it does not quite make a play, it can certainly help. It will persuade some people to see it—this is where the pure joy of being a critic lies."[34]

Despite such brouhaha, stage producers long ago adopted techniques to "Times-proof" their shows and investments. Some simply keep their productions on tour until they become profitable, making New York just the last stop on a national circuit. Others, including Joseph Papp, have taken large advertisements in the *Times* the day after a new show opens to publish other reviews from critics invited to respond to the new play. On several occasions, black theatre critics reviewing new black plays have been given much wider exposure by appearing in these counter-criticism ads than they would have otherwise had. Many believe the idea has merits. Readers can get more than one view of the new work, though certainly the reviews in the ads are still a bit suspect (despite disclaimers of prior editing) because of their identification with the producer.

Any discussion of the *Times* must include a word from Walter Kerr, the Sunday drama critic since 1967 who won the Pulitzer Prize for Criticism. Kerr explained his current perspective in a recent column:

> My own ideal but rarely realized notion of what the audience-reviewer relationship ought to be is a conversation about something *both* had seen, not a preemptory command to get going or keep out. I realize, of course, that no one who wishes to write about theatre can possibly wait until absolutely everybody's beat him to it; but if there's a consensus in the air that suggests more and more spectators are determined to attend no matter what *anybody* says, then the reviewer is relieved of his burden of functioning as a shopping service and is free to chat, to compare notes—the audience having already proclaimed its own freedom.

Constructive criticism: play-doctors make house calls to theatres.

Theatre makers with weak productions desperately crave specific reactions and advice from critics on how to turn a certain failure into a modest success. Not only are critics-cum-play-doctors expected to tell a playwright or director what's wrong with their ailing production, but they are also asked to prescribe remedies for it. As sort of living Band-Aids, these critics have allied themselves with the theatre in efforts to patch up the infirm.

Norman Nadel, Scripps-Howard critic whose reviews appear in 17 newspapers with a combined readership of 2.5 million, and

Elliott Norton, of the *Boston Herald American*, are the two most famous and proficient practitioners of this trade. Critics in try-out towns such as Philadelphia and New Haven also are known to write constructive criticism to help "improve" shows enroute to Broadway.

Nadel agonizes over his role as "play-doctor" but believes that such criticism can help both the production and the audience and is basically good for the state of the art. "No one *has* to accept what I say," he hedges.

Some theatre people reject the practice flatly. Broadway director Larry Arrick states, "From 200 plays I've directed and that have been reviewed, I've never learned anything that helped me in my work." Off-Broadway director Andre Gregory is more damning: "I never get constructive criticism from critics. When Jerzy Grotowski or Peter Brook see our work, they can tell us what's right and wrong with it in two minutes. The most ordinary person in the normal audience can give better criticism than a critic."

Other critics also oppose play-doctoring. Jay Novick explained his reason why in *Yale/Theatre*:

> I don't write for performers. The point is not to tell an actor you did this and should have done that, or to tell a writer you did this and you should have done that, because this reduces all your other readers to eavesdroppers. Essentially, you're talking to the public and what you say is, first of all, intended for them.[35]

Theatre critic John Simon is also negative on this count:

> To the casual laymen, constructive criticism would be, "Go easy on him, he's doing his best." But this is the worst fallacy of all: it assumes that art does not really matter. If a surgeon's patients die on him, one after the other, does one excuse him by saying he did his best?

Simon's point, however, fails to consider what the producer's purpose really is. In some instances, producers are bent on some insidious personal goal or are simply trying to cash in on a contrived production. They may be trying hard to accomplish misdirected objectives, but it's up to a responsible critic to blow the whistle on these "rip-off artists."

Critic John Lahr—whose criterion for great theatre is simply "astonish me"—preaches involvement with theatre people, but not play-doctoring. He believes critics should read scripts before seeing new plays, talk with theatre friends about the production and participate in its process, but he adds: "Like all affairs of the heart, criticism should be violent, beautiful, omnivorous, intimate, unfair and a totally absorbing passion."

Perhaps at the other extreme from the constructive critics are those who take no responsibility for the theatre and its problems, preferring to remain professional outsiders. These critics never read scripts, attend rehearsals, go backstage after a show or exhibit intimate knowledge of its workings in their reviews. In their attempts to retain purity as a private person with one's own opinions, they also rarely write anything of value to readers or the theatre.

The private game of drama criticism.

Drama critics—rooted in the "high brow" school—express contempt for everything: theatre, reviewers and readers. Former *New Republic* critic Eric Bentley, for instance, assails Broadway reviewing this way:

> You take a highly educated critic and you take the ordinary Broadway play, and the contest is too uneven. There's nothing to criticize, it's too easily a target, and becomes an unworthy exercise for the reviewer. It doesn't require his education, his faculties, to explain that this little nothing is a little nothing.[36]

Robert Brustein, of the Yale Drama School, lambasts reviewers mercilessly,

> Never before have a handful of reviews possessed so much power and lacked so much authority. . . . It is almost as if the theatre had been abandoned by men and women of intelligence and taste, and delivered over wholesale to the publicists, the proselytisers and the performers.[37]

Writing mostly for obscure periodicals, quarterlies and scholarly journals, drama critics are rigidly pessimistic: sick theatre is rooted in a sick society, the commercial theatre is fundamentally corrupt and Broadway has lost its sense of purpose and direction. To smokescreen such an orthodoxy, drama critics concentrate on scripts as literature and dramatic history in their tomes.

Their preference of text to performance leaves them wide open for attack by those who care about theatre. Their arrogance and scorn for "bad things" closes readers off from further discussion of the subject.

Despite all this, Stanley Kauffmann has risen to their defense: "The best drama critics have changed the world in which the best theatre exists, have helped to alter the air it breathes."

Perhaps. But one wonders if politicians and the Environmental Protection Agency don't have more influence.

• • • •

Best wisecrack: When asked what he thought of a particular play, critic and playwright George S. Kaufman once remarked: "I don't know. I saw it under bad conditions. The curtain was up."

• • • •

"There's no function for a critic where intellect has no status," observed Eric Bentley, drama critic of *The New Republic* from 1952 to 1956.

> Real criticism is, trying not to be overwhelmed by the enthusiasms of the moment, as they're promoted by the publicity business, but saying, is it *really* good? Criticism will always have the force of the child in the story about the emperor's new clothes, because there will always be naked emperors who everybody says are wearing the Crown jewels.[38]

• • • •

Although the *Guinness Book of Records* cites Wolcott Gibbs' single word review of the farce "Wham" (he said "Ouch.") as the shortest dramatic criticism in history, Clive Barnes, then writing for the London *Daily Express*, tied the record. He said of a production called "The Cupboard": "Bare."

• • • •

Like many other theatre people, playwright Dale Wasserman believes critics are "an auxiliary stream of publicity for the theatre." Actor Kevin O'Connor also admits: "Everyone in the arts uses reviews, if they are favorable, as publicity."

• • • •

At the 1974 organizational meeting of the American Theatre Critics Association, a new national group formed to stimulate greater communication among critics, the central issue of contention was exclusivity of membership.

• • • •

At the National Critics Institute, a tutorial short course for budding critics held in conjunction with the National Playwright's Conference at the Eugene O'Neill Memorial Theatre Center in Waterford, Connecticut, founder Ernie Schier, drama critic of the Philadelphia *Bulletin*, tells his charges: "Any decent piece of criticism should be a letter to the world." Co-worker Lawrence DeVine, of the Detroit *Free Press* cryptically adds: "Two qualities I look for in the best critics and people: dependability and believeability."

• • • •

As for the young, who would normally be expected to swell the ranks of serious theatre critics, providing new energy, insight and commitment, they seem peculiarly indifferent to the profession—mostly, I would guess, because they have no exciting models to imitate.

says Robert Brustein, whose Yale Drama School offers one of the few programs of study for critics. "There is nothing like an exemplary critic to generate enthusiasm for the practice of criticism, the fact is that very few writers on the theatre are setting very good examples these days."[39]

• • • •

"There's always something in a play that someone loves and critics must find out what that is on their own," Briton Martin Esslin, head of the BBC's radio drama division and a theatre critic who regularly lectures in America, says.

If one believes, as I fervently do, that the theatre can greatly enhance a society's understanding of itself, can contribute to a deepening of men's capacity to feel and refine the emotions— that, in brief, the theatre can contribute to raise the quality of life in a society—and if one believes, as I fervently do, that one cannot have a good theatre without an informed, knowledgeable audience, and that to the formation of such an audience good critics are essential, then surely one is justified in occasionally appealing for higher standards of theatre criticism.

MUSIC

Has rock revived music criticism?

Music criticism in the daily press has changed very little in the past 75 years, says composer and critic Virgil Thomson. "The attitudes adopted for reacting to music or used in observing it, the styles considered acceptable for writing about it, even the types of reviewer appointed to major papers—none of these has gone through notable change."

Thomson also says the amount of space devoted to music criticism and reportage has actually been reduced over the years because of the decline in the number of newspapers as well as the competition for space with other arts. "Today there are too few newspapers in any city to sustain a controversy or even to reflect a consensus," he writes in *The New York Times*.[40] "Consequently, the tone of newspaper criticism is blander and less urgent."

While noting that criticism has not expanded or evolved, Thomson observes that the composition and performance of music has increased. "Reviewing, unless it is an interplay between facts correctly stated and ideas about them fairly arrived at, makes no point," he continues.

> Contemporary composition is where reviewing comes to life. Complaining about interpreters or rooting for them, however legitimate, is just fidgeting. Criticism joins the history of its art only when it joins battle, for or against, with the music of its time.

In assessing the state of music criticism, Thomson says that "weekly magazines still produce, as they have always done, our most readable reports on music, whether as studies of composers' works and temperaments or as straight concert coverage." He also cites a short list of writers he regularly reads: Andrew Porter in *The New Yorker*, Leighton Kerner in the *Village Voice*, Herbert Kupferman in the *National Observer*, Robert Craft in the *New York Review of Books*, Irving Kolodin in *Saturday Review*, Alan Rich in *New York* and B. H. Haggin, formerly in *The New Republic*.

Two other noted composers were less kind to critics. Charles Ives so detested critics he tagged them with his most despicable label: Rollos. Igor Stravinsky also railed at critics who "misinform the public and delay comprehension. They do not see how a music phrase is constructed, do not know how music is written; they are incompetent in the techniques of contemporary musical language."

• • • •

"Critics are the eunuchs of art; they talk about what they cannot do," wrote Russian pianist Vladimir de Pachmann.

Martin Bernheimer, chief music critic of the *Los Angeles Times*, is quick with a hoary rejoinder, "You don't have to be able to lay an egg to know if you've been served a rotten one."

• • • •

"I am not sure that music criticism—unlike, say, movie criticism—is a young man's job," writes Alan Rich in *New York*.[41] "The perspective of a lifetime of dealing with performers and music itself cannot be synthesized overnight in a man who hasn't been through it all himself."

• • • •

John Yohalem, of the *San Francisco Phoenix,* believes today's music critics face difficult new challenges:

> The focus of music criticism has certainly been altered by the LP and its by-products, the expansion of the repertory in all directions and the disaffection of much of the public with new music, left behind by the pace of innovation. The modern critic is less a debater on the nature of a Platonic orthodoxy than a catalogue of possible approaches.

• • • •

Noted music critic Winston Dean lists eight prerequisites for critics to make qualified responses:

- A knowledge of the technical and theoretical principles of music.
- A knowledge of musical history and scholarship.
- A wide general education covering as many as possible of the subjects with which music can be shown to have a point of direct contact.
- The ability to think straight and to write in a clear and stimulating manner.
- An insight into the workings of the creative imagination.
- An integrated philosophy of life of his own.
- An enduring inquisitiveness and willingness to learn.
- An acceptance of his own limitations, both individual and generic.

• • • •

New York Times critic Harold C. Schonberg, who often sprinkles baseball lingo into his reviews, once confessed in a Sunday column that not only was he a baseball fan but he also evaluated his skills as a player: "second base—good field, fair hit, weak throwing arm."

• • • •

"When critics disagree it seems to provoke outrage in a large sector of the public for which any uncertainty is unsettling," writes *New York Times* second-string music critic Donald Henahan.[42] "But critics know in their bones when they all agree they are usually following some leader and when that happens all but the leader have rendered themselves unnecessary."

Henahan further rationalizes, not only disagreeing with his peers, but also with himself:

> The periodic dissent against one's own ideas that dismays many readers is in this view not merely a critic's disease but a way of dealing with the only world anybody can know, a world in which formal purity and emotional messiness are simultaneous, mutually reinforcing truths.

His point is that critics have failed to find a final answer to what music is because there is none, but that some can argue— even with themselves—more interestingly than others over the issue.

• • • •

Critics need new criteria for evaluating new music, Alan Rich has postulated, because the concept of melody and harmony doesn't work with it. "The standards of evaluating new music have nothing to do with musical language," Rich says. "They have to do with the assurance and eloquence with which the composer chooses to use that language."[43] While Rich says he finds a great deal of new music personally exciting, he also readily says that "There are areas in my gut that a great, rolling melody in the old-fashioned sense can engage, and that cannot be satisfied any other way."[44]

• • • •

In his Sunday columns, Harold C. Schonberg often takes to the lectern to educate his *Times* readers about the intricacies of music appreciation. On one occasion, he explained the musical idea:

> Music is a much more mysterious art than painting or poetry. It acts powerfully, but nobody knows exactly why or how it acts. And it acts powerfully in proportion to the composer's vision. When we hear music, any music, we are subjected to a complicated series of reactions. But the most important of these reactions, I believe, is the identification with the mind of the creator. It is there that "idea" is so important. Depending on the strength of the composer's mind—on his ability to impress on your mind, unforgettably, his personality and the material (or ideas) of the composition at hand—the music lives or dies.[45]

At another time, he tackled the conflict between composers and performers over musical interpretation:

> a process in which a composer's ideas—his mind, if you will— are refracted through the prism of the performer's mind. And every performer necessarily has to have a different mind be-

cause, no matter how he tries to get back to the original, he nevertheless is bringing to it his own background, his own tastes, his own knowledge, his own view of life.[46]

• • • •

Eh? What's that? The second-string music critic of the Philadelphia *Inquirer* wears a conspicuous hearing aid? Yes.

• • • •

Famous last words: "That pinched high C was for Harold Schonberg," stage-whispered New York City Opera tenor Michele Molese to a Lincoln Center audience, just before he was fired. Molese, annoyed with his reviews, had earlier pulled the same trick in New Orleans, citing the critic there.

• • • •

At an institute the Music Critics Association annually conducts to train new professionals, *New York* critic Alan Rich stressed the investigative reporting role he believes all critics must perform.

> It seems to me that, at a time when music—as the most expensive of the performing arts—is in deep financial trouble in almost every city across the map, the critic's role vis-a-vis this situation has to be drastically rethought and strengthened,

he wrote afterwards.[47]

• • • •

Norman Nadel, Scripps-Howard music critic, has been taking copies of the musical scores of the works to be performed to concerts he attends for 15 years. Other critics are not so diligent. Most New York critics were caught skimping on their homework in October 1975 when they wrote rave reviews of a series of concerts by Marie-Francoise Bucquet. A few days after the events, staff pianist of the New York Philharmonic Paul Jacobs publicly embarrassed the gushing critics when he announced that Miss Bucquet's performances of piano music by Schoenberg, Webern and Berg were nothing less than "a mishmash of improvisation, distorted rhythms and wrong notes."

• • • •

Bostonian George Frazier, who is credited with writing the first jazz column in a daily newspaper, rated performers on the basis of the attribute "duende," which he defined as "charisma to the nth power, heightened panache or overpowering presence." Some musicians who had it: Frank Sinatra, Benny Goodman, Miles Davis, Billie Holiday, Elvis Presley, Tina Turner. Some who didn't: Artie Shaw, Diana Ross, Aretha Franklin.

• • • •

Robert Christgau, the *Village Voice's* self-proclaimed Dean of American rock critics, believes that he and his colleagues are collectively striving for a new form of critical writing, which includes increased subjectivity on the part of the reviewer, a more lively style of expression and a refusal to concentrate on the work as if it were a given and as if it were the locus of the artistic experience. What is instead? The relationship between work, artist and audience, Christgau insists.

• • • •

Rock music devotees tend to be firmly anti-critical, arguing that music should be heard and felt, not analyzed and criticized. Writing in *Commentary*, Barry Gewen explained why rock criticism had so little value to fans:

> Because rock is a new cultural phenomenon, there are no accepted critical standards, no canons of taste or established traditions to draw on. We are all equally in the dark, with little but our personal impressions to guide us, and the result for criticism is a large degree of subjectivism. What can a writer offer us except his own opinion, and then how do we know what that opinion is worth?[48]

• • • •

Jerry Garcia, of the Grateful Dead, once wisecracked that it took more time to read most record reviews in *Rolling Stone* than it did to play the albums, and they said less.

• • • •

John Rockwell is pained by how little rock writers know about music:

> A lack of acquaintance with the technical aspects of the art or the traditions of other kinds of music, serious and popular, is common in the rock press. It is an unfamiliarity shared by many of the rock musicians themselves, though, and it is no doubt part of the process by which rock has begun to demythologize some of the more hieratic elements of the serious contemporary music scene.[49]

• • • •

"Rock magazines have as much interest in new work and artists as the record companies," free lance music critic Tom Nolan
says. "They are much more likely to rave about something than
put it down because they have to try to keep up the air of excitement in order to sell their publications."

• • • •

Dr. Demento, aka Barry Hansen, a pioneer rock critic and
now a syndicated disc jockey, observed of rock criticism's development:

> Rock criticism now leaps at you from every newsstand. It's a
> flourishing, profitable institution that has played an intangible
> but obvious role in converting rock from its relatively small-
> change status of earlier times to the billion dollar baby it is
> today.[50]

• • • •

On occasion, critics become cynical about their role. The
commercialism of the Avant Garde Festival of 1974 caused Tom
Johnson, of the *Village Voice*, to make this reassessment:

> Ideally, a critic should feel like an independent person, who
> writes according to his sensibilities, and has little direct effect
> on economics. But sometimes I feel like I'm just part of a big and
> highly impersonal publicity machine, which takes in new works
> of art, creates images for them, and spews them out into all the
> galleries and auditoriums across the country. If someone hap-
> pens to make an important artistic discovery or develop some
> extraordinary skill, and if the public really derives some satis-
> faction from an event, that is all well and good, but it is really
> incidental to the basic process, which has to do with eco-
> nomics.[51]

• • • •

While *Rolling Stone* critic Dave Marsh hedged on whether
rock criticism had become more important than rock, he leveled
some harsh words at his colleagues in the rock press:

> Little rock criticism is concerned with music, because most
> rock critics are less concerned with the sound than sociology. . . .
> There's good reason for this though. Most rock isn't worth dis-
> cussing except as phenomenon, a result of working within a re-
> strictive format. But it cripples criticism, when everything is
> seen as event, nothing as art. At some point at least, the critic
> must deal with the work itself, rather than the circumstances
> surrounding it. A glance at any group of record reviews will tell
> you that most critics see the sound as a secondary issue. Gossip,

event, phenomenon, psychology, lyric writing, all take precedence over music.

But most criticism has struck out lately, even as an analysis of phenomenon. This is partly because most critics fail to understand the basic rock phenomenon of the Seventies: it is now a huge business.[52]

As the rock industry soared over the $2 billion mark and a series of scandals erupted in 1973, Richard Goldstein spoke out on the naivete of critics: "For a critic to maintain an intense righteousness about his musical taste while ignoring its economic consequences shows a sense of powerlessness which is childish and fraudulent."

• • • •

Although a few rock journalists dig into the shenanigans of the music industry that supports them, most conveniently ignore corrupt practices and conflicts of interest. Writing in the *Village Voice*, Geoffrey Stokes turned in this exposé on his own peers:

The rock industry's cozy clubbiness would be the envy of the most cynically corrupt political machine. In its simplest form, it comes down to this: record companies hire rock writers as publicists; the same writers then publish favorable articles about their clients. And, you and I, the poor slobs who buy records, have no way of knowing who's on the take.[53]

• • • •

When just more than 100 rock writers from across the country met in Memphis in May 1973 to establish a national association which would help improve their lot (most earned less than $50 a month from writing, they complained), it was seriously suggested that they launch their organization with funds generated from benefit concerts by rock groups they'd reviewed. "Many groups owe us favors," someone piped up. "We've done more for them than they deserve." The group's efforts to form fizzled.

• • • •

When Bruce Springsteen landed on the covers of both *Time* and *Newsweek* and his "Born to Run" album neared platinum (a million sales), New York critics were crowing about their vital role in his success story. They said he was the first rock star in history to be propelled into fame and fortune by critics. Robert Christgau, speaking for the "rock-crit establishment," said that phenomenal sales resulted from widespread, unanimous raves given Springsteen.

It was true that Springsteen did receive more critical coverage in a short period than any other performer in recent times, but Christgau and others failed to mention that Columbia Records had invested a large stake in boosting Springsteen's career. Columbia laid out $150,000 to promote the album, about ten times more than the usual advertising and promotion budget.

Whatever illusions the critics fostered for king-making, Henry Edwards dashed them in *The New York Times:*

> Whether a new-born rock-critic establishment exists or not, several major record company officials declare that they will still continue their policy of rarely quoting rock critics in their ads. The reasons? Many members of the record-buying public, they have discovered, cannot identify *any* rock critic by name. Furthermore, rock critics in general are perceived as untrustworthy, having overpraised too many mediocre disks. Then, too, the public is confused by the widely diverging points of view and even the inability to handle the English language demonstrated by some of those who write about rock. In sum, a significant portion of the record-buying public looks upon rock-music criticism as more an entertainment than something to be taken too seriously.[54]

● ● ● ●

Despite its pre-eminence among pop music publications, *Rolling Stone* has seldom cast its editorial eye on criticism. Chet Flippo did squeeze in some cogent comments in a book review:

> The greatest disappointment of rock journalism is that it has produced so few genuine critics. Record reviewers abound in every corner ("This's, uhm, a good album") but critics—those who can knowledgeably judge a work of music and write about it in a way that entertains and makes sense—are a near-extinct species.[55]

Flippo cited a tidy half-dozen critics who met his rigorous standards: Robert Christgau, Jon Landau, Greil Marcus, Dave Marsh, Lester Bangs and Ellen Willis.

> They share a few attributes which loosely describe critics. They retain their enthusiasm for the music. They have an instinct for understanding and appreciating the place that popular rock occupies in the general scheme of things. Despite personal quirks and eccentricities, they have built-in gyroscopes that keep everything in perspective (none of them got excited about Jobriath). And, they know the music backward and forward.

Colleague Jon Landau, as he left *Rolling Stone*, wrote more extensively about his trade:

I find the biggest problem with rock criticism is the lack of any criticism. . . .

Rock criticism is too limited in scope. There are many ways to deal with a record; rock critics generally employ too few of them. Most rock critics have a background in literature, journalism or the social sciences. Few of them have a background in music. As a result, most rock criticism spends too much time dealing with a record's literary qualities and not enough with the musical ones.

Rock critics enjoy writing about Joni Mitchell, Neil Young and Sly Stone because they can think of things to say about them. This is because a great deal of what these people say can be gleaned from their lyrics and their stance. This doesn't mean that critics only think of good things to say about them. But the more time they invest in writing about someone, the more likely the net point of view will be sympathetic,

Landau continued.

At its worst this syndrome turns rock criticism into lyric reviewing. Again, this is because for most of us it's easier to talk about lyrics, which, like us, are verbal and familiar, than music, which is not. . . . At the same time, most rock critics are not comfortable writing about something whose virtues are primarily musical. . . . Albums with primarily musical virtues must suffer as a result.

"Lest I be misunderstood," he concluded,

I am not advocating a classical-music school of criticism. I'm not interested in reviews that emphasize merely technical or musical matters. The critic doesn't have to tell us whether the singer is in pitch, or the guitar in tune, or whether the solo is in some way innovative—although these things can be interesting and useful to know. I do feel that the music is the center of most rock and critics must always try to deal with it as such, rather than making it an appendage of a discussion of the artist's lyrics, stance or presumed personality.[56]

Unfortunately, Landau did not stick around to follow his advice, but left the charge to his colleagues as he headed off for other chores.

TELEVISION

Is television criticism restricted by the medium?

Compared to other popular culture forms, television criticism is still in its infancy and struggling to find its métier. Its development, dating from the rebirth of the medium in the late 1940s, was somewhat constrained by the transitory and free nature of broadcasting. A review of a show that viewers will not have a chance to see again was said to have negligible value to those who missed it. Alternatively, many reviews were often little more than what Jackie Gleason called "describing traffic accidents to eye-witnesses."

Attempts to apply the standards of drama criticism to television were futile. Most critics looking at network shows (90 per cent of their attention is still directed at "extraordinary" national shows) conceded that TV acting was fine and that technically productions were excellent but that scripts and plots were improbable and characters absurd. These problems remain today for both viewers and critics.

"Television, conservatively speaking is at least 90 per cent trash," John J. O'Connor tells his *New York Times* readers. "A reviewer new to the medium gets the picture quickly. The naive might demand a steady flow of masterpieces. The practical will be grateful for occasional successes."

O'Connor believes that TV criticism, like that for all popular culture, must follow a horizontal plane and consider genre:

> Quality is an element that should be found in any type of programming, from news to entertainment. "The Mary Tyler Moore Show," a situation comedy, has quality in its writing, casting and direction. "Ironsides," a detective series, has quality. "60 Minutes," a news magazine, has quality. There is nothing wrong with any particular genre.[57]

Implicitly, he rejects vertical appraisal or placing high-brow intellectual shows at the top of the scale and low-brow entertainment shows at the bottom as an invalid critical approach for TV or all popular culture.

O'Connor sees the critic's role as being pragmatic and catalytic:

> Television is not a thing without context. It demands scrutiny far beyond the obvious level of whether one program makes for good or bad entertainment. The critic does not have to devise the right answers. This is not necessarily his job. He might, though, at least occasionally, stumble on the right questions.

● ● ● ●

Fifty-eight television critics writing for newspapers in 40 major cities were surveyed in 1973 about their duties, attitudes and opinions on the effects of their work. The study, conducted by the late Dr. Charles S. Steinberg, professor of communications at

Hunter College of the City University of New York, reported these insightful findings:

1. What kind of newspaper work were you engaged in before writing about television?

Only a third (34%) indicated any previous experience either working in, or writing about, the mass media—television, radio, film or theatre. The remainder had no previous experience in the field they cover, though all were journalists.

2. Did you ask to cover television, or was the assignment offered to you?

One-third (34%) made specific requests for the TV beat. The rest were offered, assigned or as one put it "ordered" to assume the TV duties.

3. Do you cover television exclusively, or other media as well?

Slightly more than half (55%) cover television exclusively, 24% cover both television and radio, and the rest are responsible for television and other assignments such as business reporting, youth news, a weekly veterans column and a host of popular arts.

4. Do you do only reviews, or features and news as well?

Not a single "critic" devoted his time exclusively to television criticism. Every respondent also wrote features, interviews, personality pieces and news.

5. Do you think that covering television is a full-time job?

The respondents overwhelmingly (95%) said yes.

6. How do you view your primary function: as critic or reporter?

In view of the wide spectrum of assignments, it is not surprising that relatively few (28%) see themselves primarily as critics. One-third are more comfortable with "reporter," while 29% prefer a combination title "critic and reporter." The remainder prefer to be called "television editor."

7. What is your primary obligation to the reader, critical judgment or reporting?

The greatest percentage of replies (38%) look upon their obligation primarily as reporting. About a third (31%) believe that their obligation involves both judgment and criticism, 21% view their function in terms of rendering critical judgment and the remainder are undecided.

8. In your opinion are press junkets helpful in covering the medium?

A substantial number (62%) of the major TV press across the country do accept invitations for network press junkets. The 17% who do not cannot because of the policy of their newspapers. Of those who attend the annual junkets, 72% believe they are helpful to them in securing copy and ideas, while 19% believe junkets are occasionally helpful.

9. Should newspapers send reviewers to the coast instead of the networks?

Almost two-thirds (62%) would prefer to be sent to the network press junkets by their own newspapers, while 17% are opposed to their newspaper sending them.

10. Do you get adequate information service from the networks and local stations?

While 91% believe they get adequate service from the networks, only 60% are satisfied with the service from stations in their respective cities.

11. Are critics occasionally under pressure to write favorable reviews?

Despite a close working relationship between the critics and the press departments of the networks and local stations, 79% of the critics say they are never under pressure to write a favorable review. About 17% say such pressure is occasionally exerted.

12. Do you think it is a service to the viewer to pre-review programs?

Three-fourths believe pre-reviewing is a service to their readers, 16% say that it is on special occasions and 7% believe that it is not.

13. Is it your policy to run pre-reviews when possible?

Since the networks instituted policies permitting critics to pre-review shows, 72% have adopted the practice. Only 16% of the papers queried do not run pre-reviews at all.

14. In your opinion, which has the greater effect on the reader—movie or television reviews?

Three-fourths of the respondents (74%) are convinced that movie reviews have "greater effect" than TV criticism, 19% believe that the television review is more important in terms of effect, and 3% see movie and TV reviews as identical in effect.

15. What effect do you think television criticism has on those who program television?

Here the reviewers clearly reveal a sense of frustration, Steinberg says. Only 3% see "considerable effect," 60% believe they have "some effect," the rest are of the opinion that they have "little or no effect."

16. Do you think that favorable reviews can keep a program on the air, even though the ratings are not high?

More than half (55%) do not believe that good reviews can offset low ratings. Slightly fewer than a third (31%) think that, rarely, critical acclaim will prevent a program from being cancelled. The remainder believe that "on occasion" an acclaimed program will survive low ratings.

17. Do you think that television criticism has any general effect on the policy decisions of the F.C.C., network or local station executives?

Only 7% believe that their writing has any effect on the Federal Communications Commission, 34% think they have some effect and 57% believe they have no general effect.

Conversely, 53% think that TV criticism does have some effect on network executives, while 36% think it has no general effect.

On local station executives, 43% of the critics believe their work has "significant effect," while 40% believe they have only "some effect." About 16% think they have no effect.

18. Do you feel that your column has effect, in terms of taste, on the reader?

About 45% do think that what they have to say has effect on viewer taste, 31% see slight effect and 10% see no effect whatever.

19. Do you look upon your job as prestigious?

Despite admitted frustrations, slightly more than half of the critics polled (52%) see their job as prestigious, while 34% do not believe that it is.

Despite the rather downbeat statistics in his survey, Dr. Steinberg, a former CBS vice-president, was optimistic about television criticism in his overall assessment:

> When television does move toward developing its own aesthetic, criticism of television may take on a significance comparable to criticism of other media such as theatre, books and films. The television critic's review may one day have comparable significance and impact to the press notices that are so important to the success or failure of the opening night on Broadway.[58]

Dr. Steinberg more realistically stated: "Television, the most powerful and pervasive of mass media, has not generated interest in serious criticism either from the industry or the viewer."

● ● ● ●

When they were all writing TV criticism in the early 1970s, Gary Deeb of the *Chicago Tribune,* Norman Mark of the *Daily News* and Ron Powers of the *Sun-Times* were known in the industry collectively as "The Chicago Problem."

Ron Powers set the pace for the trio:

> It's impossible to talk about radio and television in America without talking about American life. No other critic on a news-

paper deals with a medium that reflects so directly the personality, character, hopes, fantasies, distractions, myths and delusions of the American people.

In his six columns a week, Powers raised such consumer issues as how commercials were put together and needled the industry on its use of ratings and power politics.

Because he envisioned the critic's role as open-ended, he wrote about much more than prime-time entertainment. For his efforts, he received a Pulitzer Prize for criticism in 1973. Yet, his hard-nosed reporting and criticism rankled both readers and those in the industry and Powers eventually left the television beat. Later, he explained his departure this way: "TV critics are always shooting at the same sitting ducks. I just got worn out with it."

For his part, Norman Mark was the first critic to pin down TV's harmful effect on children. In his regular *Daily News* column, he probed through the entire Surgeon General's report and asserted that evidence showed TV violence and aggressive behavior were positively related, hence the report was far more damning than the summary which appeared in *The New York Times* revealed.

Mark also infuriated television executives and other critics when he attacked the pack journalism mentality and mushy criticism on display at the annual West Coast junkets sponsored by the networks. Such audacity caused ABC to ban Mark and his two fellow Chicagoans from the junket one year, but Mark boldly showed up at the Hollywood bash anyway.

In early 1976, after leaving TV writing, he explained why: "I simply got tired of punching pillows that never punched back."

Gary Deeb, who remains on the job with the *Tribune* and is now syndicated in 60 other newspapers around the country, is also an aggressive reporter-critic: "Reviewing programs is the least important part of the job. I love to expose fraudulent, shoddy practices."

In an article in *Variety* headlined "The Hack Pack," Deeb turned his investigative scorn on fellow critics, whom he called "fuzzy-headed boobs whose minds were sealed at birth. . . . Far too many TV critics are continuing the mindless—and anti-journalistic—practice of grinding out fan-rot nonsense culled directly from network press releases and writing up fluffy and soporific phone interviews with fifth-billed stars of 'Movie of the Week' or spending hours in the unwarranted creation of 'Mailbox Columns' filled with phony queries (Is it true David Cassidy has a skin condition and won't let anyone take his picture?). . . . Most of these unprofessional hacks are merely products of foolish newspaper management that demand—directly or indirectly—that the TV beat be covered in a frothy, show-biz-y manner. After all, the thinking goes, television is cheap entertainment and not too much significance should be attached to it."[59]

The dissolution of the Chicago triumvirate is especially regrettable since Powers, Mark and Deeb seemed well on their way to producing television criticism that was respected as examples of quality American journalism.

• • • •

It's ironic that network news personnel are forbidden to go on junkets, but the press information offices of the same networks annually arrange such junkets for television critics working for newspapers. Surely an axiom lies therein.

• • • •

"Television doesn't care about the quality of their shows, only ratings," snipes Terrence O'Flaherty of the *San Francisco Chronicle.*

> Why are we advising those people how to run their business? They are multi-millionaires. Television is a huge success. The people love it and don't want to change it. If anyone reading his favorite columnist wrote down all his comments on how to make a good show and then went to Hollywood and did all those things, he would go broke without a doubt.

• • • •

At least one television critic has clout, or so a Long Island station thought. *Newsday*'s Marvin Kitman, whose incisive criticism is streaked with deft zaniness, blasted the ineptitude and incompetence of WSNL, Channel 67, when the New Islip station attempted to break into the Long Island market. In six stinging columns, Kitman twitted the station for erecting its antennae in such a way that its reception was fine in Connecticut and in the Atlantic Ocean, but pitifully weak on Long Island. WSNL was incensed by Kitman's witty comments at their expense and promptly brought a libel suit for a whopping $15 million. Yet the claim has never been pursued since the station failed and early depositions in the case virtually proved the factualness of Kitman's charges.

• • • •

"Somebody must be responsible for looking at the whole," believes Jack Gould, retired *New York Times* critic and now a special assignment writer for the *Los Angeles Times.* Yet, despite his insistence that critics strive for comprehensive and meaningful criticism, he also acknowledges the frustration and presumption of trying to deal with all kinds of fare: "The cultural conceit of the television critic is unparalleled in its fundamental arrogance."

Further, Gould has long recognized the repercussions of his task:

> A television show is not judged for itself, as is the case in the theatre, movies, books or records. It is weighed against the appeal of the two competing attractions in the same time period. A low or high rating can affect the ratings of shows coming before or after the presentation. By extension, one bad rating can influence the statistical value of an entire evening of television. And a bad evening can wreck a week. Along the way the revenue is affected.[60]

● ● ● ●

When the Television Critics' Association (TVCA) was formed in mid-1978, the organization set very modest goals, indeed, setting up interviews with industry representatives to broaden critics' perspectives. But, after all of the group's efforts were put into scheduling a single day's worth of additional interviews at the annual network junket to Los Angeles, some of the "new breed" of TV critics began to question its worth. The group had already rejected including a code of ethics in its charter. They were making no attempts to convince "uneducated" newspaper editors that the TV beat could no longer be covered adequately by the office hack. In short, the group, headed by Lee Winfrey of the *Philadelphia Inquirer*, was accused of halting leadership. Happily, the group made no plans to give out annual awards.

● ● ● ●

A cartoon in *Broadcasting* magazine perhaps best stated the industry view of critics. It showed an editor saying to a cub reporter: "You're going to start at the bottom. I'm making you the television critic."

● ● ● ●

Three research efforts add tidbits to our understanding of TV criticism:

The Louis Harris survey found that TV critics tend to be slightly different from other types of critics in being more often Protestant and less left of center politically. This selective factor, Harris analysts observe, is related to the "popular" aspect of the medium.

In polling 50 randomly chosen Philadelphians, researcher Joseph Turow concluded: "It must be admitted that even the people of this highly educated sample do not think much about television criticism."[61]

In an unpublished University of Pennsylvania thesis, Susan Louise Fry concluded from her study of influential readers of criticism:

> Critics appear to be somewhat self-deluded, believing they are taking a scholarly, comprehensive approach to television and its effects on the public when they are actually most competent as a specific source of "feedback" to TV programming directors and people within the broadcasting industry.[62]

● ● ● ●

Despite the pervasiveness of broadcasting, less than 100 journalists criticize it. As the Steinberg survey found, nearly all critics have other related chores. This practice leads them into a bind, insists John J. O'Connor: "The type of person who reviews the shows, interviews stars and has to put together a column or little briefs about what's going on in the industry is drawn into a type of involvement in the industry that lessens his objectivity."

Considering the large number of outlets for criticism and the few employed to write it, most newspapers routinely rely on the wire service critics—Jay Sharbutt of Associated Press and Rick Du Brow of United Press International—to serve their readers. Somehow it seems fitting that the largest number of people are exposed to the wire service critics, yet it's safe to say their superficial reviews do little to improve the state of the art of criticism.

● ● ● ●

"Because the criticism exchange between print and broadcasting is a one-way street," CBS News gray-beard Eric Sevareid told a Washington Journalism Center audience,

> I am finally violating Ed Murrow's old precept that one never, but never replies to critics.
>
> TV critics in the papers tell us day in and day out what is wrong with us. Let me return the favor, and suggest they stop trying to be renaissance men. They function as critics of everything on the screen—drama, soap operas, science programs, musical shows, sociological documentaries, our political coverage— the works. Let the papers assign their science writers to our science coverage, their political writers to our political coverage, their drama critics to the TV dramas and so on.
>
> Let me suggest something else. That they add a second measurement to their critiques. . . . On news, documentaries and especially coverage of live events, it seems the newspaper critic

must also be a reporter; he must, if he can, go behind the scenes and find out why we do certain things and do not do other things; there is usually a reason. In the early days, critics like John Crosby and Marya Mannes would do that. A few, like Arthur Unger on the *Christian Science Monitor,* still do that; but very few.

Let me also suggest a little less hypocrisy and a little more consistency. I'll give an example from my own recent experience, by no means a unique example, to explain what I mean. Last season (1975) I did seven hours of conversations with some of the experienced, wisest minds around: Willy Brandt, John McCloy, George Kennan, Leo Rosten, Robert Hutchins and others. Not prime time, not a vast audience; but the reaction from viewers was wonderful. Hundreds of letters, many expressing gratitude that they had been given something that made them think. Some from historians wanting transcripts for their own writings and teachings.

Now this, we thought, really ought to please the generality of the newspaper critics who deplore the scarcity of this kind of things on the commercial networks. What happened? The *Monitor,* the *Los Angeles Times* rose to it gratifyingly. A few scattered smaller papers did. I don't remember a line in the news magazines or the two Washington daily papers. The *TV Guide* critic presumed to analyze my motive in putting on John McCloy—without of course, asking me about it—and not only got it wrong, he got it precisely backwards. The intellectually inclined *New York Times* critic had a paragraph saying it was nice to have something of substance during TV's summer dog days; he did not suggest the nature of the substance. *The New Republic* critic, in a patronizing summation of the series, was more bemused by the fact that I wore a turtle neck sweater in these informal conversations than by anything else.

How do you extract scarce air time from a network for this kind of program if you not only can't show vast ratings, which nobody expected, but you can't even show a good press reaction? We had only that gratifying heap of letters. On the strength of it we will do more of these hours and because we think we have an obligation to them.[63]

● ● ● ●

"Most critics are expected to love what they cover, appreciate the theatre or art or what have you," says Ron Aldridge, TV critic of the *Charlotte* (N.C.) *Observer.* "But television critics are different; they are expected to hate TV because all newspaper people hate TV. The best critics—like Gary Deeb or Ben Brown of Tampa—love television; that's why they write about it so interestingly."

● ● ● ●

ART

Did Tom Wolfe misjudge art criticism?

In April 1974, *New York Times* art critic Hilton Kramer stirred up a storm with this passage:

> Realism does not lack its partisans but it does rather conspicuously lack a persuasive theory. And, given the nature of our intellectual commerce with works of art, to lack a persuasive theory is to lack something crucial—the means by which our experience of individual works is joined to our understanding of the values they signify.

The controversy erupted a year later when social critic-pop journalist Tom Wolfe seized Kramer's statement and converted it into dogma in the cover story of *Harper*'s. In an article (and subsequent book) titled "The Painted Word," Wolfe postulated that abstract paintings are no more than illustrations to the critical theories that attempt to elucidate them. He states his premise as: "Modern Art has become completely literary: the paintings and other works exist only to illustrate the text." He further predicts that in the year 2000 there will be a retrospective museum exhibition of the American Art of 1945–75 and that the three seminal artists of the period will prove to be Clement Greenberg, Harold Rosenberg and Leo Steinberg, all of whom are CRITICS. Wolfe foresees museum walls covered with huge copy blocks presenting passages of 'berg-criticism accompanied by tiny reproductions of the work of Morris Louis, Kenneth Noland and other leading illustrators of the word.

In his unique sociological style—glib and seductive—Wolfe argues that art has been reduced to the status object batted around in a complex social game by pretentiously aristocratic collectors. His article concludes by saying that future art historians and intellectuals will look back on the era of The Painted Word with "sniggers, laughter and good-humored amazement."

Wolfe's interpretation of Kramer's statement understandably stirred hostile reactions from readers, critics and artists:

Kramer's colleague, John Russell, quickly came to the rescue and stated that Wolfe had simply misread that statement and offered his own "perfectly clear" interpretation:

> Serious art aims to tell us something that we urgently need to know. Unserious art does not; it may give us pleasure of a momentary kind, but it does not set before us a system of values by

which we ourselves may be changed and enriched. Without such a system art is trivial, unanchored, unresonant.[64]

Book critic Christopher Lehmann-Haupt called Wolfe's notion "profoundly anti-intellectual—a rejection of abstract thinking because of the style in which it was made concrete." *Minneapolis Tribune* art critic Mike Steele said that Wolfe had missed the point:

> Theory isn't to blame for the present state of modern art. . . . The alternative to esoteric art is not Tom Wolfe middlebrow kitsch but rather the embracing of theory in the interests of communication. This means a will on the part of artists to communicate with audiences and a concomitant will on the part of audiences to champion artists.[65]

David Bourdon of the *Village Voice* called Wolfe's ideas a melange of fact, distortion and wishful thinking:

> What Wolfe fails to realize is that art criticism dates much faster than the works of art it interprets. Most art critics realize that their writing is strictly provisional, that the chances are a million to one that their work will end up as a footnote rather than a blowup on a museum wall. As Leo Steinberg once observed: "Critical writings and systems of aesthetics, if they are more than a generation or so old, come to sound quaint and ineffectual or, at their worst, pernicious in false doctrine."[66]

Harpers' readers also cried Wolfe. John Penney of Boston wrote: "Tom Wolfe has no understanding of painting. To see the dissolution of visual concepts into the printed word is a pompous idea that only a writer could invent. Perhaps the article is a joke?" New York gallery owner Andre Emmerich said Wolfe's depiction of the art world was "askew."

While Hilton Kramer apparently ignored Wolfe's re-interpretation, he may not have been as misread as Russell would have us believe. His position is a little more clear when considering his 1973 comments in a book review of "Letters of Roger Fry":

> Critics are sometimes remembered, if they are remembered at all, for their dogmatism rather than for their labors of illumination. Their theories are invoked as evidence of a fatal narrow-mindedness, while their concrete analysis of particular artists and works of art—where a critic's real contribution to a deeper understanding of art is likely to be found—are forgotten. Complex perceptions, arduously achieved, are thus reduced to caricature, and dismissed as rude simplifications.[67]

Yet this writer finds Wolfe's view fantastically wrong-headed for another reason: the state of art criticism itself. Let's begin with an assessment of the principal critics Wolfe cites.

Clement Greenberg, a formalist who relies on "aesthetic intuition" as his method of evaluation, also holds that satisfaction or dissatisfaction from art is simply a "verdict of taste." As a proponent of Immanuel Kant's position that the "judgment of taste" always "precedes" the "pleasure" gained from the aesthetic "object," he defined his standards in *Arts Magazine:*

> This state of exalted cognitiveness or consciousness *is* aesthetic value or quality. Inferior art, inferior aesthetic experience shows itself in failing to induce this state sufficiently. But all art, all aesthetic experience, good and bad, promises or intimates a promise of it. And it's only aesthetic intuition—taste—that can tell to what extent the promise is kept.[68]

Greenberg's "aesthetic intuition" was certainly lambasted by Rosalind Krauss in 1974 when she revealed in *Art in America* that he had authorized the removal of paint, thereby altering the visual appearance, from certain sculptures by David Smith. As an executor of Smith's estate (the artist died in 1965), Greenberg admitted his role in a practice that Smith himself had called "vandalism." Needless to say, Greenberg's complicity in this affair created a furor in art circles and no doubt eroded his reputation as a critic.

Or consider the heretical views of Harold Rosenberg, the *New Yorker* critic who coined the term "action painting" and underpinned it with the philosophy of French existentialism: "Not only have the qualities of art objects become increasingly irrelevant in judging art but the objects themselves are losing importance."

A defender of avant garde artists in the 1940s and 50s, Rosenberg now appears to have carried pluralism to its extreme: "Post-Art." He now attacks and discourages curiosity in all new work because he finds it impossible to define. He abhors Pop, minimal, process and conceptual art, New Realism and all the rest. Rosenberg has only enthusiasm left for artists in the 1946 to 1953 period of the New York School and thus stands frozen in time while the art world moves on without him.

His position becomes a little more clear when one learns that over the years he accepted paintings as gifts from artists he admired (an ethical practice sharply rapped by Sophy Burnham in her book, *The Art Crowd*). Now, he admits that these painters have become famous—their reputations no doubt in some measure improved by his own praise of their (his) work—and his collection has greatly increased in value, at least worth a small fortune. Has this form of corruption and his anti-art posture affected his credibility as a critic? Unquestionably, yes.

Further, Rosenberg is also anti-critic: "Artists are the best writers about art." Critics are bankrupt, he says, because, "one price of freedom is a lack of leadership and refusal to recognize authority."

Leo Steinberg, a critic with a cautious, academic sensibility who is determined to "let the world in again," prefers to write about the "Twentieth Century art" of Rodin, Picasso, Jasper Johns and Robert Rauschenberg, artists whose work meets his criterion that "representation is a central aesthetic function in all art." (Disapproving of critics, Picasso once said: "Those trying to explain pictures are as a rule completely mistaken.") Yet, almost unbelievably, Steinberg refuses to confront modern abstract art, much less new forms. Can such an authority actually outlast the great abstract artists of the day, as Wolfe so boldly postulates?

Perhaps Wolfe is bent on elevating the status of art criticism. If so, he faces considerable opposition from all quarters.

Nowhere as in art criticism are critics more disaffected with their roles. Even John Canaday, who became "embattled" and left art reviewing for the restaurant beat in the *New York Times*, is disenchanted with the game critics play:

> Who needed critics?—until the 19th century when a separation took place between the artist and the public in a society so complex that an artist's reflections of the segment of life he understood best were frequently incomprehensible to people in general, who were inadequately conditioned to respond to the unfamiliar except with puzzlement or resentment. Critics (witness Baudelaire) became missionary teachers, middlemen between artist and public, and by the time we woke up to something called modern art we had so much to catch up with that critics were justified in thinking of the public as one vast freshman class in art appreciation.
>
> For the kind of critic who thinks of himself as an educator, this was a happy state of affairs. But it was based on the assumption that art is something that happens naturally, an assumption that no longer holds. Artists are no longer magic vessels, but computers programmed to synthesize a product determined by a synthesized demand. Critics are no longer middlemen, but members of a self-annointed incestuous caucus devoted to intramural oneupmanship.[69]

As Canaday rather shortsightedly but rightly observes, art criticism has not developed significantly over the years. In a June 1940 newsletter, a group of New York artists called American Abstract Artists voiced complaints still heard today:

Not only painters and sculptors in our particular traditions, but artists generally, including musicians, writers and architects, are challenged by the deplorable level of American criticism. If anyone is to raise this it must be those most directly concerned—the artists themselves.

The artists did note, however, that the critics are not entirely to blame: "Their superiors are doubtless responsible as well for the dreary mediocrity. Is it too much to ask that vast organizations such as the *New York Times* should take into their employ at least one critic with a modest schooling behind him?"

Artists today acknowledge that the art world is more diverse and complex than ever before and that the critic's job is more difficult. In the current period of pluralism, critics have no dominant movement to champion. Even trend-spotting has become relatively unimportant, believed Thomas B. Hess, the late art critic of *New York:* "Any critic who tries to tell you what is going to happen is propagandizing." The increased output of artists also presents greater problems of selection for critics. While as many as 200 art exhibitions may open in New York during a month, only 20 will get reviewed. "Art critics do not seem very interested in trying to cope with cultural abundance and stylistic multiplicity," says critic Lawrence Alloway of *The Nation.* "Their tendency is to cut off tiny corners of the field."

Too, many artists now produce work that defies traditional critical analysis—applying the old standards of harmony, unity, balance and so on—and orthodox critics are at a loss on how to approach it, much less what to say about it. Of video art, for example, *Newsweek* art critic Douglas Davis notes, "Critics often don't like fleeting art like ephemeral video images."

In addition to refusing to review group shows, another problem that critics haven't coped with is collaborative efforts, in which it's impossible to say who did what part of the creation. Indeed, some art collectives not only are not concerned with the authorship of their work, but also avoid the gallery-museum-criticism network and submit their art directly to the public. Ray Johnson's correspondence art is sent directly to those on his mailing list. General Idea collective in Toronto does likewise. Some artists are committed to unconventional forms, they take the risk of presenting their ideas to the public without critical appraisal. For instance, two San Francisco artists recently staged a two-week environmental performance in an old North Beach flophouse and when *San Francisco Chronicle* critic Tom Albright came to review the "show," they refused to admit him.

Didacticism in art has always been treacherous territory for conservative elitist critics, though certainly activist-protest art attempts to disseminate propaganda. Cindy Nemser, of the *Feminist Art Journal*, elaborates on this issue:

> No attempt has been made to deal with the socially critical content of contemporary art. Those who call themselves critics have avoided dealing with this content at all cost (whether by condemning the work as rubbish, e.g., Hilton Kramer and John Canaday of the *New York Times* or by discussing only its formal aspects—as if the work had no social content, e.g., Greenberg, Michael Fried, et al.). If this art has any importance it also has social significance and this significance must be made clear to the public. Critics and art historians must be willing to stand up and deal truthfully with all aspects of the work and not only with its stylistic characteristics.[70]

Elitist criticism in a time of democratized art obviously presents conflicts. Lawrence Alloway, who admits a penchant for popular culture and believes critics should be descriptive and permissive, rejects the elitist critics' practice of evoking nostalgic absolutes as a way of coping:

> For example, Hilton Kramer and Emily Genauer write for newspapers not in terms of the mass audience who will read them but in terms of elite values of quality and greatness. Ideas based on an archaic and absolute notion of elites are not adequate for a twentieth-century culture of urban complexity.[71]

Alloway believes that art cannot be isolated from the rest of society.

John Russell, who after 25 years as art critic on *The Sunday Times* of London moved to the *New York Times*, also believes that "art people who only write about art have something wrong with them." His own interests include French translating, travel writing and literary and music criticism.

Wolfe also ignores another salient point about art criticism that threatens his contention. If the maxim, "Clear writing is clear thinking," holds, a random reading of art critics will show that the craft is cliché-ridden, bogged down in semantics and suffering from malaise, abstruseness, arrogance, confusion and just plain silliness. Cindy Nemser states the case succinctly:

> Collectors, at whom these writings are aimed, must be convinced that they are being sold great and meaningful works of art. Therefore, enterprising editors encourage their writers to make up esoteric theories about the most simplistic images and present their theses to the readership in the most confused, jargon-ridden, unreadable prose. The idea behind these strategies being that most people are completely intimidated by writings they cannot comprehend, believing that it is all too deep

and intellectual for any but the most profound minds. Therefore any critic who wishes to write in a clearer, readable style is accused of either being a simpleton or a philistine.[72]

Judith Goldman of *Art News* also concedes that art writing lacks literariness and humanism, but believes it's more intelligible now than during the 1960s. While Nemser wants to rid art criticism of its esoteric jargon, she doesn't want it reduced to the level of pap and admits it's difficult for writers to pursue that narrow line between the two.

Nemser, who has long complained about the unhappy lot of the independent, free lance art critic, has other gripes: ridiculously low pay for reviews and impenetrable cliquishness. Editors of periodicals only use a handful of critics they can depend on to write favorable reviews of shows exhibited in galleries who also advertise in their publications, she charges.

Despite Wolfe's dreams of critical power and glory, many critics are openly depressed with their trade. Former *New York* critic Barbara Rose drew hisses from a SoHo audience of artists when she admitted: "I do not enjoy writing about art now, under the present circumstances. Art isn't interesting and you can't have interesting criticism until after the fact." She also attacked the "star system," a process in which critics began heaping praise on a few celebrity artists during the 1960s (it continues today) and neglecting unknown artists. "Young artists have to have critics, too," she says. "The problem is that no one wants to be a critic these days."

> Criticism as a profession is among the lowest paid and most reviled occupations an educated person can have. No art critic—including the most celebrated—can support him or herself by writing criticism. The result is that serious art criticism is in danger of extinction,

Rose adds.

Lucy Lippard has also given up writing conventional art criticism. Her views in *Art Rite* certainly deny Wolfe's thesis:

> I've never had much faith in art criticism as a primary form because you are leaning on somebody else's work. It's not that it can't be a positive parasitic process, not that you can't bring new insights to the work, or get out the artist's intentions better than the artist himself or herself might be able to do, but I can't think of any criticism that has ever stood up in the long run as a real parallel to art. Some of the critics we respect the most didn't write good criticism—they were good poets or something. It's self indulgence when you come right down to it, you like something and you enjoy defining it with words. I don't finally

know what the hell criticism does for anybody except the artist and the writer.[73]

Lippard, who began writing New Criticism in historically grounded and formally analytical style, wants criticism to adapt itself to the new realities:

> I wish criticism could be loosened up to the point where it would really follow the art almost blindly, not in a sense of no criteria, but blindly into the esthetic, drawing back only to elucidate or complain, but for the most part riding with the art. Like criticism on Olitski should be all mushy, and on Judd all straight and trim. I'd like to be able to write good stream of consciousness criticism. I don't think that all that academic transitional stuff should be necessary.[74]

Robert Hughes, an Australian who came to *Time* via London, believes that critics must constantly ask themselves, "Why am I doing this?" The usual answer, he says, is "to aid people to think analytically about their own reactions to works of art," but also acknowledges that critics go through phases of disillusionment with criticism and some move on to "creative" roles.

British critic Edward Lucie-Smith believes critics become disillusioned when they realize, after attempting to cope with rapid change in art, their own limited span of effectiveness:

> After a period of years experience fails them, art seems to move away from them. What can confidently be interpreted gives way to the gnomic. The explanations given for this rather disturbing phenomenon really add up to one thing only—even the most gifted critic, in some cranny of subconscious, becomes tired, and even perhaps frightened, of being constantly at risk in the way that his profession demands.[75]

Hughes says he copes with the pace required by being selective and writing positively. "You can't write about art effectively in a condemning way. The ideal is to write only what turns you on. Enthusiasm should aid writing so you can turn others on. Of course, the mechanics and politics of the art world have to be written about, too."

It should be obvious, then, that this writer finds art criticism rife with pitfalls and problems and nowhere close to achieving the stature Tom Wolfe assigns it. Certainly art criticism is not totally bankrupt. If readers recognize that critics favor specialized interests, they can learn about art from them just as satisfactorily as they can from looking at art itself. But criticism is not a substitute for art. The merit of Wolfe's provocative article is that it calls attention to the verbal support system that art requires. By being outrageous, he calls for measures to correct current excesses. One such measure would be pluralistic criticism which would follow the art, as Lippard suggests. The amount and spectrum of art criticism must be expanded to accommodate the changes in the art world and society.

New critics such as Peter Plagens, John Perrault, Jack Burnham, Cindy Nemser and others can certainly write about new art that the formalists can't seem to understand or evaluate. They must be loose in order to deal with trickster artists who have serious messages hidden in Dada-style humorous works or with the stream of androgynous art of the likes of Linda Benglis. Critics can help the public demysticize art if they are only willing to communicate what they see.

Painter Barnett Newman perhaps suggests the route:

> What I wish to do is plead for passionate criticism for the sake of the passionate itself. Just as passion reveals the artist, so does it reveal the critic. . . . To write passionately, the critic must invest, or, to use a more accurate word, he must create his criticism so that it reveals a work of art, through the critic's feelings.

● ● ● ●

Will the *real* Jack Connor please stand up? Why, it's Robert Taylor, art critic of the *Boston Globe.* Taylor reportedly wrote an exposé about an art scandal at the Museum of Fine Arts for a Boston magazine, after the misdealings had already been reported in the London press. Taylor's article appeared under the pseudonym of Jack Connor.

● ● ● ●

As an awareness of sexual discrimination swept the country in the early 1970s, a content analysis of the five national art magazines and four major newspapers revealed that women artists were much less written about—either in reviews or articles—than men.[76] The study, conducted by June Wayne of Los Angeles' Tamarind Lithography Workshop, found that 92 per cent of the reviews in *Art in America* dealt with male artists while 96 per cent of the articles in *Art News* were on men. *Crafts Horizons* had the most balanced ratio, 56 per cent of the 1,720 reviews were about men.

In the *New York Times*, 82 per cent of 236 reviews during a randomly selected 26-week period were about male artists, while the male percentages at the *Los Angeles Times* and *San Francisco Chronicle* were 84 per cent of 344 reviews and 86 per cent of 292 reviews, respectively.

While this revelation only documented what those in the art

world already knew—the media devote more coverage to men because the galleries and museums also give more space to them—Ms. Wayne's research also illuminated the general paucity of art coverage in the media, a neglect that affects every artist.

• • • •

Artforum, by consensus the leading intellectual art journal with a circulation of about 16,000, is both feared and loathed.

Since *Artforum* publishes more reviews than the three other major art magazines put together, with a bias toward formalist artists whose work fits its theoretical ideas, unconventional new artists fear its power. "The *Artforum* mafia dictates the taste of 80 per cent of the art world," says technological artist James Seawright. "Their critics favor work about which anything can be said, so they don't have to worry about being contradicted or whether they're right or wrong." Lucas Samaras also worries about its clout: "A lot of us find we are victims of *Artforum*. We have to find ways to survive."

The loathing began in December 1975 when Hilton Kramer and David Bourdon attacked the magazine for its "muddled and strident Marxism" and "sociopolitical ideology." The critics' volleys were triggered by a series of articles that editors John Coplans and Max Kozloff said "address themselves to unfree conditions in art (Nazi, Maoist, American television, Napoleonic painting) and potently illuminated art's bondage to strong governmental, corporate and museological agencies . . . dissent to which modern artists are generally committed."

In defending their position, Coplans and Kozloff further wrote:

> We believe that if criticism fails to illuminate the dilemmas with which artists and viewers are entangled, it merely supports the market. We're all creatures of ideology. Our problem is to guard against being too alienated or acculturated by our beliefs. This requires a delicate balance. Whether it deals with past or current cultures, institutions or works of art, the criticism that observes such a balance is one we applaud.[77]

One of the three associate editors who resigned in protest of *Artforum*'s new direction, Joseph Masheck, observed what bothers most readers of the publication: "people still can't read the stuff and if they could, they would only find disillusionment."

• • • •

Unlike critics in other fields, art critics often ally themselves with the art establishment on various projects as a means of livelihood. Many critics hire on with museums to curate a show that the museum wants to organize. Many also write catalogues, monographs and museum bulletins. While their association need not taint their criticism, it causes them to be suspect of ethical conflicts.

• • • •

"The highest purpose of art is precisely to provide the connoisseur with the opportunity to gain that satisfaction which he experiences in 'forming an opinion' and in criticism," wrote August Strindberg in a brilliantly satirical essay, "How to become an art connoisseur in sixty minutes," which was first published in 1877.

• • • •

"Art critics tend to not take themselves very seriously, on the one hand, and far too seriously, on the other," says Sophy Burnham, author of *The Art Crowd*. "Writing incomprehensible gobbledegook pleases the artist but makes no sense to ordinary people. There are too many damn critics around not taking seriously the fact that they have said, 'I'm a critic. I have a certain knowledge. I am going to do my homework, I am going to research. I have an intellectual discipline. Then I will tell you something about my work and my understanding of this artistic work.' The critic who doesn't understand that he is used in some way as a threshing agent to separate the worst from the best is being naive. A critic has a true function: to help people understand things. If he doesn't take his work seriously, then he should not be a critic. Not many critics think they have a *real* job to be done."

• • • •

"In the best days of art, there were no art critics," Oscar Wilde observed.

• • • •

After winning the 1974 Pulitzer Prize for criticism, Emily Genauer of *The New York Post*, reflected on her 40-year career of seeing some 50,000 works of art a year and her motivation to carry on:

> The craft of criticism is the best route for keeping awake and alive. Someone—I can't remember who wrote that life needs two forces to sustain it, though they are in total conflict. One is the need for the old, the continuing, the familiar, the dependable, the tried and known. The other is the need for the new, the unknown, the different.

Decades of functioning as an art critic have guaranteed that my life would have both these "conflicting" forces in great and balanced supply. Art itself, art as an idea and way of life, art as the embodiment and measure of value, is the continuing element.

Masterpieces of the old and more recent past are the home base I must always return to. They're the familiar, the tried, the known, as indeed is the art world itself, which is to say the galleries and museums. Galleries, rather than places to be ducked because the years have made them seem overfamiliar, remain oases to be sought out in an ugly, dirty city.

Total, continuing immersion in the world of creativity is the most effective antidote I can find to the encircling, overwhelming corruption of our time. In comparison with what goes in politics, the maneuverings of dealers, collectors, museums are child's play.

But if the old and familiar are important to me, the new is no less so. Each day I set out on my gallery rounds knowing for certain I'll see something I've never seen before. It may not be good. It may be meretricious. But it will be new. And while newness itself need not be a virtue, openness to it most certainly is. It carries over into other areas. It gives me a tolerance for and capacity to enjoy the new and strange overflow into life outside art.[78]

● ● ● ●

Although photography has increasingly been woven into the fabric of 20th-century art, as *New York Times* photography writer A. D. Coleman says, "There is hardly an art critic today competent to discuss photography as a branch of printmaking, much less as a creative graphic medium with a unique and distinctive field of ideas.

"This lack of knowledgeability of the art critics in regard to photography does not stop with them," Coleman laments. "It is transmitted to both the audience and the artists. Such a situation is not merely regrettable, but damaging to all concerned."

● ● ● ●

Critics with specialties other than painting and sculpture are increasingly being demanded. British art historian and critic Garth Clark told a ceramics conference at Bennington College in mid-1977 that "the need for cogent and informed criticism is high" in the field of ceramics.

● ● ● ●

DANCE

Can dance criticism win its media niche?

As dance audiences swelled from one million in 1965 to more than 11 million in just ten years, dance criticism also proliferated, though its development and improvement has been more gradual.

Journalism first recognized dance criticism as a specialized field when the *New York Times* hired John Martin as its regular reviewer in 1927. Aside from Margaret Lloyd of the *Christian Science Monitor* and Edwin Denby of the *New York Herald-Tribune* and others, most early critics were little more than boosters of the art. Though some modern reviewers are still raving dance fans, responsible criticism is on the increase. But cautions Michael Steinberg, former music and dance critic of the *Boston Globe*, "dance criticism on most newspapers is now where music criticism was 70 years ago."

Dance critics, apparently sensitive to their low status in "culture gulch" and upset over how little editorial space was being allotted to writing about this boom in dance activity and interest, met in New York, in June 1974, to form a new national organization. The resulting Dance Critics Association was formed "to encourage excellence in dance writing through education, research and the exchange of ideas."

One item of business was to survey the 110 participants in order to get a better view of the dance critic's life. The poll revealed that most critics worked part-time or free-lance for monthly magazines. Only two full-time dance critics were reportedly employed on major newspapers: Anna Kisselgoff of the *New York Times* and George Gelles of the *Washington Star-News*. Most critics said they covered less than five concerts a month and the majority confessed they earned less than $600 a year from writing dance criticism. And, although 62 per cent of the respondents said they had taken dance classes before beginning to write criticism, more than half expressed a need for more training in review writing.

"There is a special function of dance criticism that is perhaps different from criticism of the other arts," observes Deborah Jowitt, dancer, choreographer and dance critic for the *Village Voice*. "Because of the often-lamented ephemeralness of dance, we don't have an accessible, easy-to-read notation system. The dance critic has more of a commitment to history than perhaps any critics from the other arts. I don't wish to give self-inflated ideas of writing for posterity because I write in a very immediate, quick style for the *Voice*. Dance critics must write immediate history, near history, so there will be some sense of what a work looked like, of what it seemed to do and of what the central idea was. I feel more of a commitment to describing in some evocative way than other critics."

Clive Barnes, who covers about 300 dance performances a year for the *New York Post*, worries about how anyone can keep up with the rapidly expanding "establishment" dance scene, much less the new experimental work. "With so much activity, every critic has to be highly selective in what he chooses to see," he says. "The limit of what I can cover is a pity."

During his ten-year tenure with the *Times*, Barnes often discussed criticism with his readers:

> To describe dance movements to someone who hasn't seen it is almost like describing smoke to a blind man. . . . How can you analyze something you have difficulty in describing? This is the heart of the problem. At times it tends to make critics write about the story of ballets rather than the ballets themselves, and to reduce the primary art of choreography to the secondary art of stage direction. . . . Dance critics tend to give undue emphasis to the non-dance elements of any ballet. This is the almost inevitable cop-out.[79]

Barnes also believes that critics ought to be able to discern, describe and evaluate differences between two different productions of a standard classic and that that skill is acquired only by attending performance after performance of the same work.

Yet he acknowledges that that task creates a pitfall:

> One of the difficulties of dance criticism is that of familiarity breeding acceptance. You see a certain ballet—10, 20, 30 times— and after the first impressions, the first impact, has worn off, the ballet itself becomes remarkably difficult to see. You take it for granted and, more dangerously, you take your earlier opinions for granted. At worst, you see the ballet almost as a symbol of what you once thought of it.[80]

In commenting on popular vs. critical success, he says: "If I were an artist and I had the choice of having the critics with me or the public with me, I would choose the public every time. Critics buy remarkably few tickets."[81]

While dancers may get infuriated by his biases, he is candid: "To be perfectly honest, I do not like ethnic dance."

Barnes also is optimistic about the future vigor of the dance but warns: "During the next decade, we are going to need sharper critical standards."

Speaking to the Dance Society in New York, Anna Kisselgoff called the space problem for the arts at the *New York Times* "serious." She reported that only nine columns were devoted to cultural news a day and that drama, film, and TV were considered more important than dance. Space limitations necessitated short reviews, she said, and occasionally her reviews are still not published because of the lack of room.

Of her audience, Miss Kisselgoff said:

Film reviews are read by almost everybody but dance reviews are not. I write for people interested in dance. The person I write for first is the copy editor, who doesn't understand dance language so I can't use French or any technical terms or get too academic about it. Dance is a repertory art and the editors just don't understand that I must review the same works over and over again. It's difficult to explain why it's important to review different casts and continually evaluate performers to see if they improve or not. . . .

I do think of myself as a reporter and try to tell the reader what happened onstage the night before. I want to describe and analyze a work so you can make up your own mind about it. Of course, I give my opinion. But sometimes, when I see something for the first time, I can't make up my mind and so a vague review is really an honest reflection of my opinion. . . .

I'm more interested in choreography and stress it more than performance if a work is a premiere. When it's not a premiere, I don't have to rehash the content and stress the performance. Performance can make a bad ballet good and a good one even better. . . .

I may be pedantic about certain standards, but I don't think dancers should add their own innovations to the choreography in the same way that Beverly Sills shouldn't be permitted to break into a pop tune in the middle of an opera. . . .

The audience's reactions to works plays no part in influencing my review, although I often mention audience reception to works. . . .

One doesn't have to take dance to be a critic. It may make you too aware of technical difficulties of performing. . . .

I don't have favorite dancers or groups or schools. I don't have a favorite anything.[82]

The current generation of dance critics is the first one not totally identified with dance, says Marcia Siegal, who writes for *New York* and elsewhere. She also charges the dance press with putting pressure on critics to write favorably so they can help build audiences and gain grant support for dance companies. "Dance publications emphasize pure description but a critic's job is not only to describe. The balance should be changed toward emphasizing the meaning of works."

Dance critic William Moore, writing in *The Feet*, a monthly arts and dance magazine, believes critics should love and understand their subject and be advocates for it:

> A good critic does not evaluate or criticize in the limited journalistic sense. He educates the public in a field in which it has little or no knowledge. The object of a good critic is to enlighten the public to the art of which he writes. A good critic understands the artist-creator and what he is trying to do, and assists the public in understanding the artists who are (if worth their salt) always working in areas far in advance of the general public.[83]

● ● ● ●

"Even though dance companies still think critics should give teacherly advice, critics shouldn't be in the business of telling dancers how to improve their work," lectures Deborah Jowitt, herself a dancer, teacher and critic for the *Village Voice*.

● ● ● ●

When Alan M. Kriegsman won the 1976 Pulitzer Prize for criticism, it was the first time a dance critic had been so honored. Kriegsman writes about dance, music, television, films and theatre for the *Washington Post*

BOOKS

Is book reviewing "pure?"

Book reviewing style has changed little since Margaret Elizabeth Ohlson noted the two kinds of reviews in 1932: "The reviewer uses the book as a springboard and writes an essay on whatever the book suggests to him or else he makes the book the principle topic of his discussion and subordinates himself." Miss Ohlson observed in her Columbia University thesis, "The first is more interesting for it is the product of a personality but the second is more just to the author and to the reader who seeks information."

● ● ● ●

Richard Kluger, former editor of the now-defunct *Book Week*, former publisher and book critic, describes the relationship between publishers and reviewers as "symbiotic, largely honorable, occasionally treacherous, conducive to paranoia among publishers, conducive to overeating by reviewers and essential in view of the chaos of the marketplace."

In assessing the field in *American Libraries*, Kluger found:

> Most daily newspapers across the country give the shortest shrift imaginable to book reviewing. Only a couple of dozen papers pay a living wage to reasonably astute men and women whose principal task is the evaluation of books; most papers settle for 'canned' or syndicated reviews or ignore books entirely (though most of the better dailies pay lip service to the muse of literature by throwing in a book page to break up the glut of ads in their bloated Sunday editions).
>
> Still, the reviewing ranks are robust enough for most publishers to view them as adversaries and necessary evils (when they pan a perfectly lovely new book) as well as collaborators and enlightened oracles (when they love that same lovely new book) in the ongoing task of bringing written words of lasting or fleeting value to the American reader. Perceptive or cloddish, sensitive or peevish, reviewers wield enormous power by virtue of the hard facts of the tradebook marketplace: too many titles are contesting for their day in the sun. Without receiving reviewers' scrutiny (friendly or hostile) and barring a heavy outlay of advertising or promotional money by the publisher (usually impossible except in the case of titles for which the publisher has high sales hopes), any given title is likely to pass over the face of the earth like a shadow, unheard of, unlamented, and with a life expectancy comparable to that of a fruit fly in a blizzard.[84]

In addition to the large amount of free space that publishers receive for their products, they also mine reviews for quotations that can be used in advertisements, Kluger says.

> Many publishers find themselves reading reviews backward since that key quotable phrase is more often than not found (when it is there at all) at the bottom of the review. Thus, book reviewers serve the additional, if indirect, function of being the main advertising copywriters of the book trade.

Publishers regularly wine-and-dine reviewers as a way to inform them of their new titles or to introduce them to authors. "Most reviewers accept this hospitality for what it is and enjoy themselves without feeling in any way compromised," Kluger adds. He also says that in recent times reviewers have even begun to reciprocate in picking up the tab on such occasions.

Eliot Fremont-Smith, book critic of the *Village Voice*, confirms the operational integrity of the field:

> I know of no other endeavor in which the presumption and habit of honesty is so deeply engrained. . . . There is an overriding tradition, upheld in theory and practice by both publishers and reviewers, that virtually guarantees the latter's critical independence. . . . Overt publisher pressures for favorable reviews are extremely rare, and when they do occur are easily frowned away, which may make the business unique.[85]

Fremont-Smith acknowledges that reviewers are involved in some literary "political" games involving honesty: "The compromises here, which are all too common, have mainly to do with critical backscratching of friends, lovers, colleagues and other ambition-determined importances—or its opposite, the kicking of enemies, real, imagined, and advantageous."

As 1978 president of the National Book Critics Circle, Fremont-Smith has harsh comments on the standards of his colleagues: "I think that many of us . . . are too content with what we do. There is not enough thought in our work. We are notoriously inaccurate, and rarely correct ourselves, much less express a change of mind and probably play too much to the industry—regular shills at Christmas—however inadvertently, and rely on the industry too much for what's going on in books. The swiping from flap copy, PW (Publishers Weekly), press releases and *The Times* reviews is only the scandalous tip of the iceberg. And we are, for our own good, probably too gentlemanly or ladylike about our performances; there is hardly any frank back-and-forth commentary among us in print about the responsibilities, problems, and performances of individual critics and review media."

Nonetheless, Fremont-Smith is convinced that professional book reviewing is "more intellectually sophisticated and with-it now than it ever was."

• • • •

Pre-reviewing is considered the most important stage of literary criticism. The industry rule-of-thumb is that while good reviews may not make a book a success and bad reviews may not cause one to falter, no reviews insure failure. With about 40,000 new books appearing each year, selecting which ones will get reviewed is the major chore for book editors and staff critics. Even the *New York Times Book Review* considers only about 2,200 books a year in its pages, while *Time* and *Newsweek* must pare their list down to less than 300. Barbara Bannon, "Forecasts" editor of the influential trade magazine *Publishers Weekly*, says her criterion for evaluating new commercial fiction is simple: "The only instinct I can go on is the old-fashioned pull of good story-telling."

• • • •

Despite the fact that Jacqueline Susann's 1966 book, "Valley of the Dolls," was received by book critics with almost unanimous scorn, the book became the best-selling novel of all times—17 million copies sold in hardcover and paperback, according to the "Guinness Book of Records." The late Miss Susann said she believed that reviewers panned successful writers just out of jealousy, envy and spite.

• • • •

Free lance book reviewers are rarely paid more than a free book and a byline for their work, though that compensation seems to be enough for most. Even at the *New York Times Book Review* section, which by all accounts is the most important book reviewing medium in the country, writers are only paid between $100 and $350. Yet free books for editors at major publications can represent a sizable extra benefit. For example, one magazine critic said he receives about 5,000 books a year from publishers, which would be worth more than $30,000 if purchased at retail prices.

• • • •

The National Book Critics Circle, an organization formed in 1974 "to raise the quality of book reviewing in all media and to encourage public appreciation of book criticism," presented its first annual awards for books written by Americans and published in 1975 in January 1976. The four literary awards—the first ever given in the U.S. to authors by book critics—were selected by the group's membership of 300. The group proposed their "critics' choices" awards as an alternative to best-seller lists which were dubbed as "the biggest fake and rip-off in publishing."

But the NBCC also besmirched its own reputation when it was reported that there was more to meeting at the Algonquin Hotel than the literary tradition of Dorothy Parker, Alexander Woollcott and Robert Benchley. It seems that the hotel, eager for publicity which might result from the association, not only supplied a free meeting room for the critics but also ponied up gratis drinks to lubricate the decision-making machinery.

• • • •

Literary critic Edmund Wilson customarily sent all request-seekers this standardized rejection slip:

Edmund Wilson Regrets that it Is Impossible for Him to:

Read Manuscripts,

Write Articles or Books to Order,

Write Forewords or Introductions,

Make Statements for Publicity Purposes,

Do any Kind of Editorial Work,

Judge Literary Contests,

Give Interviews,

Conduct Educational Courses,

Deliver Lectures,

Give Talks or Make Speeches,

Broadcast or Appear on Television,

Take Part in Writers' Congresses,

Answer Questionnaires,

Contribute to or Take Part in Symposiums or "Panels" of Any Kind,

Contribute Manuscripts for Sales,

Donate Copies of His Books to Libraries,

Autograph Books for Strangers,

Allow His Name to be Used on Letterheads,

Supply Personal Information about Himself

Supply Photographs of Himself,

Supply Opinions on Literary or Other Subjects.

• • • •

RESTAURANTS

A new menu for restaurant reviewing?

"Restaurant criticism, as practiced in the mass media of this country, is outmoded and misdirected," says William Rice of the *Washington Post*.

Rice believes that Craig Claiborne set the prevailing tone for restaurant reviewing during his 1957–1971 stint on the *New York Times*. Claiborne mainly plied his trade in New York's luxury restaurants, emphasizing haute cuisine. His writing was marked by a highly personalized style that often stirred up controversy (which editors liked).

While the *Times* gave Clairborne "total candor" and a virtually unlimited budget for dining and travel, Rice notes "few other publications have been willing to do that."

The paucity of serious restaurant criticism even in large urban centers disturbs Rice. Serious critics choose the restaurants they will review, pay for what they eat and are allowed to write something harsh if so moved, he explains.

"A further responsibility, if reports are to be a useful service to readers, is to insure the anonymity of the critic," Rice writes in *Media & Consumer.*[86] "In smaller cities, this may mean resorting to a pseudonym. Some contend that even if a critic is known, little can be done to improve his meal when he arrives unannounced. I disagree, but base the case for critical anonymity on something many who eat out value more than food—attitude and quality of service. That can change in an instant."

Rice believes that a serious restaurant critic ought to provide the consumer with a representative guide to restaurants "that are cheap as well as dear, large as well as intimate, plebian as well as haute cuisine."

During his seven-month tour of duty as the *New York Times* restaurant critic, John L. Hess perfectly filled Rice's ideal model. He wrote about steak and hamburger places, the goulash circuit, "glop peddlers" and "maso-chic" (the cult of rude service), and the relationship between architecture and the quality of food. He also exposed the use of pre-cooked frozen foods on the menus of expensive restaurants.

Hess' philosophy of reviewing called for knocking only those successful restaurants that don't measure up. "There's no sense of kicking somebody who's already down," he says. Criticism can help restaurants, he feels, but there is little of it: "Ninety-nine per cent of writing on restaurants is gush. Food writing is a bloody scandal because most food writers are underqualified and underpaid. Publishers think that anybody can write about food because everyone eats. But editors also know that not everyone who can hear can write a concert review."

Hess also puts down restaurant guides:

A rip-off and an outrage and out of date by the time they are published. That includes *The New York Times Restaurant Guide* as well. No one maintains a staff to check and maintain proper standards. To put out a good restaurant guide would cost about $100,000 a year, and it probably wouldn't sell enough copies to make it profitable, so no one is willing to do it.

In early 1974, Hess resigned his position as restaurant critic and food writing to return to general reporting. He said the reasons he wanted off the beat: "bad food my wife and I have had to endure and the editors' resistance to a consumerist approach." In a parting quip to his readers, he wrote: "Never put faith in anybody who enjoys being a restaurant critic."

Hess was replaced by former art critic John Canaday, who returned to the Claiborne mold in his Friday reviews. In his early days on the job, Canaday explained the *Times'* rating system of stars: * good, ** very good, *** excellent and **** extraordinary. "Stars are used in an effort to average food, service, surroundings and price within a single symbol," he wrote.

Rice believes serious critics eschew such symbols: "They encourage superficial judgments and comparisons and undermine the written word."

Rice also abhors the disgraceful editorial policy of some publications to highlight in sugary prose the restaurants that advertise.

Lois Dwan, restaurant columnist of the *Los Angeles Times'* "Calendar" section, also knocks the coercive business practice of giving restaurants "free advertising" under the guise of criticism but says that criticism is emerging slowly because aloof policies and nonexistent guidelines require a cautious approach:

> There are no helpful theories of criticism and no rules. Judgment is subjective, a matter of one's own taste. One's own taste may be augmented by the lore of great restaurants, knowledge of classical procedures, and palate memories of the sublime, but these are imprecise and cloudy measures to be used as the basis for judgment or even agreement.

Writing in *The Review of Southern California Journalism*,[87] Dwan clarified her own position and basis for optimism for the field:

> My instructions from the *Los Angeles Times* were "to tell people where to go, not where not to go." I have modified this policy, but only to the extent of including unfavorable comment on a restaurant that otherwise has merit. In other words, I leave the dogs alone.
>
> Most of us try to work anonymously and to write objectively. Although we are not entirely convinced that our function is to attack—the theory that the restaurant ignored will be the restaurant that withers away is not invalid—we are taking a stronger stand than has ever before been made in Los Angeles.

Fellow Californian Paul Wallach, who writes a weekly restaurant column in the *Newporter News*, disagrees with Dwan's assessment and forecasts:

> Any discussion of standards for a "good" restaurant column is meaningless at this point without an organized consumer protest, a Ralph Nader of gastronomy, an industry leader or influential media columnist willing to lead the crusade. Few newspapers are willing to experiment with integrity in restaurant

criticism, however high their standards in other departments; they're apprehensive about suffering the almost certain loss of advertising revenue today for a potential gain in advertising and respectability at some time in the future. Their reluctance means the public will continue to be bilked and conned. The future just isn't mouthwatering.[88]

• • • •

Donald Dresden, restaurant critic of the *Washington Post*'s "Potomac" magazine, publishes his credentials at the end of his review, no doubt to enhance his authority in the eyes of readers: "Dresden, a graduate of le Cordon Bleu Academie de Cuisine de Paris, is the author of two books and writes frequently for gourmet publications."

• • • •

New York magazine publishes two restaurant columns: The "Insatiable Critic" for sophisticated clientele and "The Underground Gourmet" for middlebrow palates. Since critics often make as many as four visits to a restaurant before writing about it, they often suffer from such occupational hazards as overeating and indigestion. "Insatiable" critic Gael Greene, who prefers to dine with a small group so she can sample what the others order, says: "It's hard to keep tasting things to see if they're good. You have to pay attention to service and other details that you would normally shut out of your mind. Sometimes I come out of a restaurant feeling like I haven't eaten because I've been so busy tasting."[89]

• • • •

Don't trust any restaurant guide, including this one, Jim Quinn of Philadelphia advises readers in the introduction to his guide book, *Word of Mouth*. Quinn urges readers, armed with healthy suspicion, to:

> Pick a cheap restaurant with a decent grade and stop by. Look at the decor; is it anything like the one described in the book? Look at the menu and compare prices, item by item; are they anywhere near the prices reported in the book? If all this is so—and it should be—you can be sure that you're in a place which hasn't changed since the review was written.
>
> That doesn't mean you'll agree with everything the review has to say. Maybe you'll hit a better (or worse) night than I did. But at least you've got a guide book which represents a single year's testing, and a single (maybe idiosyncratic) point of view,

and you should be able to use it as you'd use any other guide, as a kind of sounding board to form your own opinions against.

• • • •

Current *New York Times* critic Mimi Sheraton tries to preserve her anonymity among restaurateurs by always appearing in public in disguises such as huge sunglasses and floppy hats.

• • • •

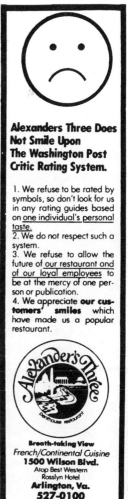

ARCHITECTURE

Will architecture criticism ever surface?

The built world, "covered" by no more than a half a dozen architecture critics in once-a-week columns, remains all but invisible in the press, charges Jane Holtz Kay, architecture and urban design critic for *The Nation*.

Among the handful of staff journalists who write about architecture are Paul Goldberger of *The New York Times*, John Pastier of the *Los Angeles Times*, Wolf Von Eckardt of the *Washington Post*, Rob Cuscaden of the *Chicago Sun-Times*, Paul Gapp of the

Chicago Tribune, Tom Hine of the *Philadelphia Inquirer,* plus a few contributing writers such as William Marlin in the *Christian Science Monitor,* Robert Campbell in *The Boston Globe,* and Thomas Creighton in the *Honolulu Advertiser.* (Clearly, architects who try to free lance lack credibility because of the apparent conflict of interest they represent.

Aside from Peter Blake, architect, editor of *Architecture Plus* and critic for *New York,* and Kay of *The Nation,* general-interest magazines have yet to show any commitment to the field. The trade press, which mainly circulates among architects, is rarely critical of anything.

As a result, Kay writes in *Columbia Journalism Review:*

> Regular coverage of our surroundings remains where it has for the last decades—swinging between handouts on the real estate page and in-and-out critics whose columns are tucked under film or book reviews in "Arts."[90]

One problem that architecture critics coming from backgrounds in art history have, says Walter F. Wagner, Jr., editor of *Architectural Record,* is seeing new buildings mainly as aesthetic performances.

Not so, says Paul Goldberger, of *The New York Times.* "My own job is more and more defined in terms of just writing about what's there, not waiting until Phillip Johnson comes up with an important building and then writing about it as a single isolated object. Rather, I write about streets and old buildings that are part of the fabric of the city and public housing projects."

John Pastier, a transplanted New Yorker, takes a much wider view of the critic's role. A sampling of his writing reveals a commitment to improving Los Angeles' urban life:

> In considering a city council ban on newsracks, Pastier urged redesigning and coordinating all street furniture—trash baskets, traffic lights, street signs, telephone booths, bus shelters, street lights and public benches—"for aesthetic and functional improvement." He even advocated the installation of public drinking fountains and toilets, while nostalgically pleading for the increase of news kiosks manned by live vendors as an important urban amenity.[91]

Architecture critics are not only concerned with new buildings but preservation of old ones that serve as representative samples of past styles so continuity exists within the built environment. Ada Louise Huxtable, now on the editorial board of *The New York Times,* is still the champion of preservations causes throughout the country. Her message packs a punch, as this example illustrates: "See the 116-year-old historic house. See it knocked down. See the hamburger stand in its place. Pow. America, of thee I sing; sweet land of the Burger King."

Paul Goldberger offers a simple process for evaluating architecture—search for a message:

> There are three different kinds of messages transmitted by a building and the best architecture is able to communicate to the viewer in each category.
>
> 1. The Building as object. What does the building look like? Is it pleasurable? What is the emotional reaction you have to the building as a pure object? Is it totally new to you, or does it call to mind some sort of historical precedent? Evaluate the facade— is there a reason the building looks as it does, or is it merely an architect's whim?
>
> 2. . . . An object among objects. Broaden your visual field; stop looking at a building as an isolated object. What message is the building communicating to its neighboring buildings? Does it want to stand apart in the city or does it respect the line of the street or perhaps continue a cornice line from its neighbors?
>
> 3. . . . As interior space. A building's use of interior space may be the quintessential architectural message. Look at a building's interior space from a practical standpoint. Do rooms connect logically with one another? Do you always have a sense of where you are in relation to the building as a whole or does the arrangement of rooms strike you as capricious and more concerned with some sort of abstract pattern than with rational use?
>
> There is another aspect to the evaluation of a building's interior—the nature of the space itself. As with the facade, the best place to begin is with your own very personal reactions. Does the room make you feel grand and ennobled? Does it humble you? Do you feel driven to the center or do you feel compelled to stay around the edges? Do you want to stand still or does it make you want to move? Rooms can do any of these things and work or any of these things and not work. Because the perception of space is so personal, it is best to trust your own feelings here.[92]

NOTES FOR CHAPTER 6

[1] Advertisement, *Variety*, April 23, 1975, page 23 and *Variety* April 30, 1975, page 21.

[2] "Which Movies Make Money," by Stephen Farber, *The New York Times*, August 17, 1975, page 16, Section II.

[3] Memo to Mazursky: Don't Get Personal, by Stephen Farber, *The New York Times*, page 17, Section II.

[4] "Exclusive Interview: Andrew Sarris," by Maurice Peterson, *Metropolitan Review*, March 12, 1972.

[5] "Prospero at the Cinema," Andrew Sarris, *Village Voice*, Dec. 20, 1976, page 61.

[6] "On Being an Elitist Critic," by John Simon, *The New Leader*, Oct. 27, 1975, page 23.

[7] "John Simon on the Record," by Philip Nobile, (*More*), June, 1976, page 11.

[8] Pauline Kael, *I Lost It At the Movies* (Boston: Little, Brown and Company, 1965), page 309.

[9] Ibid., page 308.

[10] "Notes on Heart and Mind," by Pauline Kael, *The New Yorker*, Jan. 23, 1971, page 76.

[11] Pauline Kael, *Miss Kiss Bang Bang*, (Boston: Little, Brown & Co., 1968), page 21.

[12] Pauline Kael, *Deeper Into Movies* (Boston: Little, Brown & Co., 1973), page 345.

[13] "Pauline Kael Lost It All At the Movies," by Richard Gilman, *Village Voice*, June 7, 1976, page 40.

[14] Cleon Daniel King, "A Profile of Pauline Kael," unpublished honors thesis, University of Georgia, 1976.

[15] "Dreamstyle, Bondstyle, Turnstile: Surface is All in the Genre Films," by Bruce Cook, *The National Observer*, Dec. 21, 1974, p. 18.

[16] "New Film-Reviewing System Needed," by Don Carle Gillette, *The Journal of the Producers Guild of America*, Sept. 1972, p. 31.

[17] Interview with Mario Puzo, *New York*, August 21, 1972, p. 29.

[18] "How to Read Critics for Fun & Profit," by Clifford A. Ridley, *The National Observer*, Jan. 1, 1972, p. 16.

[19] "The Ruling Class," by Stanley Kauffmann, *The New Republic*, Sept. 16, 1972, p. 22.

[20] "Advice to Readers and Critics," by Otis Ferguson, *Film Comment*, Sept. 1973, p. 15.

[21] "Yesterday's Heroes, Today's Has-Beens?" by Stephen Farber, *The New York Times*, Jan. 7, 1973, Movie page, Section II.

[22] Harold Clurman, *The Divine Pastime* (New York: Macmillan Publishing Co., 1974), page I.

[23] Norman Mailer, *Existential Errands* (Boston: Little, Brown and Co., 1972), page 62.

[24] "Theatre and Drama Criticism: Some Notes," by Stanley Kauffmann, *Yale/Theatre*, Vol. 4, No. 2, Spring 1973, pp. 15–16.

[25] *Op. cit.*, pp. 2–4.

[26] "The New York Drama Critics," by Martin Gottfried, *Yale/Theatre*, Vol. 4, No. 2, Spring 1973, page 90.

[27] *Op. cit.*, page 2.

[28] "Putting Down a David Merrick Put-On," by Dan Sullivan, *The Los Angeles Times*, July 13, 1969, "Calendar," page 30.

[29] "An Open Letter to a Producer," by Dan Sullivan, *The Los Angeles Times*, Sept. 15, 1971, "Calendar," page 32.

[30] "A Tepid Evening and a Warm Letter," by Dan Sullivan, *The Los Angeles Times*, Feb. 21, 1971, "Calendar," page 26.

[31] "On Criticism," by Eric Bentley and Julius Novick, *Yale/Theatre*, Vol. 4, No. 2, Spring 1973, pp. 23–36.

[32] "High Noon on 44th St.—Critic Barnes Faces the Dramatists," *Intellectual Digest*, Oct. 1971, pp. 75–80.

[33] "Eder/Or: Is There Too Much Power on the Aisle?", Ross Wetzsteon, *Village Voice*, March 28, 1977, page 97.

[34] "My First Season on the Aisle," Richard Eder, *The New York Times Magazine*, July 16, 1978, pages 17–18.

[35] *Op. cit.*, page 35.

[36] "Portrait of the Critic as a Young Brechtian," by Eric Bentley, *Theatre Quarterly*, No. 2, 1976, pp. 8–9.

[37] "A Crisis in Criticism," by Robert Brustein, *Plays & Players*, Fall 1973, p. 61.

[38] *Op. cit.*, page 11.

[39] *Ibid.*, p. 60.

[40] "A Drench of Music, but a Drought of Critics," by Virgil Thomson, *The New York Times*, Oct. 27, 1974, p. 1, Section II.

[41] "The Ten Best Unpublished Stories of 1971," by Alan Rich, *New York*, Jan. 3, 1972, p. 56.

[42] "Hanslick Proved a Critic Can Change His Mind," by Donald Henahan, *The New York Times*, Nov. 2, 1975, Music page, Section II.

[43] "The Only Thing We Have to Fear," by Alan Rich, *New York*, March 6, 1972, p. 66.

[44] "Nothing for Everyone," by Alan Rich, *New York*, June 10, 1972, p. 64.

[45] "Does Anybody Know What a Musical Idea Is?" by Harold C. Schonberg, *The New York Times*, Feb. 1, 1976, Music page, Section II.

[46] "Interpretation: What Is It?" by Harold C. Schonberg, *The New York Times*, Dec. 10, 1972, Music page, Section II.

[47] "Life Out There: Westward the Course in Criticism," by Alan Rich, *New York*, Sept. 3, 1973, p. 56.

[48] "Rock Criticism," by Garry Gewen, *Commentary*, June 1970, pp. 93–96.

[49] "The Literati of Anticulture," by John Rockwell, *The New York Times*, Dec. 26, 1973, p. 37.

[50] "Rock Reaches a Critical Juncture," by Barry Hansen (Dr. Demento), *Circular*, Vol. 6, No. 34, Oct. 21, 1974.

[51] "Music Convention Without Buyers," by Tom Johnson, *Village Voice*, Nov. 21, 1974, p. 106.

[52] "The Critics' Critic," by Dave Marsh, *Rolling Stone*, Dec. 16, 1976, page 37.

[53] "Nothing but the 'nice truth,'" by Geoffrey Stokes, *Village Voice*, Jan. 24, 1974, p. 67.

[54] "Who Cares About Rock Critics," by Henry Edwards, *The New York Times*, Feb. 15, 1976, p. 20, Section II.

[55] "If You Wanna Dance With Me," by Chet Flippo, *Rolling Stone*, May 9, 1974, p. 72.

[56] "Come Writers and Critics Who Prophesize With Your Pen," by Jon Landau, *Rolling Stone*, March 11, 1976, p. 20.

[57] "There's Gold in That There Trash," by John J. O'Connor, *The New York Times*, March 28, 1971, TV page, Section II.

[58] "Television Critics—A Survey," by Charles S. Steinberg, a report issued on Sept. 12, 1973. Published in *Variety*.

[59] "TV Critics—the Hack Pack," by Gary Deeb, *Variety*, Jan. 9, 1974, page 104.

[60] "TV Has Hit Its Peak Popularity," by Jack Gould, *The Los Angeles Times*, Nov. 23, 1975, page 13.

[61] "Criticism as Support for the Status Quo: The Desired Role of Television Critics in the Eyes of Philadelphians," by Joseph Turow, unpublished seminar paper, University of Pennsylvania, May 21, 1973.

[62] "A Survey of Two Specialized Segments of the Audience for Television Criticism in Philadelphia," by Susan Louise Fry, unpublished Master's Thesis, University of Pennsylvania, 1970.

[63] Remarks Before the Washington Journalism Center, by Eric Sevareid, June 3, 1976.

[64] "The Painted Word," by John Russell, *The New York Times Book Review*, June 15, 1976, page 4.

[65] "Wolfe's middlebrow kitsch isn't an alternative to art," by Mike Steele, *Minneapolis Tribune*, June 15, 1975, page 11D.

66 "Who Does Tom Wolfe Think He Is?" by David Bourdon, *Village Voice*, April 7, 1975, page 56.

67 "Bloomsbury's Art Critic," by Hilton Kramer, *The New York Times*, April 27, 1973, page 62.

68 "Seminar One," by Clement Greenberg, *Arts Magazine*, Nov. 1973, page 44–46.

69 "The Art World Today: Manufacturers, Dealers and Investors," by John Canaday, *The New York Times*, Aug. 18, 1974, Art page, Section II.

70 "The Artist in Today's Society," by Cindy Nemser, *Feminist Art Journal*, Fall 1973, page 19.

71 "The Function of the Art Critic," by Lawrence Alloway, *The New York University Education Quarterly*, Spring 1974, pages 24–28.

72 "A Critic's Lot is Not a Happy One," by Cindy Nemser, *Feminist Art Journal*, April 1972, page 9.

73 "Freelancing the Dragon," by Lucy Lippard, *Art Rite*, No. 5, Spring 1974, page 16.

74 *Ibid.*

75 "Problems of the Working Critic of the Modern Visual Arts," by Edward Lucie-Smith, *British Journal of Aesthetics*, Vol. 11, No. 3, Summer 1971, page 245.

76 "No Fair Play for the Fair Sex," by Grace Glueck, *The New York Times*, June 11, 1972, Art page, Section II.

77 "Artform Versus Kramer," letter to the editor by John Coplans and Max Kozloff, *The New York Times*, Jan. 4, 1976, page 22.

78 "Art & the Artist," by Emily Genauer, *New York Post*, May 11, 1974, page 34.

79 "Describing Dance Is Like . . . ," by Clive Barnes, *The New York Times*, Jan. 27, 1974, Page 4, Section II.

80 "Must There Be a Story?" by Clive Barnes, *The New York Times*, March 14, 1971, Dance page, Section II.

81 "He's Loved, but Not by Critics," by Clive Barnes, *The New York Times*, Feb. 24, 1974, page 8, Section II.

82 "Dance from a Reviewer's Point of View," talk by Anna Kisselgoff, to the Dance Society, April 15, 1974.

83 "How to be a Good Critic of Dance," by William Moore, *The Feet*, June 1973, page 22.

84 "Such Good Friends," by Richard Kruger, *American Libraries*, Jan. 1973, pp. 20–25.

85 "A Critical Conspiracy, But Where's the Smoking Gun?" by Eliot Fremont-Smith, *Village Voice*, March 10, 1975, p. 32.

86 "What's a Reviewer to Write? Restaurant Criticism's Coming of Age," by William Rice, *Media & Consumer*, Sept. 1973, pp. 8–9.

87 "The Emerging Restaurant Critic," by Lois Dwan, *The Review of Southern California Journalism*, Feb. 1972, pp. 2–3.

88 "The Restaurant Critic: Consider Now His Murky Depths," by Paul Wallach, *The Review of Southern California Journalism*, Feb. 1972, pp. 4–6.

89 "Food Critics' Rating Can Play Crucial Role in Restaurant Success," by Peggy J. Murrell, *The Wall Street Journal*, Nov. 2, 1970, p. 15.

90 "Architecture and design—who cares?" by Jane Holtz Kay, *Columbia Journalism Review*, July/August 1975, pp. 30–36.

91 "Buying News Off the Rack," by John Pastier, *Los Angeles Times*, Dec. 16, 1974, pp. 1 & 8–9, Part IV.

92 "Buildings Speak to Us; Here's How to Listen," by Paul Goldberger, *The New York Times*, April 25, 1976, page 16, Section II.

Make Money Writing Short Paragraphs

by LAWRENCE CHRISTON

Are YOU:

Pusillanimous, power-hungry, waspish, namby-pamby, handicapped, repressed, an *artiste manque?*

Would YOU Like To:

Meet members of the same or opposite sex? Feel important? Hang around celebrities? Get your name in print and see yourself quoted in ads? Go to cultural events on the cuff? Earn money for your opinions, whether considered or not? Improve your chances of becoming one of Andy Warhol's World-Famous People for 15 minutes? Enjoy job security regardless of puerility or senility? Give parties with the assurance that everyone will show up? Turn hatred to your advantage?

Can YOU Say:

"A delicious, delightful, delectable evening!"
"Certainly the most fun-filled disaster movie I've ever seen!"
"A mournful wail that haunts long after the curtain drops."
"Tacky, tacky, tacky."
"If you don't see anything else this year, see this."
Or, "If you don't see anything else this year, don't see this either."
"Erotic, bawdy, sensual. Couldn't leave my seat. A grabber."
"The show was good, too"?

Then You, Too,

Can BE A CRITIC

The Famous Critics School of Westport, Conn., is for you! The Board of Directors of the Famous Critics School is comprised of leading professionals and academicians who have designed a comprehensive, authoritative and inexpensive (cheap) curriculum that will allow any eligible candidate to become a full-fledged critic within five (5) days. The comprehensive list of courses will teach you all there is to know about writing and professional criticism. Courses, subjects and themes include:
—Writing Good, I through V inclusive
—Invective, and How to Unleash It
—Quotable Quoting
—How to Convert Ambiguity Into the Appearance of Fairness and Ignorance Into the Illusion of Knowledge
—Mixed Metaphors and How to Season Them
—Surefire Intermission Quips
—How to Develop Inscrutability
—How to Cover an Event Through Which You've Slept
—The Compleat Guide to Prating (a compulsory text)

—Musical Criticism for the Tone Deaf; Art Criticism for the Color Blind
—Principles of Currying Favor
—The Uses and Abuses of Conflict of Interest
—How to Foment Controversy
—Typing Essentials

The Famous Critics School is founded and staffed by people who are basically just like you, leaders in their fields who understand your hopes and what it takes to realize them. You will benefit from decades of experience of people who have clawed their way to success and are now willing to impart their knowledge. All you need to do is send $300 and an introductory letter to Famous Critics School in Westport, Conn., describing yourself and your background, your education (if any), your destructive motives, and include a sample of your writing (or printing, clear if possible). The FCS will critique your work and return an application and spelling test—the completion of which is the FCS's only entrance requirement. This simple procedure may mean fame for you, even if you don't wish to finish the complete course. The FCS's lessons in intimidating others and the importance of self-importance will benefit you for a lifetime. Here are what some Famous Critics School alumni have written:

"I find people tend to listen to me now, whereas before they didn't."
—E.W., Houston

"At the lectern of a cultural awards banquet, I was drunk, told stupid jokes and didn't know my fly was open. The following year I was elected president of the Hackensack Drama Critics Circle."
—L.G., Dumont

"I used to be a 98-pound weakling and couldn't lift weights because of my asthma. Your course has given me the means to protect myself and satisfy my lust for power. I get lots of girls, too."
—M.O., Dubuque

"A producer was hassling me in the lobby once and I told him 'One cannot be too careful in choosing one's enemies,' which is a line from Oscar Wilde that I learned at the Famous Critics School. Now I am widely known as the possessor of a rapier-like wit, and nobody fools with me."
—W.K., New York

"I am a small female and member of a minority. Now 22 different ethnic, cultural and sexual minority groups claim me as their spokesperson."
—Gloria, 412-7711

"I saved $500 in choice seats and free parking privileges in 1976."
—Orgon, Mission Beach

ADDISON SKOLD

Founder of Famous Critics School

These are just some of the thousands of endorsements the Famous Critics School has received over the years. Be the first on your block to profit by this unique program. Remember, you need not be professionally qualified—why should the artist have exclusive rights on outrage and thwarted innocence? Act now! Our limited introductory offer includes a free two-volume set hot off the Alumni Press, "The Art History of Cincinnati," and "The ABC's of Aesthetics, a Lay Guide to the Abstruse." Don't Delay! Clip and fill out the coupon below and mail it today!!

Note: The Famous Critics School is an affirmative action institution that does not discriminate on the basis of race, religion, creed, sex, political affiliation, nationality, intellectual capacity or talent.

YES, the Famous Critics School of Westport, Conn., is for me!!!!
Name . . . .
Address . . . .
*Credit Card No. . . . .
*Cash also accepted.
Christon is a local critic and humorist.

7

A CHECKLIST OF
13 QUESTIONS FOR
EVALUATING CRITICS

1. Does the critic offer adequate description, interpretation and evaluation to satisfy readers?

Description.

Just as sports fans enjoy reading about sporting events they have witnessed, so too, a large portion of the readers of criticism like to read the critic's account of his experience with the arts event. Like sports writers, critics face the bind of writing descriptively enough so that those attuned readers who did·not witness the work first hand will be able to recreate it in their mind and yet not so detailed that those who were there will get bored with its replay. For those who were on hand, the critic must be the uncommon observer, supplying an overview and yet citing details of interest and significance. Additionally critics must write for readers who rarely experience the arts but who have a social interest in keeping up. A critic's description, then, must serve different types of readers with different informational needs.

Interpretation.

As uncommon observers, critics are also charged with the responsibility of analyzing, interpreting and illuminating the arts.

This intellectual activity requires puzzling out the artist's message, if one is intended. For example, Alan M. Kreigsman, Pulitzer-Prize winning critic of the *Washington Post*, offered new insights into Bernardo Bertolucci's controversial film of 1973 when he wrote:

> "Last Tango in Paris" is much more apt to strike one as compelling when viewed as a study of contemporary emotional needs and barriers than as an essay on offbeat sex. From this perspective, both the film's aspirations and its failings seem worthier of respect.

Kreigsman's interpretation deals with the film's message and intent, not just its story line. Fundamental to effective functioning, a critic must decide what any work of art should do. The most salient view is that art only assumes relevancy if it stimulates new ideas and initiates change in people's lives. Since artists generally work with ideas—their statements or attitudes toward the culture or view of the world—critics must not only apprehend what the artist is saying and interpret or clarify it if it is vague, but also they must discuss and challenge those ideas.

Evaluation.

Like those in the arts public, critics base their primary reactions to a work on emotional responses or intuition or gut instincts. But they must also give a more detailed reaction than "I like it," or "I don't like it," though these simplistic verdicts should be apparent in their reviews. A critic's personal preference represents only one person's subjective tastes, but if readers believe that one person's tastes and opinions are just as good or valid as another's, since no two are the same, the whole notion that criticism offers any value is negated.

A useful critic must offer a clear statement of a critical judgment that represents intellectual thought and analysis or the collective "we." While an individual may be content with his or her "feeling" about a work, a critic must struggle with possible conflicts between taste and critical judgment.

"Criticism is not a matter of right vs. wrong, good vs. bad, or thumbs up, thumbs down," says Chicago critic Mary Knoblauch. "There is no absolute final judgment, only a series of defensible positions taken on a particular work." Judgmental positions stem from comparing one work with other efforts and assessing the historical significance of both.

While some readers expect critics to guide them toward improving their tastes, others are quite content in knowing what they like. Nonetheless, the best critics state both a personal preference for or against the work being reviewed as well as a critical evaluation of its worth.

To fulfill both these emotional and intellectual responsibilities to their readers, about 98 per cent of critics rely on Goethe's threepoint formula for analysis, says Sandra Schmidt Oddo, a New York drama critic who has studied critics:

1. What has the artist tried to do?
2. How well has he done it?
3. Was it worth doing?

Since readers are presumably more interested in the actual experience of the art work than its technique of production, critics must balance the elements of description, interpretation and evaluation in their reviews in order to serve a broad segment of their audience.

2. Does the critic's review seem full of fresh reporting and observations?

Most critics have their review half written before they see the work, chides *Variety*'s Carroll Carroll. "Critics on TV, especially, have semi-frozen reviews in their heads that are thawed out on the way back to the studio." Carroll rightly observes that too many critics rely on background material culled from public relations handouts or their past reviews of previous work by the artist so that their reviews appear more canned than fresh.

Critics must focus on the work under consideration and draw examples from it to make their points. The practice of attempting to tie in extraneous information most often appears far-fetched and fails.

3. Does the critic draw from his/her personal experience and storehouse of information and relate previous examples to the present?

The best criticism has an autobiographical flavor and critics shouldn't hesitate to tap their own experience on occasion when it adds to the discussion.

Similarly, a good memory is an important asset for a critic. Critics not only have to memorize each new experience for instant recall, but also keep in mind a virtual audio-video library of these experiences for comparisons. The best critics seem to have the best memories, not only for trivial details but for the emotional tenor of a work of art.

4. Does the critic express his viewpoint with confidence and passion as well as with clarity?

Passionate responses reveal a critic's enthusiasm for both criticism and art. Excessive passion can lead to the pitfall of over-praise or overkill. Most works of art barely invite comment, critics say, so hyper-reactions and inflated vocabulary are obviously misleading.

A critic's confidence is also easy to detect from careful readings. Some critics are afraid of making "wrong" decisions because they simply are not confident in their own judgments. Their writing reflects the tentativeness and often relies on weak innuendo, cleverly concealed qualifiers and evasive verb tenses, such as "presumably," "might have," "must have known," "surely," "perhaps," "indeed," "rather," "I presume" or "I gather" and of course, "I dare say."

Other moods such as contempt, sarcasm and sentimental adulation can be monitored by persistent reading of a critic's output.

5. Is the critic's writing style communicative?

In the same way that the style of English tea service differs from that of the traditional Japanese ceremony, critics exhibit a wide range of writing styles that reflect their own character. It is axiomatic to say that the best critics are also the best writers. Conversely, excellent critics are never bad writers. No matter how acute their perceptions or how accurate their evaluations, they would mean little if they were not written in a lively, readable style.

Critics as writers, like any artist, exhibit characteristic weaknesses. A few suffer from logorrhea, or writing more than anyone would ever want to know about the work. Some proffer dry and academic prose that is tedious and uncommunicative. Lazy critics substitute clichés for original and precise expression. Among the overused phrases that appear in critical reviews are: truth to tell, need no introduction, got off to a flying start, happily enough, conjured up, comes alive, delicately wrought, a pure delight, modicum of truth, sublime heights, part and parcel, gala event, comes unglued, and if last night's audience is any indication. . . .

The critical language has also been debased by the practice of blurb ads, in which advertising hypes and inflates the significance of selected words or key phrases. The process makes about as much sense as rating olives in size by such terms as select, medium, large extra large, mammoth, giant, jumbo, colossal, super colossal and super supreme.

Weak criticism, like any bad writing, has other apparent shortcomings—poor organization, syntactical clashing of words, overwriting, straining for novelty and frequent use of jargon.

Quality criticism must have the characteristics of both reportage—accuracy, completeness, timeliness, balance and emphasis—and literature—conciseness, clarity, unity and general effectiveness. In addition, criticism should reflect evocative qualities such as color and vitality, imagination, a sense of humor and, of course, readability.

The overall tone of the publication affects the style of critics, too. For example, Jerry Bailey's folksiness in the *Nashville Tennessean*—"With a voice as country as cows and plows, Miss (Barbara) Lea should blend as naturally with (Porter) Wagoner as biscuits and gravy"—would hardly appeal to readers of the *Boston Globe*. And the informal style of the *Los Angeles Times*, with its free use of such popular idioms as "din-din break," "scruffy digs," and "godawful," would seem out of place in the staid *New York Times*. Other New Yorkers, however, are addicted to the gabby and sassy style of *New York* and *Village Voice* critics. Music critic Andrew Porter occasionally uses descriptive words that are imaginative and startling, if eccentric. In his *New Yorker* column, he has called a violin concerto "delicately jeweled" and a performance of a Mozart symphony "plump, bland smooth-jowled."

Each publication strives to print criticism written in a conversational manner for their readers, full of warmth, familiarity, spontaneity and even populist energy.

Critics who are either snobbish or intentionally talk down to their readers are never as effective as those who try to initiate a discussion of a work by making the first statement about it. Readers can easily become aware of who the critic is talking to by considering the tone and style of the remarks. The best critics have their readers foremost in mind.

6. Does the critic frequently use reference points outside the field?

Critics who say they are guided by their "seat of the pants" generally write one-dimensional reviews that fail to deal with the world beyond the art object being considered. The best critics are not so narrow-minded; they use a variety of critical approaches borrowed from other disciplines. For example, literary criticism, the oldest type, yields five classical approaches, according to Wilbur S. Scott:

- Moral criticism, dating from Plato, judges a work's moral worth to humanity and how art affects man.
- Psychological criticism, linked to Freud, permits the critic to interpret the art by analyzing the unconscious drives, emotional motivation and stated intentions of the artist-creator.
- Sociological criticism ties a work of art to the social milieu and judges it in view of contemporary political and economic values and society's intellectual atmosphere.
- Archetypal criticism, stemming from Jung's collective unconscious, attempts to discover the universal social patterns of men unrelated to a particular time. Myths and rituals are of primary concern.
- Formalistic criticism or aesthetic judgment focuses on an internal analysis of style: the composition of a film frame or the structure of a poem. Stylistic artists often earn high praise from formalistic critics, even though the content of the art may be quite banal.

From film criticism, the auteur or single author approach, can also be applied to other popular arts. So can structuralism (without ideological bias), which comes from the study of semantics and anthropology.

In short, the best critics work in a pluralistic manner, using whichever approach seems most suited to the subject. It's important for critics not to get so lost or involved in their field that they fail to put it in perspective with the rest of life. Readers are not so consumed. If critics are, their value becomes moot.

The ideal critic is objective—free of psychological bias and prejudice as humanly possible—says communications theorist Ernest G. Bormann. But one wonders if it is either possible or desirable to purge the elements that infuse life into works of artists from critics? Such purity is mythical.

7. Does the critic's vocabulary reflect his standards of evaluating art?

Yes, but . . . Critics acknowledge that they shoot from the hip. The pressure of deadline writing and, in some instances, laziness are factors that must be considered when analyzing critical vocabulary.

Trite and mushy words are all too common in reviews. While

they help establish an overall impression, their meaning is imprecise. Such phrases include: magnificent, stunning, inimitable, electrifying, dynamic and masterly on the positive side and pedestrian, contrived (all art is), superficial, effete, pretentious and tedious on the negative. The critic apparently believes readers share his understanding of these words, but that's impossible.

Further, the notion of specific standards is hazy at best. Henri Peyre quite rightly says:

> I doubt any critic can ever tell you, in general and in the abstract, what his standards are, because these are always flexible and because every network has to be evaluated for its own sake and in itself and not according to the pre-existing standards or to the current fashions. We do not really know what "gre itness" is; when we sense it somewhere it may be there independently from all qualities customarily called valuable: structure, harmony, power of characterization, imagery, depth, etc.

8. Is the critic open and straightforward about his point of view or ideological commitments?

Generally, the more explicitly he states his positions the better. The public can tolerate all varieties of views if they are told directly, instead of having critics pretend that such perspectives don't affect their writing.

If a critic concentrates on one type of work to the extent he ignores others, that bias must be kept in mind in further readings. More subtly, a critic may consistently rave about an artist or type of work and rant about opposing schools. In such cases, readers must examine the critic's reasons for praising or denouncing work.

9. Do critics have any known or covert conflicts of interests that may compromise their writing about a particular subject?

The more "pure" a critic is the better. The fewer friends and enemies he has in the arts the more honest his work. Criticism written to either please or antagonize certain readers (prominent figures, funding institutions and so forth) also reflect a bias. So does any critic's association with any special interest group in the field. Personal and professional motivations and influences may not only affect the critic's attitudes and judgments but also invalidate his criticism in the eyes of readers.

10. Who should the critic serve—himself or his readers?

The best critics serve their readers first. Critics have to be willing to take risks: to express their world view and lay out their lives and intellect and call attention to works that they deem important, though they may be controversial and not immediately popular with audiences.

One way to tell if a critic is interested in something other than self-aggrandizement is how frequently he fights for unfashionable causes. Sometimes critics must lead a fight against community standards which restrict the development of certain kinds of art. To be effective a critic must resist the temptation to write down to this constituency so he won't alienate the very readers he hopes to convince.

Beware of the "I" syndrome (the "I think, I believe, I feel . . .") which has infected criticism (perhaps from New Journalism, which features the writer as the central figure, instead of the subject). A critic always writing in the first person, warns Vincent Canby, has

> less interest in the work being criticized than in displaying himself, desperately, by standing in front of the subject. This kind of critic is likely to think of himself in terms of his clout, his effectiveness in persuading as many people as possible to hold exactly the same opinions as he does.

11. Does the critic appear to take his writing and himself seriously?

Gene Shalit has come to represent the critic-as-comic type. Shalit's playfulness with words is ingenious and ingenuous. His quips tend to trivialize his subjects. His sneering cracks lack the bite of serious censure and his credibility is impaired when he fails to convince his audience that he loves the arts and is dedicated to their improvement—a goal that improves the quality of life for all. This type of critic, whose ego and personal image are more important than his subjects, resorts to grand-standing to build his own superstar reputation at the expense of a particular work and culture in general.

High-brow critics, such as John Simon, are often intrigued by witticisms, puns and cleverly reworked phrases as a form of intellectual gamesmanship. Simon, for example, has flippantly called: "2001: A Space Odyssey," a "shaggy God story." It's a sign he's not as serious as he might be.

Among movie critics, Pauline Kael always is sober-sided and tirelessly thorough. As a result, her criticism is worth reading and a reliable measure of her concern about the field.

Most critics, though, don't take themselves seriously and their writing shows that lack of concern.

12. Can readers detect lazy and worn-out critics by looking at their work?

Certainly. Commitment and dedication to the arts are generally reflected in a critic's productivity as well as the quality of his product. The best criticism requires lots of physical energy.

Clive Barnes' work schedule sets the pace. He writes six or seven daily reviews each week on the ten theatre and dance events he attends and does a Sunday dance column. In addition, he reads shortened versions of his reviews on the *New York Times* radio station five days a week, lectures occasionally and even writes free lance articles for other publications when asked. Barnes has been working at this clip for ten years and shows no signs of flagging enthusiasm for his craft or the arts.

13. How can readers learn to use critics to serve them?

Rarely is there universal critical opinion on any work of art and readers can become confused if they try to believe every critic they read. While readers must assume the responsibility for choosing a critic they can use as a guide, they should not make their selection on the basis of whether they agree with that critic or not. In fact, critics with whom one disagrees may be the most illuminating and exhilarating to read. They may offer a peculiar relationship with art that broadens one's own perspective, relate historical lore or legend that's relevant or make pertinent comparisons one didn't think of or simply impart their feelings with captivating intensity. The critic's verdict is generally the least important of considerations.

On the whole, a critic's reviews reflect a consistent personality and sensibility. By reading a critic's work long enough—say, several months—readers can learn the critic's temperament and biases and then calibrate their own tastes in relation to them. For those who find they agree with his views, they can begin to rely on him as a barometer in helping make decisions on what they want to see or avoid. Even those who consistently disagree can do the same thing by reversing his index.

The best check is to see a new work when it first is announced and then comparing one's own view with that of the critic after you both have shared the experience. Subtleties and special interests will be apparent as one learns both about one's self and his critic.

8

THE FUTURE
OF CRITICISM

In assaying the state of the art, a few critics agree that some criticism today is of higher quality than the art form being criticized. Most, however, believe the issue is sophistic. *Newsweek*'s Zimmerman is crystal clear: "I'd rather see a good movie than read a good review." *Time*'s Kalem takes a longer view: "Nine hundred and ninety-nine reviews are better than the work they deal with, but one masterpiece is worth a thousand reviews."

The philosophical orientation of critics is an important clue on how fast and in what direction the field will develop. In the 1974 survey, critics were asked if they believed a reviewer should go beyond appreciation, evaluation and box-office guidance to attempt to change the social context in which the popular arts live in the world. The muddled results—41 per cent responded "Yes," 33 per cent said "No" and about 26 per cent failed to answer—are less than encouraging. Generally, art, architecture and music critics most often agreed with this idealistic goal, while drama, film and book critics were pessimistic over either the aim or its accomplishment. Television critics, as usual, were evenly divided on the matter.

David Elliott, of the *Chicago Daily News*, led the majority who favored aggressive, society-based criticism: "This may be the most important and difficult duty a critic has."

Critics at the *Los Angeles Times* share the philosophy of entertainment editor Charles Champlin: "Critics by definition almost are optimists, idealists and perfectionists. They espouse failing candidates and lost causes, always in the hopes of making a better world." John Pastier adds: "One cannot separate arts from society; to criticize one is to criticize the other." Digby Diehl agrees: "Criticism of art is criticism of the entire culture."

Other critics succinctly stated their world view as well as their assessment of art. *Newsday's* Joseph Gelmis responded: "Art changes the context by altering how we *see.* As a critic, I'm committed to recognizing and supporting excellence because Art is the best social criticism. If I was an artist, I'd be interested in depicting my own visions." Mike Steele, of the *Minneapolis Tribune,* is equally adamant about the arts' role: "When the arts remove themselves from a social context they are treated as aberrant and superfluous, though often pretty, adjuncts to it, like bridge clubs or softball teams. And, social context doesn't necessarily relate only to content."

Charles Benbow, of the *St. Petersburg Times,* believes criticism should probe societal issues raised by the arts: "Critics shouldn't try to sever the tie of art with life but should point out the element in society that provides the climate and nourishment for the art—such as violence,"

Michael Feingold, of the *Village Voice,* takes an activist position: "One has to try and do as much as one can—change the world, change and improve the arts and change the relationship between the two."

Many critics agree with the stance but are skeptical it can be executed with effective frequency. "Such influence is rare," says Fred W. Wright, Jr., of the *St. Petersburg Independent.* "So is the talent to exert such influence." New York art critic Peter Frank also believes few critics are powerful enough to affect such change. Paul Zimmerman says critics who write with "passion and intelligence" alter the social context of the arts "to some small extent involuntarily." James Auer, of the *Milwaukee Journal,* also argues that the process of change is gradual, not revolutionary: "In a way, we do this simply by diverting toward the arts the time of the general reader who would otherwise be spending his time with sports or something else."

Lawrence DeVine, of the *Detroit Free Press,* is cautiously optimistic on what critics can contribute: "Properly supplied with valid, valuable criticism, audiences ought to demand better quality stuff—which would then affect their lives. One hopes." Mary Nic Shenk, of the *St. Petersburg Times,* notes that despite the idealistic vision of critics they still must work through editors who may not share that view.

The sternest warning of why critics must assume the broad-est possible view of their role comes from Robert Jennings, music critic of the Memphis *Commercial Appeal:* "Unless the 'social con-text' is soon drastically changed, the arts—popular or oth-erwise—will be unable to survive."

Among those who don't think critics should try to alter the social context of the arts is Leslie Cross, book editor of the *Mil-waukee Journal*, who says, "That's not the reviewer's responsi-bility in my field. But a social conscience is not to be despised."

Four Washington critics concur. Robert Evett of the *Star-News* says simply that "critics are not Sunday school teachers." Colleague David Richards thinks critics should respond to social issues only in connection with a given work and not as policy. Ir-ving Lowens believes critics might work toward such goals as private individuals, but not in their official roles as critics. Rich-ard L. Coe of the *Post* also says such work can be done subtly but not in actual reviews.

Archer Winston, veteran film critic of the *New York Post*, is similarly conservative: "That's for the politician, the revolu-tionary." Others just insist that such an expanded role is doomed to frustration. Ted Kalem says such critics "might as well charge a stone wall." The late Jack Harris, UPI critic for 34 years before he died in 1974, said such an effort would be "futile." Another crusty veteran, Hobe Morrison of *Variety*, advises: "Critics shouldn't take themselves so seriously. Too much is made of critics and criticism. Most of us should ignore critics and make our own choices. Our own are the only ones that should matter to us."

Of the nay-sayers, Alan Rich's comment is the most tem-pered: "Critics can't change, but they can make audiences aware of possible areas in which change should be considered."

In addition to a wider role, critics polled by Louis Harris predicted major changes in methods and content of criticism. They expect criticism to have an increasingly youthful orienta-tion and to be more informal, honest, irreverent, vigorous and funny, and less pedantic and Puritanical.

In many ways, the critics now appearing on television are al-ready carving out the path of that new direction. As the only critic on network TV, Gene Shalit uses dramatic antics—he took a fly swatter after "Superfly"—and verbal wit—his review of "Si-lent Movie" ran through adjectives beginning with each letter of the alphabet—to impress and entertain his estimated six million viewers in the New York area plus the millions of others who watched him on 140 affiliated stations across the country.

Shalit's zany style has already encouraged imitators who are even more outrageous. For example, in Washington, D.C., Davey

Marlin-Jones mixes in magic tricks as he reviews movies and theatre for his WTOP-TV audience. Or on St. Louis' KPRL-TV, Gentry Trotter has become the quintessential performer-critic, resorting to costume and props related to productions he's reviewing. For "Jaws," he appeared entangled in seaweed clutching a live fish. In terms of sheer bluster, Trotter offers an act that would be difficult to follow.

While Shalit and others are certainly aware of the limitations of their 90-second or 200-word reviews, they recognize that television is becoming the most popular forum for criticism since the majority of the American public already relies on the medium as its main daily source of news. Yet as the trend toward entertainer-critics spreads to cities across the nation, the need to offer serious, intellectual criticism of the arts still is not being filled in most places.

One program innovation worth imitating elsewhere surfaced in 1973 on public television in the Washington, D.C., area. The weekly, half-hour show, produced by WETA and called "The Critics," featured four critics representing drama and dance, the visual arts, film and music plus guest critics from other fields who held spontaneous discussions on their experiences and interests in the Washington arts scene. Each show covered a wide range of arts activity, providing information on upcoming events and recommendations or things to see and do. All four critics witnessed as many events to be discussed as possible and therefore brought interdisciplinary viewpoints to bear on each work. Ruth Leon, cultural programming director of the host station, said the show worked because the critics "believed in the unity of all the forms of creative expression and the necessity of involving others in the enjoyment and appreciation of the arts." Although the WETA-TV show was not re-funded after 35 weeks, the idea has been picked up by public stations in Baltimore, New York, and elsewhere.

The critic's forum type of show effectively counters the criticism that readers often make about a medium that only offers a single critic's viewpoint on a subject. Some newspapers do attempt to publish diverse expressions of opinion, so the local critic does not have a monopoly voice on the local arts. Taking the initiative from the Music Critics Association, which began encouraging critics to swap posts for a short period some years ago, other groups of critics could also arrange such exchanges. Not only do such opportunities offer critics a fresh perspective on their craft, they also offer readers a different voice and new insights into the local arts scene.

Another innovation pioneered at the *Village Voice* by drama critics Michael Smith and Arthur Sainer and film critics Andrew

Sarris and Molly Haskell is the collaborative-dialogue review. The two participating critics both witness the same event and then discuss it in a conversational style. A transcript of their remarks is edited and published as a review. Such an original form of reviewing engages the reader and gives multiple viewpoints at the same time.

The media could also stimulate more audience participation with critics if they regularly published letters-to-the-editor on arts subjects, perhaps in the Sunday entertainment section.

One newspaper actively soliciting reader feedback to help shape its service role is the *Miami Herald*. Lively arts editor Hunter George recently conducted a reader poll to ask what they liked about the paper's entertainment coverage and what they wanted improved. In publishing the survey responses, George wrote: "You want to know more about what's going to be coming up locally, and you want to know what we think of it when it gets here. Through calendars and personal columns by our writers, we are going to try to give you this information."

George said the survey, while not scientifically conducted, brought in hundreds of responses—completed questionnaires and letters from readers—and not only reinforced their commitment to do more local coverage of the arts, but also specified the arts interests of readers (movies were tops, then theatre, art, music, etc.).

"We're not making any drastic changes in our coverage but we're running more columns by the music, art and theatre critics and started a new art featurette called 'Studio Hopping,' which spotlights various local artists and their work," George said afterwards.

Another reader complaint about arts criticism is provincialism, which could easily be remedied. If readers are to keep up with the national arts scene, then newspapers must provide some coverage of events elsewhere. Wire service copy on the arts is the obvious solution, yet most metropolitan papers rarely use wire service reviews. Many medium-size and small dailies regularly devote 25 per cent of their arts space to wire service coverage (some go as high as 50 per cent) but the trend in major outlets is definitely to run more locally written criticism.

Since wire services are the least expensive way for most papers to share news of events, one wonders why the Associated Press and United Press International (and other syndicates) limit their critical coverage to the New York area. Cultural critics in each region of the country could file stories and expand the range of reviews, at a time when the arts themselves appear to be decentralizing. Arts readers in St. Louis, for instance, would be just as interested in staying informed about major events in nearby Chicago, Kansas City or Dallas as faraway New York or Los Angeles. Expanded coverage can certainly help put local work in a national perspective.

Expanded arts coverage might also abate some of the criticism that the media are only filled with "bad" or depressing news. More cultural coverage might begin to correct that imbalance that readers perceive.

One idea the *New York Times* has instituted to expand its cultural commitment is its "Critics Notebook" columns. Based on the journalist's notebook concept, in which the writer reports all sorts of behind-the-scenes tidbits of information not usable in traditional stories, the *Times'* critics have considered the influence of applause at concerts, the tastes of jazz audiences, notes on European opera, counter-commercials on television and a host of other minor concerns and developments.

Consumerism in the arts should also increase in the future. Some critics have long preached and practiced such an approach in their criticism. The late Ralph Gleason, for example, wrote:

> Reviewers should campaign for adequate working conditions for artists, adequate economic participation, comfortable places for audiences, good lighting and all the rest. They should be mortal enemies of sloppy performances, sloppy ticket sales, sloppy buildings and anything else that involves a public event. They should be unbribeable and report honestly with a crusading spirit. They should be the guardian to protect the public from anything fly-by-night promoters and exploiters might want to do.

Finally, regular critiques of critics should be instituted in the journalism reviews so that performance can be regularly monitored and the field can be improved.

Thus, the future of all criticism remains "undetermined," because just as Louis Reeves Harrison wrote about film criticism in the Jan. 31, 1914 issue of *The Motion Picture World:*

> A good critic must be able to collect evidence of power successfully exercised and use it to guide this new art out of a labyrinth of mediocrity. Such men will be hard to find as long as production is more sincerely commercial than artistic. Improvement is bound to come in the course of keen competition, but there is a present need for clearer vision.

As always, the ever-challenging job of the critic is and will be, as Alan Rich says, "to do battle with apathy, the art's worst enemy."

APPENDIX

List of Critics Evaluated by Readers (in Research Study)

Drama

1. Clive Barnes, of *The New York Times*, reviewing "Via Galac-
   tica"
2. Richard L. Coe, of *The Washington Post*, reviewing "National
   Lampoon's Lemmings"
3. David Richards, of *Washington Star-News*, reviewing "The
   Member of the Wedding"
4. T. E. Kalem, of *Time*, reviewing "Shenandoah"
5. Edith Oliver, of *The New Yorker*, reviewing "The Hot L Baltimore"
6. John Simon, of *New York*, reviewing "The Ritz"

Music

1. Robert Christgau, of *Newsday*, reviewing Carly Simon
2. John S. Wilson, of *The New York Times*, reviewing Barbara
   Cook
3. Don Heckman, of *The New York Times*, reviewing Elvis Presley
4. John Rockwell, of *The New York Times*, reviewing the Allman
   Brothers
5. Harold C. Schonberg, of *The New York Times*, reviewing the
   Metropolitan Opera's "Boris Godunov"

Film
1. Charles Champlin, of the *Los Angeles Times*, reviewing "Alice Doesn't Live Here Anymore"
2. Liz Smith, of *Cosmopolitan*, reviewing "The Exorcist"
3. Arthur Cooper, of *Newsweek*, reviewing "Lost Horizon"
4. Rex Reed, of the *New York Daily News*, reviewing "The Great Gatsby"
5. Vincent Canby, of *The New York Times*, reviewing "Chinatown"
6. Jay Cocks, of *Time*, reviewing "The Sting"

Art
1. Robert Hughes, of *Time*, reviewing Joseph Raffael
2. John Russell, of *The New York Times*, reviewing Claes Oldenburg
3. Hilton Kramer, of *The New York Times*, reviewing the Whitney's "The Flowering of American Folk Art 1776–1876"
4. Paul Richard, of *The Washington Post*, reviewing James Rosenquist

Dance
1. Michael Iachetta, of the *New York Daily News*, reviewing the Joffrey Ballet's "N.Y. Export: Opus Jazz"
2. Anna Kisselgoff, of *The New York Times*, reviewing Paul Taylor with Nureyev
3. Clive Barnes, of *The New York Times*, reviewing Merce Cunningham
4. Arlene Croce, of *The New Yorker*, reviewing Twyla Tharp

Television
1. Paul Jones, of *The Atlanta Constitution*, reviewing drama "Death Be Not Proud"
2. Marvin Kitman, of *Newsday*, reviewing series "The New Temperatures Rising"
3. Cecil Smith of the *Los Angeles Times*, reviewing drama "After the Fall"
4. Richard Schickel, of *Time*, reviewing documentary "The Corporation"
5. John J. O'Connor, of *The New York Times*, reviewing drama "The Glass Menagerie"

SCHOOL OF JOURNALISM
THE UNIVERSITY OF GEORGIA
ATHENS. GEORGIA 30601

In an effort to improve public understanding of criticism, and with the aid of a foundation grant, I am commencing a study of the critics of the popular arts. As you might guess, current original material in this area is scarce so I am going to the best sources I know: professional reviewers/ critics.

I would prefer to gather material by talking with you about your work, opinions and ideas but neither time nor budget permits that thorough approach. So I have put together some questions in my areas of concern and would appreciate your candid response to each. Other facts, anecdotes, views are certainly welcome, too. I'm more interested in qualitative responses that can be quoted than adding up numbers and trying to determine the significance of the tallies. (However, if you prefer, your response can and will be kept confidential and only used as general information without attribution.) If you don't have room enough for complete answers in the space provided, kindly use the reverse side of each sheet. Include clippings of your work, if you think it makes the point.

Obviously the success of this undertaking is tied to the cooperation and assistance of the working critics I contact. I believe the finished project will serve the media, critics and readers if it helps open the dialogue about the role, process and influence of popular arts criticism.

For these reasons, I am asking you to take a few minutes to fill in the enclosed questionnaire and return it to me in the envelope provided. I do appreciate your generous gift of time and your support of this study project. Many thanks.

Sincerely,

John W. English
Assistant Professor of Journalism
Critics Project Coordinator

Return to: Critics Project
266 Barrack Hill Rd.
Ridgefield, Conn. 06877

"A Study of Popular Arts Criticism"

Name_____ Publication/medium_____

1. How many years have you worked as a reviewer/critic?_____

2. In your work, what percentage of your time is devoted to criticism?_____%
What other journalistic duties are you assigned?_____

3. Which of the arts do you regularly cover? Please rank 1,2,3, etc.

   Visual arts:____Television;____Film;____Art;____Architecture;____Photography;____Interior design

   Performing arts:____Pop music;____Classical music;____Records;____Theatre;____Dance;
   ____Cabaret;____Specials, such as circuses, ice shows, etc.

   Other:____books;____restaurants;_____

4. How much space are the arts allotted daily?_____pages or _____columns

5. How many reviews do you usually write a week?_____

6. Do you write analysis critiques for a Sunday arts section? ____Yes. ____No.

7. How much wire service or syndicated copy on the arts do you use weekly?
   _____/_____ per cent of local copy to wire service copy

8. How much time do you usually have to prepare reviews? ____less than 2 hours;____2 to 5 hrs;
   ____5 to 8 hrs.;____more than 8 hrs.

9. Is this time to prepare adequate or not?____Yes.____No.
   Ideally how much time would you need?_____.

10. How would you characterize your medium's editorial image?
   ____liberal;____middle of the road;____conservative;____other_____

11. How aware are you of your publication's editorial philosophy, tone or style when writing
   your reviews? ____very aware, restricts personal expression;____aware, but of little
   influence;____aware, but of no influence;____not aware.

12. How many editors process your copy before it is in print?_____Briefly describe the
   copy flow:_____.

13. How often--frequently, occasionally, rarely or never--is your copy edited for:
   a. length only, trimmed to fit?_____
   b. major revisions?_____
   c. minor changes?_____.

14. In general, what is your impression of a copy editor's work on your reviews?
   ____weaken the impact;____destroy my personal style of expression;____improve and
   clarify copy;____make little difference.

15. What element do you consider the most important part of a review? Rank 1,2,3.
   ____description of work;____analysis or interpretation of work;____evaluation of work
   ____other_____

16. Do your editors have any restrictions on what (or whom) you can review? Or do you have a
   completely free hand in choosing what to write about? For example, can you review a
   presentation of an advertiser who hasn't paid his bill? Can you review off-beat political
   works? Sexual works? ____Free hand. Restrictions:_____.

17. If you can consistently exercise selective judgment over your review subjects, do you tend to review only the best works you find and avoid the worst, thus affecting the overall tenor of your criticism?_____

18. Over the years, how would you assess your total output? _____ % favorable reviews
_____ % mixed reviews
_____ % unfavorable reviews.

19. What do you perceive your role as critic to be? Rank 1,2,3.
_____reporter of artistic events;_____promoter of the arts;_____educator;
_____arbiter of taste;_____advisor to artists;_____feedback to producers;
_____others:_____.

20. What part of your job gives the most satisfaction?_____
_____What gives the least satisfaction?_____

21. What attributes or characteristics would you consider most important for a critic to possess? Please rank 1,2,3, etc.
_____knowledgeable in the arts;_____talented writer;_____excellent teacher
_____consistent viewpoint;_____interesting personality or character
_____responsive to reader & community needs;_____highly intellectual
_____high moral values; _____ability to perceive & respond to arts
_____others:_____.

22. What is your response to this statement: A critic must not be concerned with "What do I think of this?" but "What is my relation to this?"_____
_____

23. How does your salary compare with peers covering business or politics?
_____higher than others;_____the same range;_____lower;_____don't know.

24. Do you do investigative reporting in the arts? _____Yes. Any examples?_____
_____No. Does someone else do this work?_____

25. Do you do stories on the economics of the arts industry? For example, articles on financial problems, success stories, pressures, etc. _____Yes. _____No. Comment?

26. If the deficit in the arts is expected to grow, do you think reviewers/critics can do anything to help remedy the crises? _____Yes. What?_____
_____No. Why not?_____.

27. Should critics be concerned about cultural facilities--concert halls, theatres, museums, libraries--in his community and write about them? _____Yes. _____No.

28. Does the source of a cultural work affect your evaluation of it? Some critics say they are easier on local amateurs and tougher on distant corporate products. _____ No.
_____Yes. Explain:_____.

29. Do you try to determine the social relevance of a work? _____Yes. _____No.
Is it important to put a work's message in a timely sociological context?
_____highly important;_____usually not important;_____depends on message;_____not concerned

30. Do you ever write about why a cultural work was produced, even though it seems to have little critical relevance? _____Yes. _____No. Example?

31. Briefly describe the audience of your medium:

32. When you prepare a review, what types of readers do you have in mind? Please rank 1,2,3.
_____peers (other journalists);_____artists involved;_____arts public who shared event;
_____arts public who didn't share event but are attuned;_____those who rarely attend arts events but are interested;_____casual readers with little arts interest;_____producers & those in entertainment industry; _____others:_____.

33. In your reviews, do you try to indicate or define the type of audience for which a work might be intended, best suited or most appealing? _____Yes, if specialized. _____No.

34. Do you write reviews to serve as a consumer guide? _____Yes. _____No.

35. Do you have any evidence that your reviews have any effect--positive or negative--on local audiences? eg. box office records, ratings, etc.?

36. Do you have any evidence that your reviews have any effect on producers or creators of the works you review?

37. Do you ever write about criticism to explain the process to readers?
_____Yes. Examples?   _____No. Why?

38. Please cite your three favorite or best critical reviews:
    1.
    2.
    3.

39. Do you prefer a private screening or dress rehearsal to witnessing an event with a typical audience? _____Yes. _____No (prefer audience). Comment?
    Do you include comments on audience and its reactions in your review? _____Yes. _____No.

40. What sources do you generally use as background material in a review? Check applicable:
_____personal experience;_____reportage of others;_____press releases;_____interviews
with principals;_____reference works;_____others:_____

41. Do public relations activities of arts interests ever affect what you write about?
    Yes   No
    ____ ____ promotion tours of celebrities
    ____ ____ pseudo-events, publicity stunts, etc.
    ____ ____ press releases or publicity photos
    ____ ____ direct personal contacts with agents, publicists, distributors, etc.
    ____ ____ cross-media coverage (stories in other media) exert pressure to cover
    ____ ____ massive advertising campaign enhances value of review in mind of editor

42. Do you belong to any organization of critics? _____Yes. _____No. Comment?
    If so, which ones?

43. What other reviewers/critics do you regularly read? _____

44. Do you think reviewers can have any significant influence in helping a good, though obscure work or artist gain recognition? _____Yes, can help. _____No, can't.

45. Can they thwart the success of other work? _____Yes, can thwart. _____No, can't.

46. Can reviewers educate an audience to become attuned to the arts? _____Yes. _____No.

47. Can they elevate the standards of art? _____Yes. _____No. Comment?

48. Andrew Sarris says that film criticism today is of higher quality than most films. Do you think the status of criticism has superseded any other art forms? _____Yes. _____No.Comment?

49. We often hear that the avant garde is dead. Do you think criticism has any effect on innovation in the arts?

50. Do you believe a reviewer should go beyond appreciation, evaluation and box office guidance to attempt to change the social context in which the popular arts live in the world?
_____Yes. _____No. Comment?_____.

                              Thanks.

Judge the review you just read on the following scales. Place an X in the space that most clearly reflects your degree of agreement with one of the words:

valuable	____:____:____:____:____:____:____	worthless
negative	____:____:____:____:____:____:____	positive
unpopular	____:____:____:____:____:____:____	popular
good	____:____:____:____:____:____:____	bad
strong	____:____:____:____:____:____:____	weak
complex	____:____:____:____:____:____:____	simple
lenient	____:____:____:____:____:____:____	severe
hard	____:____:____:____:____:____:____	soft
active	____:____:____:____:____:____:____	passive
confusing	____:____:____:____:____:____:____	understandable
calm	____:____:____:____:____:____:____	intense
abstract	____:____:____:____:____:____:____	concrete
interesting	____:____:____:____:____:____:____	dull
conservative	____:____:____:____:____:____:____	liberal
unclear	____:____:____:____:____:____:____	clear
authoritative	____:____:____:____:____:____:____	unauthoritative
meaningful	____:____:____:____:____:____:____	meaningless
not important	____:____:____:____:____:____:____	important
informal	____:____:____:____:____:____:____	formal
persuasive	____:____:____:____:____:____:____	not persuasive
consistent	____:____:____:____:____:____:____	changeable
stupid	____:____:____:____:____:____:____	intelligent
involved	____:____:____:____:____:____:____	cool, aloof
romantic	____:____:____:____:____:____:____	pragmatic
stale	____:____:____:____:____:____:____	fresh
not enriching	____:____:____:____:____:____:____	enriching
satisfying	____:____:____:____:____:____:____	annoying
original	____:____:____:____:____:____:____	imitative
wordy	____:____:____:____:____:____:____	succinct
appealing	____:____:____:____:____:____:____	repellent

over

Here are some other questions about the review you just read:

1. Is the critic's verdict clear? _____yes _____no

2. What would you call this review? _____Rave
   _____Mostly favorable
   _____Mixed—some favorable—
   some unfavorable
   _____Mostly unfavorable
   _____Pan

3. Did the critic: _____recommend that you attend the work
   _____recommend that you avoid the work
   _____make no recommendation

4. Did the critic specify what type of audience the work being reviewed seems intended for:
   _____Yes, audience was specified _____No

5. Which element of this review seems to be the strongest?

   _____description _____interpretation _____evaluation

6. What five evaluative words in this review do you think best convey the critic's view of the art work?

   Positive words   Negative words

INDEX